# Somerset Maugham

## A WRITER FOR ALL SEASONS
### A Biographical and Critical Study

Portrait of Somerset
Maugham by Graham
Sutherland.

*Tate Gallery, London*

# Somerset Maugham

## A WRITER FOR ALL SEASONS

A BIOGRAPHICAL AND CRITICAL STUDY

by Richard A. Cordell

Indiana University Press

Bloomington & London

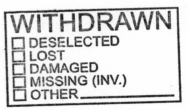

TO WILLIAM AND ALAN

PREFATORY NOTE TO SECOND EDITION

AFTER *Somerset Maugham: A Biographical and Critical Study* was written in 1959, Maugham lived on for six more years. This new edition includes an account of his last years and last writing. It is not, strictly speaking, a revised but a lengthened edition: the old edition has been left unchanged except for the new chapter carrying the story through to Maugham's death.

R. A.C.

# PREFACE

THE AUTHOR is indebted to Random House, Inc., for permission to reproduce in revised form a section of his Introduction to the Modern Library Edition of *Of Human Bondage*, 1956; and to *Modern Drama* for permission to reproduce, also in greatly revised form, an article on Somerset Maugham's plays. Two other sections of this book are revisions and extensions of parts of an earlier book on Maugham by the author.

He is also indebted to Dr. and Mrs. Nesfield and Dr. Etheridge of Whitstable, Sir Gerald Kelly and Mr. Martin Secker of London, and Mr. Gwynne Leyshon of Shrewsbury for assistance in gathering material for this book; and he is particularly grateful to Mr. Maugham and Mr. Alan Searle for providing information, checking the accuracy of details, supplying photographs, and generously answering many questions.

R. A. C.

CONTENTS

# ILLUSTRATIONS

# Somerset Maugham

## A WRITER FOR ALL SEASONS
### A Biographical and Critical Study

I

## BIOGRAPHICAL SKETCH

As the name indicates the Maughams are of Celtic extraction. Many years ago Somerset Maugham's paternal ancestors migrated from Ireland to Westmoreland, where they prospered as gentleman farmers and government officials. His great-grandfather, ruined by the Napoleonic wars, sent his son Robert Armand to London to study law. Robert rose rapidly in his profession, became an eminent barrister, and wrote a number of books on legal and moral subjects. In 1825 he founded the Incorporated Law Society, which is still in existence, and for many years he was the proprietor and editor of the *Legal Observer,* now the *Solicitor's Journal.* Robert Armand's wife was well educated; a family heirloom is her Greek edition of the New Testament, which she used on Sundays. The Robert Armand Maughams had eight children, the oldest being Robert, born in 1823, father of the writer.

Somerset Maugham's maternal ancestry is much more

imposing, if not downright spectacular. The British geneal-
ogist Patrick Montague-Smith has traced the author's
mother's descent from Edward I, King of England (died
1307) and Eleanor of Castille (died 1290), and has found
such far-off kinsmen in the family tree as Clive of India,
Sir Richard Grenville of the "Revenge," and John Churchill,
the great Duke of Marlborough. When Maugham's grandfather, Major Snell, was killed in the Indian Mutiny in 1857,
his two daughters were sent home to England in charge of
an ayah, to live with the somewhat aristocratic Snell family. The major's widow, who preferred Paris to England,
was careless and extravagant and in spite of a liberal pension and a substantial inheritance soon found herself with
little money. She was a woman of energy and spirit, however. Establishing herself in Paris, she wrote dozens of sensational novels in French, children's books, and popular
songs. Although she herself was a professional writer (the
same disdainful charge was to be made against her gifted
grandson years later), the Snells were very genteel and
were distressed when one of her daughters married Robert
Maugham, a mere solicitor.

But Robert was more than a mere solicitor. Although he
was never so eminent a lawyer as his father, who was also a
writer and editor, the firm of Maugham and Sewall was the
most celebrated and respected in Paris. The author's father
was also a cultivated man of the world, interested in art,
literature, and society. He journeyed to Asia Minor and
North Africa, where he discovered the cabalistic sign now
found on the covers of his son's books, stationery, and the
gateway to his house in southern France, Villa Mauresque;
in the Atlas Mountains the sign, possibly a stylization of the

human hand, was supposed to ward off the Evil Eye. He also collected a large library.

The young solicitor and his beautiful wife lived in an airy and attractive apartment on the third floor at Number 25, Avenue d'Antin, close enough to the Champs Elysées to provide an excellent view of that incomparable avenue. In the 1870's the Champs Elysées was lined with elegant private homes and apartments; there were no shops and only one hotel. In this area young Willie spent his first ten years, the first eight of them very happily, near the walks, gardens, boutiques where sweets were sold, Punch and Judy shows, merry-go-rounds, and the Summer Circus at Rond Point. With his older brothers he walked to the Luxembourg and the Louvre: from the beginning he was familiar with the arts, both in his home and in the galleries. Although Willie and his brothers had English governesses, they all spoke French, the servants were French, and the young Maughams played with French boys in the Champs Elysées. For his first ten years Willie was in nearly all respects a French boy himself.

In 1850 Robert Maugham had been appointed solicitor to the British Embassy, and in addition to a busy private practice he performed the extra duties until his death in 1884. His connections with the Embassy widened the Maughams' already extensive social circle. Mrs. Maugham was often referred to as the most beautiful woman in Paris, and photographs still in possession of her son show that she had great beauty indeed; she was also kind, amusing, and popular. In spite of ill health, for she had contracted tuberculosis, she was active in social life; she knew everyone in Paris worth knowing and her *salon* was brilliant. Prosper

Mérimée and Gustave Doré were her intimate friends. In the summer she took the children to a villa in Deauville for three months. There were finally six children, all boys, for according to a strange belief of the day, child-bearing was supposed to be beneficial to a woman suffering from consumption. It is ironically possible that child-bearing shortened her life. Two of the boys died very young. The youngest, William Somerset, was born on January 25, 1874.

Fate became suddenly malevolent. Mrs. Maugham died of tuberculosis in 1882. After nearly eighty years Somerset Maugham confessed that time never completely healed the wound caused by her death; he remembered her great beauty, made fragile and ethereal in her last months by the wasting disease. The three older boys were sent to school in England, but Willie remained in Paris until his father's death from cancer two years later. After his mother's death he was taken out of the French school he had been attending and sent daily to the rooms of the English clergyman attached to the British Embassy, who had the unusual task of teaching the English boy his own language. His earliest reading had been *Peau d'Ane, La Belle au Bois Dormant,* and other fairy stories read by French children. French was spoken by his parents, the servants, and most visitors to their home, for it was modish then for British residents in Paris and visitors to speak French if they could. The clergyman evidently had a sense of humor, for he taught the English boy by having him read aloud the police-court news in the London *Standard.*

Although unmistakably British in manner and appearance, Maugham has always been devoted to France, where he has chosen to spend much of his life. He has acknowledged, "It was France that educated me, France that taught me to value beauty, distinction, wit and good sense, France that taught me to write." He has said some uncomplimentary things about the French, too: their meanness and their corruptibility in government and politics. The French gourmet would be pained by his opinion that Wisconsin Camembert is as good as the French and that Australian champagne is indistinguishable from that of Rheims—except for the labels. France may have taught him to value beauty but he has said that the French have had little taste since Louis XV—in such a rash statement he ignores the *Flandre,* the *Caravelle,* the Simcas and Arondes, the new architecture of the school of Le Corbusier, the new well-designed household appliances. Nevertheless he has preferred to live in France. He says that when he crosses the Channel or the border to enter France he feels at home.

Just before his wife's death Robert was building a somewhat bizarre and expensive house outside Paris. It was never occupied and his heirs could recover only part of the vast sum expended on it. Charles, the oldest son and a lawyer, took charge of the family finances, succeeded his father in the Paris firm, and helped his brothers along whenever it was necessary. Like his parents, Charles was kind and lovable (Somerset Maugham, Sir Gerald Kelly, and others who remember him agree that he was "a saint") and he became almost as eminent as his father in his profession, although on his father's death the name of the firm was changed from Maugham and Sewall to Sewall and Maugham. After Charles retired from practice, he lived in Lausanne for some time, before settling in London for his last years.

Frederick went on to Cambridge, became a very celebrated lawyer, and finally was made Lord Chancellor and the Viscount Maugham of Hartfield. He died in 1958 at the age of ninety-one. Two of Lord Maugham's daughters and his son Robin, the present Lord Maugham, are novelists. A few years before his death Frederick published his autobiography, *The End of the Day*. In this very long book his celebrated brother William Somerset is mentioned twice, for a total of two lines.

Henry was quite unlike his three brothers, and is said to have been a prodigious bore. He was prominent at Eton and Oxford, and then like Charles and Frederick become a solicitor. He found the law distasteful, however, and left it to devote himself to writing. Evidently for his own amusement he wrote Jacobean verse plays which were never performed and two novels which no one read. He committed suicide at the age of thirty-six. When near the end of medical school Willie told Charles (then the head of the family) that he wanted to write, the latter did not discourage him but suggested that he show the manuscript of *Liza of Lambeth* to Henry. This somewhat precious *fin de siècle* aesthete, whose tastes ran to verse plays, poetry of the school of Oscar Wilde, and "Reflections," was shocked by the raw, unpoetic novel and advised his young brother to give up once and for all any ideas of authorship.

After the death of the father in 1884 there was no proper home for ten-year-old Willie in Paris, and so he was sent to live with one of his guardians, his father's brother, in Whitstable, Kent. Henry Macdonald Maugham, M.A., after serving as curate in various towns in Surrey and Kent, had become vicar of thirteenth-century All Saints' Church in

Whitstable in 1870. A more violent change of environment for the Parisian boy is hard to imagine. After a childhood in a carefree, cultivated home, bathed in warmth and affection, with his brothers and French boys as playmates, the enchanting Champs Elysées as a playground, and his only religious duty that of tipping his cap to priests whom he passed on the street, he suddenly found himself in the severely quiet home of a middle-aged, childless couple, where laughter was seldom heard and religious duties were regarded as laws of nature. Playing games, reading (anything but the Bible) or in any way amusing oneself on Sunday was viewed with grave disapproval. It is not surprising that the child was lonely and unhappy. His uncle regarded him as obstinate and uncooperative. He now declares that he was undersized and in poor health; his shyness was interpreted as sullenness (as it sometimes was). Moreover, he was afflicted with a serious speech defect, which increased his natural shyness (later he defined "shyness" as a mixture of diffidence and conceit) and isolated him from others. Evidently in Paris his stammer had been ignored in his home and in the French primary school and by his playmates, for it caused him no self-consciousness until he went to Whitstable.

The half-foreign little boy found the vicarage terrifyingly different from the gracious, sunny apartment on the Avenue d'Antin, and life there a matter of unvarying routine. His stern uncle and his aristocratic German-born wife, Sophie, daughter of Baron von Scheidlin, were not really unkind, but they were unimaginative, especially the vicar, and thoroughly incompetent to assume their new task. The novelist has described his uncle with brutal frankness in

*Of Human Bondage* and with wry humor in *Cakes and Ale*. He was not a vicious man. He was not unpopular with his parishioners, some of whom, to be sure, thought him odd, but he was self-centered and inflexible, and had the lazy man's devotion to an easy, fixed routine which protects him from disturbance. He was most inept as a guardian. Maugham has never forgotten, for example, that his uncle forced him to eat fat meat, which all but nauseated him. To the vicar it was probably a matter of discipline and thrift, but to the sensitive boy it was cruelty.

When his uncle died in 1897, the year Maugham finished medical school—Aunt Sophie had died several years before and the vicar had then married the daughter of a General Matthews of Bath—his nephew was surprised at the homage paid to his memory. During the hours of the funeral nearly all shops and offices in Whitstable were closed, fellow-churchmen came from all over England, and the local paper praised not only his services to the church, but to the community as well. Maugham had not been aware of the scope of his uncle's activities. Many years later it occurred to him that his uncle might have had a sense of humor, that when he pronounced his religious and moral clichés there may have been a twinkle in his eyes unnoticed by the rather humorless and priggish youth.

His aunt was the personification of the *gute deutsche Hausfrau* in the worst sense of the phrase: her whole life was dedicated to waiting on her egregiously pampered husband. She was generous and tenderhearted, but her wispy kindness afforded too insubstantial a refuge for the needs of the lonely orphan.

Whitstable and environs should have been a perfect com-

Somerset Maugham and his uncle at the Whitstable Vicarage, 1884.

Somerset Maugham in 1884.

Somerset Maugham

munity for a growing boy. He would have been fairly indifferent to its two thousand years of history, its economic
importance in the 1880's in the production of oysters, the
story of the seven-centuries-old church, of which his uncle
was vicar. But the seaside activities would have fascinated
him: the eighty vessels engaged in oyster-dredging; the 300
merchant vessels with Whitstable as home port; the fishing
fleet; the colliers from Newcastle; the busy ship-building
yards; the resort-like aspect of certain stretches of beach,
with Mr. Kemp's swinging boats, skiffs for hire, bathing
machines, and tea booths; the long row of fishermen's cottages with regularly spaced public houses. Absurd restric-
tions of gentility, however, insulated Willie against the real
life of the animated seaport and market town, although in
the summer he would sometimes disobey his uncle and
steal away to the harbor and beach to gaze on the forbidden vulgarities of workmen, fishermen, and trippers.

Although Whitstable has never become a resort comparable with neighboring Margate and Ramsgate, there was a
threat in Maugham's boyhood that it might become a popular holiday spot when ambitious citizens erected a number
of cottages and small hotels along the shore. The professional folk and gentry looked with distaste on such vulgar
enterprise and either ignored the summer visitors, most of
them from unfashionable boroughs of London, or treated
them with the condescension accorded to tradesmen, fishermen, chapel-goers, and other representatives of low life.
Willie was forbidden to associate in any way with these
interlopers, even with the sons of the few well-to-do Lon-
doners on holiday (he was cautioned against becoming
familiar with the young son of a wealthy London banker,

because the father was "in trade"), and of course he was carefully kept away from nearly all the Whitstable boys.

He was bewildered by the church members' feuds with local dissenters and by the preposterous snobbishness and Victorian notions of propriety which cut him off from wholesome companionship. When thousands of "foreigners," many of them from London, invaded the Kent countryside in September and early October to help harvest the hops, Willie would sometimes cycle out to the edge of a camp of workers and their families, and look with astonishment at their carefree gypsy-like life. Naturally his uncle had warned him against association with these migrant workers and their brown, dirty, and almost wildly happy children. Even as a child he craved freedom, and the easy pattern of his life in France had not prepared him for the irksome conventions of the vicarage. Memories of the pleasant years in France and the seven cheerless years in Kent have never been erased from his mind. In 1928 he established permanent residence in France, partly because of the salubrious climate of the Côte d'Azur, partly because he feels most at home in France. Since the end of the Second World War, however, he has spent a fourth of each year in England, and has occasionally visited Whitstable and wandered through the rooms and grounds of "The Old Vicarage." At times his references to England have been, for him, downright sentimental. Speaking of the Riviera, he once confessed, "Sometimes I get sick of this hot sunshine and these garish colors. I want grey skies and a soft rain falling. I want to feel under my feet the grey pavement of an English country town. I want to be able to have a row with the butcher because the steak he sent me yesterday was tough, and I want to browse around second-hand bookshops. I want to be said how d'you do to in the street by people I knew when I was a boy. And I want to have a walled garden at the back of my house and grow roses." He indulged in this bit of romanticizing more than half a century after he left Whitstable. He has tried to analyze his emotional love of England, stronger in his late years. He says that to him the very shape of England on the map has meaning and brings to mind a hundred things—the lovely countryside of Kent and Sussex, the Thames estuary and St. Paul's, lines from Shakespeare, Keats, and Collins, visions of Sir Francis Drake and Henry VIII, Tom Jones and Dr. Johnson, the beautiful posters in the ugly but friendly London railway stations.

His school years were even more wretched when he entered King's School in Canterbury, only seven miles from Whitstable. He was lonely, frightened, and plagued by his shyness and speech defect. This small public school is housed in beautiful old buildings alongside the Cathedral. Maugham has never admitted it, but his love of beauty must owe something to King's School and its environs. Canterbury is still a beautiful city, although many deplore the new postwar functional architecture of High Street. The School, Cathedral, Cloisters, and gardens achieve a simple perfection in architecture and prospect like the perfection in style Maugham strives for in his writing. Although pilgrims and sightseers have been coming to Canterbury for hundreds of years, its loveliness and treasures have not been unduly commercialized; it is not vulgarized by traffic in souvenirs and importunate guides.

Christopher Marlowe, Walter Pater, and Hugh Walpole

attended King's School. In 1884 its boys were gentlemen's sons, and the emphasis was almost entirely on the classics and games. The ritual of good form was preached and often practiced, and the rites of the Church of England were scrupulously administered. Although good form prevented cheating and dishonesty, or at least curbed them, and strict attendance at prayers and chapel was required, the boys were savage enough to torment the newcomer and make a purgatory of his first years.

The painful story of this period is faithfully recorded in *Of Human Bondage*. Willie's frail health and disinclination for games precluded the popularity he secretly longed for. That he would be tormented by his schoolmates because he stammered is understandable, for the young are thoughtlessly cruel; but that his masters should bully him and be impatient of his stammering is incredible, but true.

In his old age bitterness toward his old school has faded, and he has been able to view it more objectively, if not with the deep pride of a former student. He gave to King's School the original manuscripts of *Liza of Lambeth* and *Catalina,* his first and last novels. In 1950 he contributed a sum toward a new boathouse for the boys. In 1958 he gave King's School £10,000 toward the cost of a new science building, tangible evidence of the emergence of a rival with the classics for domination in secondary schooling. At the age of eighty-four he made a special trip from Cap Ferrat to Canterbury to open the new building, and of course was much honored as the most distinguished Old Boy of the school. He said with characteristic saltiness when interviewed on the occasion: "When I was young and travelled a good deal, I found that the English were detested all

over the world because they were so class-conscious and
sniffy. The public schools were, in my view, largely responsible for creating this class-consciousness. So I suggested
to the headmaster that I should provide a certain sum to
educate a working-class boy at King's School. But the
scheme was a flop; for one thing, working-class parents
didn't seem to want their sons contaminated. So after a
number of years I said the money should be spent on something else. Hence the Science Building." He ventured his
personal view that the public school system is bound to
die out in a generation. "I think grammar school competition
is an excellent thing. I can't see why England needs public
schools. They seem to get on all right without them in
France and Italy and the United States." These comments
were hardly of a nature to endear the benefactor to either
the staff or the boys of King's School.

It is almost certain that his bad stammer not only made
impossible his considering the law or the church as a profession, but also resulted in an introversion, or at least an
introspection, that led him to be an observer and a writer.
The anguish that his stammering brought to him was as
poignant as that inflicted by Philip Carey's club foot in
*Of Human Bondage.* In a preface written for *The Old
Wives' Tale* he remarks about Arnold Bennett's stammer,
and he is obviously writing about himself as well: "Every
one knows that Arnold was afflicted with a very bad stammer; it was painful to watch the struggle he had sometimes
to get the words out. It was torture to him. Few realized
the exhaustion it caused him to speak. What to most men
was as easy as breathing, to him was a constant strain.
It tore his nerves to pieces. Few knew the humiliation it

exposed him to, the ridicule it excited in many, the impatience it aroused . . . the minor exasperation of thinking of a good, amusing, or apt remark and not venturing to say it in case the stammer ruined it. Few knew the distressing sense it gave rise to of a bar to complete contact with other men. It may be that except for the stammer which forced him to introspection, Arnold would never have become a writer."

In recent years Maugham has been able to overcome his speech difficulty to some extent. After a series of treatments with the specialist who cured King George VI of a similar disorder, he was able by 1941 to speak in public and finally to participate in radio and television programs, and to record readings of some of his short stories. Although his religious skepticism remains undiminished, it is possible that freedom from speech trouble may have contributed to a mellowing of philosophy, a greater tranquillity, an increased tolerance noticeable in *Don Fernando, The Summing Up*, and late entries in *A Writer's Notebook*. Maugham himself insists that what we call personality has in part a physical basis.

When still in school he became rather seriously ill, and an examination showed his lungs to be affected. His alarmed guardians, remembering that his mother and an aunt had died of tuberculosis, sent him to Hyères in the South of France. Here he was happy once more. The sun shone and the days sang again. He discovered the stories of Maupassant and other French writers he had been too young to read in his early years in France. He enjoyed a common experience of adolescent boys: he fell in love with a mature woman, the wife of his tutor. After a few months he was able to return to England, but the bleak routine in Canterbury italicized in his memory the joyous, carefree life he had enjoyed on the Continent. He determined to defy his uncle, who still insisted that he go on to Oxford and prepare himself for the Church; he would get away from England for at least a year. Many young Englishmen of the time who could afford it continued their education abroad for a year after leaving preparatory school.

His uncle consented to allow him to spend his eighteenth year in Germany, since the vicar's German wife, with her aristocratic connections, could make arrangements for the boy's sojourn in Heidelberg in safe and proper surroundings. He did not become officially a member of the University, for he did not matriculate, but he took advantage of the lectures, library, and intellectual stimulation of a university community. He was happy; he felt a sense of freedom he had not known in Whitstable and Canterbury. His companions introduced him to the pleasures of art, poetry, theatre, and friendly disputation. He discovered the *Maxims* of La Rochefoucauld, and their echoes were heard for sixty years in his plays and stories. On Maugham's eighty-fifth birthday a journalist reported him as uttering a pure La Rochefoucauld: "Now that I have grown old, I realize that for most of us it is not enough to have achieved personal success. One's best friend must also have failed." Fortunately one is not obliged to accept as authentic every statement made by a columnist, and this ill-humored remark is quoted out of context.

At the University of Heidelberg Kuno Fischer's stirring lectures introduced him to the delights of philosophy and led him to read, among others, Schopenhauer. In the grubby

municipal theatre he saw his first plays, some of them shattering *avant-garde* dramas by Ibsen, Becque, and Suder-
mann. He cast off the misfit mantle of Christianity which
his uncle and masters had forced upon him. He knew the
keen delights of the free play of mind on mind and with
the arrogant intolerance of youth he exulted in his "emanci-
pation." The year at Heidelberg did other things for him.
It gave him his first serious lessons in the study of the unpredictability of man's behavior when the conduct of one
or two new companions and of fellow-lodgers in the pension surprised him completely. Standing one day on a
hill above the Rhine Valley, he was exhilarated for the
first time by a mystic, almost unbearable, feeling for beauty.
And not least of all, his brief journeys from Heidelberg
to other parts of Germany, and to Italy and Switzerland,
developed a wanderlust from which he never recovered,
and which was to have a major influence on his writing.

He returned to England determined to be a writer, but
to announce to his guardian at the age of eighteen that
he had chosen literature as his profession was unthinkable.
What to do? He firmly rejected the Church. Why did his
uncle, knowing the boy's disabling speech defect, insist
on his becoming a clergyman? It was proposed that he
become a civil servant, but his uncle and aunt had been
told that civil servants are often thrown with people who
are not gentlemen. He was indifferent to the law, already
the choice of his three surviving brothers. Uncle Henry had
heard that there was a demand for chartered accountants
and that many young gentlemen had been attracted to
accountancy. (It is still a profession of some snob appeal
in Britain, partly because of the long and expensive train-

ing period required.) So he was articled to a chartered accountant, but he loathed the work and quit it after two months. Then he himself proposed that he study medicine, and his uncle and aunt agreed—with relief. His uncle was weary of problems concerning the future of his stubborn ward, and irked by them as well. Preparation for a career in medicine was a welcome solution. Moreover by the end of the nineteenth century it was a profession for gentlemen, no longer associated with yarb-doctors and barbers, as it had been seventy-five years earlier.

He entered St. Thomas's Medical School in 1892 as a "perpetual student"—meaning that he could remain a student for life, not qualifying if he did not wish to do so. But he took the normal course and period of study and qualified in 1897. St. Thomas's Hospital is of monastic origin and dates from the thirteenth century. Its group of eight buildings, some of which were badly damaged in World War II, fronts the Thames directly across from the Houses of Parliament. Much of the work of the Hospital has always been charitable. It adjoins the Borough of Lambeth, which in the 1890's was largely a slum district. The poor were usually treated in the Out-Patients' Department, which in Maugham's student days received about 25,000 patients a year. The Medical School had, and has, a high reputation; moreover it offered the would-be author an opportunity to live in London and to gain experience of life, which he wisely felt a writer must have.

For the first two years his subjects did not greatly interest him; he studied just hard enough to pass his examinations. He kept very much apart from his fellow students, few of whom in later years, somewhat to their chagrin, could recall the shy young man who later became famous. He did, however, find young companions with sympathetic interests—writers, musicians, artists—some of them fellow lodgers. (There were no student dormitories.) He enjoyed his living quarters at 11 Vincent Square, Westminster; he formed some needed friendships with fellow boarders; and he liked Mrs. Foresman, his delightful, motherly landlady with her Cockney humor, and later drew a modified portrait of her in *Cakes and Ale*. She was kindness itself and an excellent cook; moreover she possessed the common sense and the patience and tolerance a landlady must have if she is to find her arduous calling enjoyable. Her sharp Cockney humor was a source of delight to young Maugham, who entered in his notebooks many of her sprightly comments.

He has described himself when he entered St. Thomas's: "I was eighteen. I was ignorant, ingenuous, enthusiastic and callow." In a preface he wrote late in life for a new edition of a very early novel, *Mrs. Craddock*, he remarks that he probably would dislike the young man who was then Somerset Maugham. He never suffered the harrowing poverty of Philip in *Of Human Bondage*. "I lived nearly all my student years in a boarding house for eighteen shillings a week. Indeed my weekly bill came to no more than thirty shillings, and with an allowance of fourteen pounds a month, I lived very comfortably." Vincent Square, just off busy Vauxhall Bridge Road and not far from Victoria Station, is one of London's largest squares. Although a few of its old houses remain unchanged, including Number 11, as in Berkeley Square two-thirds of the old buildings have recently been replaced with imposing new structures: Vincent House, the Royal Agricultural Society's Hall, Westminster Technical College, and three hospitals. Number 11, a house with three stories and half-basement, belongs today as it did in the 1890's to the Church Commission. During the Second World War it was occupied by WAAF's, who had supervision of a barrage balloon in the square. During the war, however, accommodation was found for the aged Mrs. Foresman until her death. In the open area now are children's playgrounds, with a cricket pitch and tennis courts. The square has a quiet refinement. There is no suggestion of a slum area, and there was probably none in Maugham's college days.

He spent much time reading widely in British and European literature, writing, and filling notebooks with character vignettes, anecdotes, observations, epigrams, and plots for stories. There is no mention in his *Notebooks* of his reading medical books in his rooms, although he must have done so to prepare for his examinations.

When at the end of his second year he became a clerk in the Out-Patients' Department, his interest in medicine quickened. Instead of theories, chemical formulas, diagrams, and drawings, here was life itself. The novelist and dramatist in him became alert. He saw life at first hand stripped of reticence, gentility, and pretense. He saw suffering, fear, despair, and terror; he saw hope, courage, and bravery. He saw demonstrated the truth of many of La Rochefoucauld's *Maxims* and wrote similar ones in his Notebook: "We learn resignation not by our own suffering but by the suffering of others." "People are never so ready to believe you as when you say things in dispraise of yourself; and you are never so much annoyed as when they take you at your word." "An acquaintance with the rudiments of physiology will teach you more about feminine character than all the philosophy and wise-saws." "Science is the consoler and healer of troubles for it teaches how little things matter and how unimportant is life with all its failures." "If women exhibit less emotion at pain, it does not prove that they bear it better but rather that they feel it less." He was confirmed in his materialism and his bent toward Zolaesque determinism. "I was glad to learn that the mind of man (itself the product of natural causes) was a function of the brain subject like the rest of the body to the laws of cause and effect, and that these laws were the same as those that governed the star and atom."

As an obstetric clerk he brought sixty-three children into the world; in wry moments since, he has pondered over the worth of that achievement. It was during this time when he worked as an *accoucheur* in the slums that he wrote his first novel, *Liza of Lambeth,* almost a transcript of a "case." He had not read Stephen Crane's *Maggie,* a similar objective slum story published in America shortly before *Liza of Lambeth.* It is written in the detached, objective manner to which only a few English novelists had been attracted, among them George Moore. Maugham has always retained a good opinion of his first novel, and it is interesting to note that he named his only child Liza. An opera based on the novel has been written but so far (1960) has not been produced. Years later he told an amusing story about his first novel. The eminent critic Edmund Gosse praised the book highly, and thereafter over a long period of years during which time *Mrs. Craddock, Of Human Bondage,* and *The Moon and Sixpence* had appeared, Gosse repeatedly complimented him on his excellent *Liza of Lambeth,* adding, "How wise you are never to have written anything else!" (Maugham had a similar experience at Harvard University when Professor George Pierce Baker, the famous teacher of drama and playwriting, told him that the only play of his he was acquainted with was *The Mollusc.*)

When *Liza of Lambeth* was published he was twenty-three and in his final year in medical school. His last long school holiday he spent in Florence gathering material for another novel, *The Making of a Saint,* which he did not write until later. In 1897, according to the medical register, he qualified as a doctor, with the M.R.C.S. and L.R.C.P.—Member of the Royal College of Surgeons, and Licentiate of the Royal College of Physicians.

Although his small allowance from his father's estate and occasional assistance from his brother Charles permitted few or no luxuries, he had by no means been an impoverished student. The holidays which he did not spend in Whitstable, where the brash young medical student found less and less in common with his uncle, who spurned the theories of evolution and science in general, he was financially able to spend on the Continent. One holiday he spent in Capri and the neighborhood of Naples. At Capri an acquaintance named Brooks succeeded in conveying to him his own glowing enthusiasm for literature. Although Maugham had long been a reader, and had methodically acquainted himself with the great English and French classics, at Capri he experienced for the first time the enchantment and excitement to be gained from the great writers.

One piece of trivial Maughamiana has completely disappeared. In 1923 students at St. Thomas's asked their celebrated alumnus to write a skit for their Christmas show. He consented and sent them a one-act play, the setting of which was a hospital lift. The characters—a physician, a nurse, a patient on a trolley, and an operating-room attendant—get jammed in the lift when the cry of "Fire!" is heard. The entertainment committee after much discussion rejected the skit as too macabre and liable to cause panic. (In an audience of medical students?) The only script has vanished.

He never practiced, but he later regretted that he had not devoted three or four years to the medical profession; he is aware that the novels he wrote during his first three years out of college were of little worth. But *Liza of Lambeth,* which was accepted at once by the first publisher it was submitted to, was just successful enough to strengthen his determination to be a writer and thrust from his mind the idea of being a ship's doctor. Although the death of his uncle in 1897 had removed the last family pressure (except discouragement from his aesthete brother Henry) against what had appeared to the vicar a preposterous calling, he had made so little money from *Liza* that his close friends considered him foolhardy for abandoning his profession. There was little or no interference or discussion from Charles and Frederick, who were now firmly established in the legal profession.

His years at St. Thomas's had been invaluable to him. They had afforded him the opportunity to live in London and gain the "experience of life" he had yearned for. His study of science engendered in him a respect for the scientific method. His native tendency toward realism was

strengthened and he was able to avoid the pale aestheti-
cism and art-for-art's sake literary fashion of the period
when he was learning his craft. His one concession to
*fin-de-siècle* elegance was in the "artistic" furnishings of
his rooms on Vincent Square. He early discovered that he
had no gift or taste for fine writing and deliberately trained
himself to write simply, clearly, and euphoniously. He read
and reread the great masters of simple, clear prose: Swift,
Dryden, and Voltaire. He once said that he would not know
how to begin a novel if he did not first reread one by Voltaire. Perhaps most of all, at St. Thomas's he acquired a
knowledge of mankind he might never have gained at
Oxford. His imagination was fired by the drama of life
and the unpredictable and uncharitable in human nature.

Except for autobiographical elements in his three greatest
novels, *Of Human Bondage, The Moon and Sixpence,* and
*Cakes and Ale,* he has as a writer made little overt use of
his professional training. The number of physicians in his
stories and plays is probably no greater than that in the
writings of other authors. One volume of short stories,
*The Mixture As Before,* bears a title with medical associa-
tions, but the book could just as appropriately be called
*Ironic Tales.*

He went abroad and wandered about Spain and Italy, for
both of which countries he has maintained a deep affection. He went first to Seville, where generous British friends
invited him to stay in their house while he wrote his second novel; they knew how slender were his royalties from
*Liza of Lambeth.* In Seville he wrote an autobiographical
novel, never published, and *The Land of the Blessed Virgin,*
an undistinguished book except for a striking description

of a bullfight. This section an English friend translated into Spanish and it was widely read in Spain. He "fell in love with Cervantes." He stayed for a time in Toledo, but strangely enough on this first visit he did not become aware of El Greco, about whom he later wrote so much. He was to discover the great artist more than ten years after this visit through reading Maurice Barrès's stimulating book on him. Materialistic as Maugham is in his philosophy, he became fascinated by the Greek-Spanish painter's metaphysical turn of mind. Later in Paris, when he learned more about painting, he was able to recognize El Greco as a precursor of the moderns with his striking distortions of the human body, and his greater concern for color than for drawing; like other great masters El Greco is able to give depth to a painting by use of color alone, but unlike them he considered surface more important than depth. When in 1913 he read Barrès's exciting book, he packed up the manuscript of his partially completed *Beauty of Ashes* (later called *Of Human Bondage*) and went at once to Spain. He saw the El Grecos, and there are echoes of his excitement in the passages in *Of Human Bondage* describing the canvases of this haunting mystic.

Finally he went to Paris, where he lived with a group of artists and writers, once sharing an apartment with Gerald, later Sir Gerald, Kelly. He was much attracted by the exciting work of the new Impressionist painters. The story that Maugham bought Renoirs, Manets, and Pissarros for a trifle sixty years ago and thus started his incomparable collection of paintings is without foundation. With an income of £250 a year at the most, he did not buy pictures. Most of the paintings now at Villa Mauresque were acquired after the Second World War. The Zoffanys and other paintings and drawings that the new pictures replaced are now in various museums.

He wrote steadily, but with little financial reward. This is not surprising, for before *Of Human Bondage* (1915) only *Liza of Lambeth* and *Mrs. Craddock* had any real merit, and the latter was too styptic for the sweet taste of the time. His Paris years, however, were fruitful. He knew Arnold Bennett, George Moore, and other writers, including that weird charlatan and sometimes amusing rogue Aleister Crowley, later to be immortalized as Cronshaw in *Of Human Bondage*; he knew many painters and sculptors. He lived in a walk-up flat on the fifth floor of a house in Montparnasse, and was an observer of, if not an active participant in, the more or less romantic *vie de Bohème*. He was in the very center of electric new movements in art and literature. He was never impoverished, but his income was small and he had only distaste for Bohemian seediness; as a result he developed a canny, healthy, lasting respect for money. He has repeatedly called money the sixth sense, without which one cannot enjoy the other five. There were times when he was almost embittered by his near-poverty, but "near-poverty" is a relative term. To some of his Paris companions Maugham seemed a young man of means.

In his impatience to gain success in his hazardous profession, and he was now in his thirties, in his letters and Notebooks he sometimes exaggerated his straitened circumstances. The statement, however, in various newspapers on his eighty-fifth birthday—even in the graver morning London papers—that he had been stony broke and starving in the years just preceding the success of *Lady Frederick* is a piece of romantic invention. He always had his £150 a year from his father's estate and between 1897 and 1908 he earned an average of £100 a year from writing. He was never really poor. He was born in a luxurious apartment in Paris, and in his boyhood he lived in the spacious, comfortable Old Vicarage and in a rather expensive school for gentlemen's sons. His eighteenth year he spent in a satisfactory pension in Heidelberg. During his five years at St. Thomas's he lodged in pleasant rooms on Vincent Square; he could have lived more cheaply in Lambeth, close to the Hospital. For the next nine years he lived in Spain, France, Italy, and London on an income with several times its purchasing power in 1960, never in squalid poverty, never in want. But he had set his sights high: he yearned for the freedoms a greatly increased income would bring him. Finally in 1908 he achieved a crashing success in the theatre when four of his plays were performed in London concurrently; three of them ran for a year, and these three were also produced with success in America.

In spite of his failure to write a successful novel or before 1908 to have his plays produced, the exciting life in Paris at the turn of the century and his friendly and stimulating companions there brought him a measure of happiness and enabled him to look back on his wretched childhood with some detachment. He wrote when he was twenty-six, "The passing years are like a mist sweeping up from the sea of time so that my memories acquire new aspects." He acknowledged that what was once brutal and harsh seemed less so in this new retrospect, and that he was now able to look on his past with astonishment and even a little contemptuous amusement. When he was twenty-eight he wrote in his Notebooks that he had found what he believed to be the basis for a comfortable philosophy of life: a humorous resignation.

With success in the theatre came not only fame, which Maugham invariably calls notoriety, but freedom to do and to write what he chose. In 1908 he declared somewhat unconvincingly that success had little effect on him, for he always expected it and it was too natural to make a fuss about. But he rejoiced at the prospect of being free, perhaps forever, of financial worry. During the next six years before the outbreak of the war he supplied the English and American theatre with a number of fashionable comedies, lived in Mayfair, and moved in social circles quite unlike those in Victoria, Lambeth, and Bohemian Paris. He fell in love with Nan, the girl to be immortalized as Rosie in *Cakes and Ale* twenty years later. In 1912 he began writing *Of Human Bondage,* which he completed in two years, and the proofs of which he corrected in Belgium in the autumn of 1914 within sound of the big guns.

On the outbreak of the war, when he was forty years old, he joined a Red Cross unit in France and served as a dresser and ambulance driver. The descriptions in his Notebooks of hospital and battlefield horrors are as raw and powerful as anything in Zola, Dos Passos, or Remarque, but he never used this grim material in his fiction. As at St. Thomas's twenty years before, he saw how men died, some stoical, some frenzied with terror. A few months later he was transferred to the Intelligence Department and acted as a secret agent, stationed for some time in Geneva. "The work appealed to my sense of romance and sense of the ridiculous," and disillusion made it more ridiculous than romantic, for many of his activities were monotonously routine. He had excellent qualifications for Intelligence: his command of French, Spanish, German, and Italian; his shrewdness and native wit; his shyness, which served to make him inconspicuous; his vocation as a writer, which afforded a useful screen for his activities—in the hotels where he stayed he gave "writing" as his profession, and carefully left manuscripts of his plays on his bedroom table, knowing that his rooms would be searched. Switzerland swarmed with spies from half a dozen countries, filling the hotels, spending money freely (Switzerland's neutrality always pays dividends), all suspicious of one another, creating a serio-ludicrous atmosphere.

At first his secret missions took him only to ports on Lake Geneva, but he was finally sent to the United States on a "mission of information"—he and the aging but still amusing Lily Langtry were ship companions across the Atlantic—and to the South Seas on a mysterious assignment, the exact nature of which is buried in the archives of the Foreign Office. On this enchanting journey he first visited Hawaii, Apia, Savaii, Fiji, Papeete, Mirea, Tetiaroa, and other exotic places he was to help make known to readers the world over. He went from island to island in the South Seas with the eyes of a spinner of tales as well as those of a minor diplomat—or whatever he was. Characters and their stories were thrust upon him almost ready-made: for example the missionary, his stiff-backed wife, and the model for Sadie Thompson. The natives with their dignity and simple pattern of life impressed him more favorably than did the British government officials, businessmen, and

planters. He concluded that one would have to go far
to find among the planters a man of culture, reading, or
distinction.

Finally, in 1917, he was sent to Russia on a fantastic mission: to attempt to persuade the Russian government to
carry on the war against Germany and not sign a separate
peace, and to help prevent the formation of a Bolshevik
government. This visit quickened his interest in Russian
fiction, especially that of Dostoievsky; he was conscious
of a similarity between Dostoievsky and El Greco.
Maugham saw an important bit of modern history in the
making when he was a spectator at the Democratic Con-
vention; he also became acquainted with Savinkow and
Kerensky.

With his mission a complete failure and his health im-
paired he returned to England, stopping en route at Chris-
tiania. Here in the National Gallery he saw a fruit piece
by Gauguin which aroused a troubling emotion in him far
different from the effect the French-Tahitian painter's
canvases had exerted on him in his Paris days. *The Moon
and Sixpence* derives partly from this delay in the Nor-
wegian capital. He returned to England stricken by an
alarming recurrence of tuberculosis, aggravated by a want
of proper nourishment in Russia. As it was still war time,
a sojourn in Davos seemed impractical, and so he entered
a sanatorium in Nordach-on-Dee, Scotland, where he lived
a rugged, semi-outdoor life until he recovered. He enjoyed
his illness. He relished the cold silence, the privacy, and
leisure after the hysteria of the war. While there he wrote
his most amusing farce, *Home and Beauty*, and planned
a novel suggested by the strange life of Paul Gauguin. He

observed his fellow patients with sympathetic curiosity and
again studied human nature subjected to unusual pressures.
As when at St. Thomas's and in army hospitals, he saw how
men behaved when they knew that death was near.

In 1916 he had married Syrie, daughter of the well-known
philanthropist Dr. Thomas Barnardo and divorced wife of
Wisconsin-born Henry (later Sir Henry) Wellcombe, a
noted scientist. The Maughams had one child, Lisa, first
married to Vincent Paravicini, son of the Swiss Minister to
England at the time of their marriage in 1936, and later
to Lord John Hope. Lisa has four children. Syrie Maugham
was a career woman, one of the most eminent interior
decorators of her day, both in England and America. She
was responsible for the vogue in the 1920's of the bare, all
white and off-white interior décor. The Maughams were
divorced in 1927, and Syrie died in 1955. Mrs. Barnardo,
Maugham's mother-in-law, died in 1944 at the age of 102.
It was suggested by Alec Waugh that the failure of
Maugham's marriage was a boon to literature, for it drove
him to travel, but he was very much on the move before his
marriage. His wanderlust dates from his year in Heidelberg, when at the age of eighteen he journeyed throughout
Germany and neighboring countries. He is probably the
most widely traveled writer in all history.

After his release from the sanatorium, Maugham made
his second trip to the East, by way of America. For the first
time he visited Chicago and the Middle West and observed
the "middle-class" Americans. He found them as strange
and impenetrable as the Chinese until he read Sinclair
Lewis's *Main Street;* unlike millions of American readers
he interpreted this novel as primarily a story and study of

class-consciousness, and it clarified for him many things in the American character. *Main Street* was not the same novel for European readers, possibly not the same novel for the Nobel Prize Committee, as it was for Americans. He went on to California and from there to Hawaii, Samoa, Tahiti, Borneo, Malaya, China, Java, Siam, and other colorful places that soon served him well in short stories, novels, plays, and travel sketches. One purpose of the journey was to gather more information about the last period of Gauguin's life in the Marquesas, where the rebel artist died. Maugham had heard about him, of course, in Paris at the turn of the century, and his strange and exciting life suggested the basis for a novel. He gathered his material, wrote the short novel rapidly, and *The Moon and Sixpence* was published in 1919. It was much better received by the critics than *Of Human Bondage* had been four years earlier.

In the decade from 1921 to 1931, he, it would seem, traveled almost continually—to the Far East, the United States, the Near East, a half dozen countries in Europe, and North Africa—yet these were the years of greatest literary productivity: the sparkling comedies, *The Circle, The Constant Wife,* and *The Breadwinner;* the best of his exotic short stories as well as *Ashenden,* based on his wartime experiences as a secret agent; the excellent travel book (his favorite among all his books), *The Gentleman in the Parlour;* the fine collection of sketches, *On a Chinese Screen;* and the best of his novels, *Cakes and Ale*. But even when traveling, Maugham was always a writer. Wherever he was, at home, on shipboard, in a hotel, in the house of a British Resident, if it was at all possible he spent his mornings reading and writing. Consequently his travels did not diminish his productivity. His journeys took him not only to easily accessible seaports and tourist centers, but to islands in the South Seas rarely visited by Europeans and Americans. He went into the interior of Malaya and Borneo, unfrequented areas in the Dutch East Indies, deep into the jungles and up strange rivers. He was once nearly drowned in a bore on the Sarawak River. He used crude native boats and carts, and often walked miles when transportation was impossible. The inconveniences and strange and sometimes revolting foods he endured with patience and humor. At many places in the East where there were no hotels he stayed with British officials or planters, all of whom he saw with the eye of a novelist as well as a grateful guest. Abusive rumors circulated that, to put it mildly, he sometimes failed to conceal adequately the models of some of the characters in his Eastern stories or to disguise their shady adventures; as a result his published tales aroused embarrassment and resentment in some places.

The mysterious and faraway East of Maugham's stories has been altered by the advent of the airplane. Whereas Maugham's planter or British Resident was six weeks away from his London *Times,* he is now only two days. In the age of jet travel, he is only a day or so from Whitehall or Piccadilly or his estranged wife in Surbiton.

During this period Maugham traveled frequently to the United States, maintained a flat in London, and fell in love again with Spain; he rarely missed a year going to Seville, Cordoba, and other beloved Iberian cities, as well as to Venice and Florence. He once seriously considered taking a flat in Florence and spending a part of each year there.

In 1928 he bought an ugly Moorish villa near the tip of Cap Ferrat, a tongue of land at one time owned almost entirely by Leopold I of Belgium, projecting into the blue Mediterranean midway between Nice and Monte Carlo— one of the spectacular beauty spots of the world. After a long search he chose to live on the Riviera as most beneficial for his still imperfect health. The house had belonged to a bishop who had lived in North Africa, and who had imposed on his French house some startling semi-Oriental exuberances. Maugham had the Moorish gimcrackery removed, both inside and outside, and the result was a rather simple square house with a beautiful, spacious patio, the bishop's one praiseworthy borrowing from the Moors. Maugham had a working library and writing room erected on the roof, the few hilly acres landscaped, a swimming pool built on an upper terrace, and a garden of tropical beauty laid out. Although north of Chicago, Cap Ferrat has orange, lemon, and avocado trees (Maugham had the first avocado tree in Europe); even banana trees grow near by, and flowers bloom the year round. Villa Mauresque is not large and pretentious. It is far more modest than the stately homes of England and the large French chateaus, but it is both exquisite and comfortable. The site is of unparalleled beauty: to the west the red Esterel mountains, Cannes, Antibes, and Nice; to the north the incomparable village of Villefranche and its harbor, and behind Villefranche the snow-hatted French Alps; to the east Cap d'Ail, Menton, and the Italian Riviera; and to the south the incredible blue of the sea.

The house is filled with the treasures he has gathered all over the world, a tribute to his eclecticism, but there is no atmosphere of a museum, only of beauty and comfort. Some of his vast collection of pictures he has given away: Graham Sutherland's satiric portrait of him is in the Tate Gallery, and his eighty theatre prints are in the Victoria and Albert Museum, waiting for the erection of Britain's National Theatre, in which they will adorn the lobby and staircases. Every room at Villa Mauresque has its master-pieces, pictures by Toulouse-Lautrec, Monet, Gauguin, Renoir, Rouault, Matisse, Pissarro, Sisley, Utrillo, Picasso; in an upper hall is Marie Laurencin's charming portrait of Maugham. There are Chinese bronzes, jade carvings, and other *objets d'art*. Books are everywhere, on the shelves built into the walls, on tables in every room; new books and periodicals arrive regularly from half a dozen countries. Yet his insatiable wanderlust has for more than thirty years made Villa Mauresque a rest station between travels to India, North Africa, Central and North America.

In 1934 he journeyed to the West Indies and spent some time at the notorious French penal colony, Devil's Island. In spite of the lurid, melodramatic stories he heard and the characters he talked with, he used little of this material in his stories. Perhaps he was discouraged when administrative officers of the colony told him of a survey they had made: almost none of the murders committed by the convicts had been motivated by jealousy, love, hatred, or revenge; most of them had murdered for pecuniary reasons. Maugham has had no inclination to write *romans policiers,* though he likes to read them.

In 1938 he made a much more memorable journey, this time to India, where eighty years before his grandfather Snell had been killed in battle. Here as an observer of people and a novelist he became fascinated by Hindu mysticism and its place in everyday Indian life. He was in no way "converted" to a mystical view of life, although sensational and irresponsible stories of Somerset Maugham's trances and other occult experiences appeared in the British and American press. He has written about the holy men, swamis, fakirs, yogis, and Indian priests with sympathy and an honest attempt to understand them. For the British in India he was able to restrain his enthusiasm. Remembering the tremendous historical changes in India in the past two decades, we find a comment made in 1938 of particular interest. He recalled that Wellington is supposed to have said that the Battle of Waterloo was won on the playing fields of Eton; expressing his usual lack of fervor for snobbish public schools, Maugham prophesied that it might be said in the future that India was lost in the public schools of England.

He wanted to write a novel about India and planned to return there in the autumn of 1939 to gather more material. "I needed to see India again. I have never been able to write anything unless I had a solid and ample store of information for my wits to work upon." Although the war thwarted his plan to return to India and to write the novel, he was able to use some of his material five years later in *The Razor's Edge*, and a section of his last book, *Points of View*, deals with a holy man he had met in India during his unforgettable visit.

After the second world war he came twice to the United States and once to Egypt, Turkey, Greece, and the Grecian Isles, but otherwise he confined his travels to yearly visits to England, Italy, Austria, Switzerland, and Germany, and occasionally to Spain. In 1959, however, after completing what he firmly declares to be his last book to be published in his lifetime, *Points of View*, he announced that he was "now free to do some real traveling again." In the autumn and winter of 1959-60 in his eighty-sixth and eighty-seventh years he journeyed to the Far East, to countries he wanted to see once again.

In 1939 when World War II broke out, the British government (Maugham has always retained his British citizenship) asked him, and he reluctantly consented, to write cheery propaganda stories about France—her ability to carry on a war to a successful conclusion, manufacture weapons of war, and maintain a patriotic enthusiasm for what might be a long period of hostilities. Propaganda articles he found very hard to write. "I sweated blood on these trivial pieces. I am a poor journalist." He did not mean that he was an imperfect observer or an untrustworthy interpreter of what he observed; he meant that it was difficult to conceal or ignore in his reports half the truth or more, but even more difficult, in fact impossible, not to try for what to him is a high excellence of style in whatever he writes. Even in these unimportant, forgettable, government-inspired articles he tried for lucidity, simplicity, and euphony. It was a ridiculous waste of time and effort, for his accounts proved to be as arid and unconvincing as he feared they would be.

Few civilians had so thorough a knowledge of actual conditions in France and England during the strange first eight months of the war. He knew well and had often talked with government leaders in both countries; in fact, some of them had been guests at Villa Mauresque. In preparing his articles he went into homes of workers and into factories and visited the strangely quiet front lines. Out of his distasteful assignment and his personal observation of what happened to France in 1940, its most tragic year in centuries, there came from him one comment which we are now inclined to consider a historical truth. Noting that the French declared that they must preserve their way of life at all costs, he wrote: "If a nation values anything more than its freedom, it will lose its freedom, and the irony of it is that if it is comfort and money that it values most, it will lose that too." In spite of his affection for France he put the blame for their humiliating collapse directly on the French people's self-conceit and smugness. The French considered the Germans *imbéciles* and could not conceive of being defeated by such *bêtes*. In 1940 Maugham declared that France would never recover and be restored to her place as one of the great powers until her people learned to look the truth in the face and see themselves as they are; "they must learn not humility, which would be useless to them, but common sense."

When France was invaded in the late spring of 1940, life at Villa Mauresque was at its most pleasant—comfortable, cultivated, and yet simple. Liza and her husband were there, and other guests had just departed. Then came the shock of the invasion. Maugham knew very well that France was far less invulnerable than her patriots and his own propaganda articles declared, and he knew, too, that his own safety, even his life, was in danger; for he was on Goebbels' black list, and the Nazi armies were racing through Holland and Belgium and into France. Goebbels had denounced Maugham on the wireless, mentioning

*Ashenden* and treating it not as fiction but as a factual
account of dastardly British methods of espionage and by
implication branding Maugham as a major enemy of the
New Order.

All Britons on the Riviera were ordered by their government to leave at once, and two colliers were provided for
their journey from Cannes, Toulon, and Marseilles to England. Along with 1,300 other British stranded in the South
of France Maugham made his way to England on one of
the grimy vessels. The account of the long, hazardous, uncomfortable voyage is found in the author's readable book
*Strictly Personal.* Although not afraid of death and believing that there is no afterlife to be concerned about, ever
since he was nearly drowned in Borneo he had had an
unreasonable fear of drowning. He had to make a decision:
if he refused to go on the collier through dangerous seas
with enemy submarines beneath and enemy planes over-
head, internment was inevitable. He found that he preferred death, even by drowning, to a Nazi concentration
camp. He had with him an ample tube of sleeping pills to
bring him his release if he should be captured by the Nazis,
but he did not want to die. He was only sixty-three, he had
more books to write, and beyond that he envisioned an old
age when he could "indulge in the luxury of leisure." So he
chose to travel on the collier. The discomforts—among
them the allowance of a pint of water a day for each passenger for washing and all other purposes—the dirt and
cinders, the crowded conditions, and the constant danger
he accepted philosophically and now scarcely remembers.
One windfall of the journey was a new game of patience
which he learned from a woman passenger.

The perilous voyage to England took three weeks, for the collier swung far west into the Atlantic to avoid enemy aircraft. The imperturbable London *Times,* which except in the columns devoted to military news ignored the war as far as possible, in amusing, characteristic understatement reported Maugham's safe arrival in England: "Mr. Somerset Maugham has arrived in London from the South of France. He is tired but otherwise in good health." While waiting in London for another government assignment, he spent his time in a most unusual manner during the Battle of Britain: he made a thorough study of the writings of Edmund Burke, particularly of his style, for he had long been fascinated by Burke's management of the English language. The result of his strange wartime occupation appeared years later as an essay in *The Vagrant Mood.*

One evening when he was a dinner guest of the Duff-Coopers in their house in Westminster, a severe air raid brought clanging fire-trucks to the street outside, anti-aircraft guns banged away, sirens screeched, and an ominous red light could be seen through a chink in the black-out curtain. When the raid began, dinner was over and the ten guests were seated in the drawing room listening to a trio playing a long sonata by Haydn. No one except him, says Maugham, appeared to pay any attention to the holocaust. When the sonata came to an end, there was polite applause and the trio played another long composition. Later Maugham's brother Frederick told him that all during the bombing he slept every night in his own bedroom on the top floor of his house on Cadogan Square, scorning the basement shelter: he would allow no pipsqueak of an Austrian paperhanger to rout him from his comfortable bed. Maugham was reminded of elements in the English character he had forgotten about.

Finally he was sent by the Minister of Information, Duff-Cooper, to the United States for the duration of the war on a vague mission of propaganda and good will. The country was still neutral, although in general sympathetic to the Allies; but there were powerful pro-German and pro-Italian organizations, as well as the many patriotic Irish societies, all of which were violently anti-British. Even more powerful and vocal were the isolationist groups, particularly in the Middle West, with noisy spokesmen in Congress. A few months after his arrival the United States entered the war, and the nature of his mission, whatever it was, changed; his new duties were easier and less awkward. Most of his pleasant wartime sojourn he spent in South Carolina in a small, comfortable house on the plantation owned by Nelson Doubleday, his American publisher. Naturally he was still a traveler and made regular journeys to New York, and in the summers fled from South Carolina heat and mosquitoes to Martha's Vineyard. From the beginning of his residence in America he made occasional cross-country trips; and treatment of his stammer was now so successful that he was able to speak before audiences— very tactfully at the beginning, when the United States was not at war. By request of the Ministry he wrote a novel attempting to depict the life of an average English family during wartime, but he disliked the commission, and the result, *The Hour Before the Dawn,* is a dull yarn about an atypical English family. The author would like to have it forgotten entirely. While in South Carolina he wrote also *The Razor's Edge,* free of all taint of propaganda. It was spectacularly successful, and brought to the author a vast amount of fan mail from American and British servicemen, thousands of whom read the novel in the widely distributed paperback edition.

*The Razor's Edge* was probably the first novel with literary value, the first "good" novel that many of these servicemen ever read—to judge by the ingenuous and touching letters that they wrote. More than fifteen years after its publication Maugham still receives letters with comments on the novel and inquiries about the free-wheeling hero, who finds himself discontented with the very kind of life most of these servicemen were inevitably to lead. They were disturbed to find their concept of the good life challenged. *The Razor's Edge*, like *Of Human Bondage*, answers few or no questions, but leads the reader to ask himself questions about good and evil, justice and injustice, fact and superstition, the good life and the wasted life. Maugham still receives an occasional request for Larry's picture, and a few correspondents have asked for his autograph.

At the end of the war Maugham presented the manuscript of *Of Human Bondage* to the Library of Congress as a token of his gratitude for the hospitality accorded him, his daughter, and his grandchildren in the United States during the war. In his address of presentation he outlined simply what he considered the purpose and justification of a novel, and the qualities of a good novel. He also related the early story of *Of Human Bondage*, the first version of which was written when he was twenty-four, and was entitled somewhat grandly *The Artistic Temperament of Stephen Carey*. Luckily no publisher would advance him the hundred pounds he demanded as a down payment, and he refused to release it for less; if this relatively feeble novel had been published, he would never have written *Of Human Bondage.*

Although he never felt that he knew Americans well enough to utilize them to any extent in his fiction, he was observant, and his conversation and notebooks contain many reflections about them. He was amused by what he calls some American delusions: that there is no class consciousness in the country; that American coffee is good; that Americans are efficient and businesslike. He also observed that American love of oratory can be nationally dangerous, perhaps because Americans are more emotional than the English and more easily stirred. He noted that though American men have hosts of acquaintances, there are few deep friendships among men. He wonders whether when an American man marries, his wife does not engulf him and demand his undivided attention. He was puzzled by the decline of the spirit of adventure in America, the spirit that made the country great. He was amused by the indifference of Americans to the cooking of the food they eat and their enormous pride in the plumbing used for its excretion. Maugham has always liked America and has had hosts of American acquaintances and a few close friends ever since his first visit in 1910. One of his nearest friends was the Californian Bertram Alanson, and as they had planned many years before, Maugham made the long journey from the Riviera to San Francisco in 1949 to celebrate his seventy-fifth birthday with Alanson.

By 1946 he was able to return to the South of France and attend to the restoration of Villa Mauresque, which emerged from the war battered and wrecked. First the Italians took over and confiscated his automobiles. Then the Germans swarmed over southern France. They made an observation post of the villa and appropriated *Sara,* the forty-five-ton fishing boat, owned by his secretary, Gerald Haxton; it had been rebuilt into something like a yacht. During the Allied invasion the house was fired upon by units of the British fleet, and later British and American troops were quartered there. Maugham found the house in a deplorable condition; even floors and stair-steps had been torn out, for what purpose he could not guess. When he asked a faithful caretaker, who had somehow managed to remain in the villa or in the neighborhood during all the wartime vicissitudes, about his dogs he had had to leave behind, the old retainer said, "Alas, they have been eaten long ago." Miraculously the Gauguin window was unharmed; most of his greatest artistic treasures and books had been hidden, and those that were stolen were discovered and returned. Many are unaware of the remarkable work done by an Allied Commission in returning books, furniture, and pictures looted from French, Dutch, and Belgian homes. A large German van, for example, would back up to a house in Nice and haul away its contents with the cynical notice printed on the side of the truck, "Gifts from the People of Nice to the Bombed-out People of Germany." Maugham's house had to be almost rebuilt and the twelve acres relandscaped; while the author traveled, the reconstruction was completed.

Before 1950 he wrote his last novels, three of the four he had planned; none of the three equals in merit his best fiction, although *The Razor's Edge* approaches it. *Then*

*And Now* proved to have little distinction. He could not bring himself to write one of the four, a novel of lower-class life in Bermondsey, perhaps meant to give a pattern to his sixty years of novel-writing which began with a story of lower-class life in Lambeth. He wandered about the borough and found that the war had destroyed much of the old Bermondsey he had known, and the welfare state had rehoused its inhabitants and lifted their status to that of the not-so-petty bourgeoisie. Was it his imagination and prejudice that led him to doubt that they had improved spiritually, to be aware of envy and malice among them? He left the stories of the new Bermondsey for the angry young men to write. His last novel was *Catalina*, for which a long devotion to Spain and the Spanish people gave him the theme; it was in Spain that he had done his first writing after leaving medical school. It is a pleasant and—let us add the condescending adjectives bestowed on his work by some of the loftier critics—a readable and competent novel, which he is able to regard with satisfaction as his final work as a novelist.

For the next ten years he devoted himself to essay-writing, mostly literary criticism. He wrote on Burke, the detective story, Goethe's fiction, French journals, Kipling, Tillotson, etc., for his own satisfaction. The pleasure he found in writing his volumes of essays was mental, not physical, for he suffered severely from what is frivolously called writer's cramp. An orthopedist finally constructed for him a *corset digital*, which was awkward and uncomfortable but which made writing possible. He has always refused to dictate.

In the early 1950's he established a fund to award £500

annually to a young British writer who had already published one book, not a drama, of outstanding promise. The purpose of the award is to encourage young writers to travel and acquaint themselves with the manners and customs of foreign countries. Maugham hoped that the young writer by widening his own experience would "extend both the basis and influence of contemporary, English literature, which because of its provincialism is of less interest abroad than it should be." Many years before, Maugham had advised the mother of a would-be young writer, "Give him £150 a year and tell him to go to the devil!" He was not being facetious; he meant what he said. Judges for the Somerset Maugham award are appointed by the Incorporated Society of Authors, Playwrights, and Composers. Maugham has not always been happy with the results, but he makes no publishable comments. After all, he had instructed the judges to look for originality and promise and "not to play for safety." On the whole, however, he has been satisfied and feels that the award has been useful to some writers, although he suspects that one or two have "used it just for a jaunt." Philosophically he repeats the old saw about leading a horse to the water.

During the 1950's he traveled as much as ever, but usually not so far from Cap Ferrat. For a number of years he spent the autumn months in England, seeing his daughter and grandchildren, friends, exhibitions of new paintings, the National Galleries, a few new plays. Soon after 1950 he recorded some stories for the phonograph, and personally introduced some cinema and television versions of his own stories; but he found such enterprises tiring and distasteful and refused substantial offers to continue. In

1959 he was surprised to receive from the U.S.S.R. a check for £300 as a token payment on the royalties accumulated for him in Russia. He was the first British writer to be recognized financially by the unpredictable Russians.

In old age, however, came greater honors than a royalty check from the U.S.S.R. Earlier he had received an honorary degree from the University of Toulouse, and in 1939 in Paris he was made a Commander of the Legion of Honor. There were notable exhibits of Maughamiana: an impressive one in America in 1951 organized by Klaus Jonas; at the Times Bookshop in London in 1954—here also Sir Gerald Kelly's and Graham Sutherland's portraits were exhibited; in San Francisco in 1958 at a national meeting of librarians; in Tokyo in 1959 on the occasion of the author's visit. In 1952 along with Dean Acheson and Sir Oliver Franks he was awarded an honorary degree from Oxford. In presenting Maugham the Public Orator drew attention to the remarkable number of chance resemblances between his precepts for writers and those of Horace in the *Ars Poetica*. In 1954 on the occasion of his eightieth birthday the gratifying climax of various events in London was a dinner tendered to him by the historic Garrick Club. In the long history of this famous club only three other members had been similarly honored: Dickens, Thackeray (Maugham's father had proposed Thackeray for membership in the Garrick), and Trollope. In the same year on the BBC there was a season of Somerset Maugham: five full-length plays, five dramatized short stories, and several other stories read in full. Also in 1954 he was received by Queen Elizabeth, who invested him with the insignia of the Order of the Companions of Honor. In 1958 Maugham, Sir Winston Churchill, and Dame Edith Sitwell were elected vice-presidents of the Royal Society of Literature.

He has said that he looks upon his life as a novel or a play with a happy ending. It is a sound observation in spite of the fact that he has had as much unhappiness and frustration as the average man; he has had to combat the threat of tuberculosis for more than seventy years, and has been afflicted with a painful speech defect all his life. He was unable to marry the one woman he felt a deep affection for, and his marriage to Syrie was a mistake from the beginning. One should not, however, exaggerate his unhappiness, for certainly he has had a rich life and has known satisfactions and triumphs denied most men. Above all, he has had a realistic philosophy that has enabled him to cope with seasons of discontent.

In his eighty-sixth year he confessed that old age brought him a great tranquillity in the sense that he was conscious of having done just about everything he ever wanted to do, seen everything he wanted to see, and had nearly every experience a man is capable of having. His assertion, "Now I am prepared to call it a day," we can accept only with reservations, for like Tennyson's Ulysses he is still curious about life and the world, still feels the urge to travel and to learn. He has never abandoned his simple belief that one tries in vain to find a meaning in life, and therefore the only meaning for life is to live. He prefers to go on living. He has achieved the kind of life pattern that he desired. He has troops of friends. His interest in reading, bridge, travel, conversation, and art is unabated. He remains a hedonist to the end and has been able to provide for himself comfort and beauty, almost regally to gratify every desire, and to escape from monotonous routine that would for him make life juiceless. His most intimate friend was of the opinion that Maugham had never been happier in his life than he was in his eighty-sixth year.

Still, like any one who reaches a great age with all his mental faculties unimpaired, he has his memories, some of them painful. In *Points of Views* he writes: "What makes old age hard to bear is not a failing of one's faculties, mental and physical, but the burden of one's memories." (How could Carl Sandburg, a wise man, dismiss the past as "a bucket of ashes"?) When Maugham was twenty-one he wrote that the more intelligent a man is, the more capable he is of suffering.

There will be at least one more book by Somerset Maugham. He is writing a volume of reminiscences which is in part so incandescent that he will not consent to its publication (perhaps it will be only privately printed) during his lifetime. His statement to reporters just before he sailed from Marseilles for Japan in 1959 that he had finished writing, that he was "an extinct volcano," was, to put it mildly, at least misleading. Nothing he has ever written has more fire in it than the autobiographical work he was engaged in writing at that time.

It is to be hoped, too, that some of his letters, always pointed and cryptic, will be published, in spite of his rather foolish request that all letters written by him be destroyed. It is good to learn that the burning of papers and manuscripts he and Alan Searle perpetrated in 1959 left some sections of his Notebooks untouched. They will not be published until after his death "and then only if my executors agree that they are worth publishing. If by then

I am entirely forgotten, they will obviously be of no inter-est." What a pity that Maugham never kept a journal like Arnold Bennett and Jules Renard, or Emerson or Thoreau! "I never wrote anything about my meetings with interest-ing and famous people. I am sorry that I didn't." He wished that he had recorded his conversations with the many dis-tinguished writers, painters, actors, statesmen, and poli-ticians he has known intimately. During the years he has entertained many of them at Villa Mauresque, some of them important, many of them well known but unimpor-tant: kings without thrones and their consorts, most of the distinguished British, French, and American writers (those who travel) of the past thirty years, Adlai Stevenson and Winston Churchill—their names would fill pages.

When Ilka Chase visited him at the time of the Grace Kelly-Prince Rainier wedding in near-by Monaco, she was, like everyone who goes to Villa Mauresque, enchanted by the Renoirs, Toulouse-Lautrecs, and the Picassos, the gracious rooms and patio of the villa, the gardens and terraced hillsides, the swimming pool that would be re-spected even in Hollywood. It occurred to her as she walked with Maugham past his orange and avocado trees: "An engaging combination of the sharp and mellow and very wise. Neither an assembly line nor a stock market nor an oil well did it, simply what came from one small skull and that one right hand . . ."

## II

## THE ENIGMATIC
## SOMERSET MAUGHAM

A GREAT deal of nonsense has been written, mostly in periodicals in a dozen or more countries, about Somerset Maugham's enigmatic personality, iconoclasm, and sardonic view of his fellow men. It is probable that no author has ever been interviewed so often and at so many different points of the globe. Wherever he has gone, and he has gone nearly everywhere, he is greeted or accosted by newspapermen and photographers. When he arrived in Japan in November 1959 a small army of journalists and a hundred photographers were waiting on the dock. When his automobile appears on a street in Nice, it is almost certain to be followed by a *Presse* car. On the rare occasions when he dines in public, he is hardly seated before reporters and cameramen appear. There is hardly a day at Villa Mauresque when curious strangers are not discovered walking in his gardens, for the entrance is open and there is no gate-keeper. Literally hundreds of American sailors

64

whose ships have put in at near-by Monaco or Villefranche have rung the doorbell of the villa and asked to see Mr. Maugham—or Mr. Moggam.

Journalists by the hundreds have all but invited themselves to Villa Mauresque, his apartment at the Dorchester in London, or wherever he may be staying, and fired questions at him, often the same questions he has been asked for the more than fifty years since his sudden success in the theatre in 1908. He is invariably as courteous to men and women of the press as he is to nearly everyone, from his chauffeur to a visiting ex-prime minister. He would agree with Charles Lamb, an author he usually finds unreadable, that the measure of a gentleman is not his behavior to a duchess, but to a parlormaid. "I am not annoyed by the questions and curiosity of newspaper reporters. That is their business." He is annoyed by strangers who force themselves on him out of mere curiosity.

In a thousand printed interviews the words "inscrutable," "enigma," "mysterious," "mask," "secretiveness," "puzling," "riddle," have been used over and over so that most readers of or about him regard him as the personification of mystery and concealment. In hundreds of articles his natural shyness and the reticence and reserve of a gentleman have been warped into the kind of theatrical arcana one finds in the Sunday supplement of a sensational newspaper.

When he was eighty-five, for example, a French journalist wrote of his "unpitying eyes and complete lack of tenderness." In a book published the same year it was asserted that he is yearning to believe in God and is ripe for conversion to Catholicism, and that he is indifferent to his family. A well-known American critic and professor of literature wrote recently that Maugham loves no one and nothing. A popular woman journalist describes his face as "unbelieving and guarded" (what is an unbelieving face?). A popular English novelist is of the opinion that Maugham fears being sympathetic, for sympathy implies condescension. One of his friends, a dramatic critic, writes of Maugham's "thick skin," which led him to "write obituaries for the human race." Harold Nicolson feels that Maugham is at times straining toward the Atman or imperishable Soul (whatever that means). One could quote such remarks by the hundreds. The absurd charge has been made that he discourages biographies because he wishes to be regarded as a man of mystery. Just before his first book was published he made an acute observation that may throw further light on his objection to a "life." He noted that people marvel at the romantic lives of writers, whereas they should marvel at their gift of expression. It is the man who is important; many things that happen to a writer are of profound interest to him but would pass unnoticed in the life of the average man. "It is the man they happen to that makes their significance."

Although Maugham wants no biography and has asked that all letters written by him be destroyed, he himself has written freely of the lives of other authors and has not refrained from including disreputable details of characters and shabby episodes in their lives. In *Ten Great Novels*, of example, one learns more about the quixotic behavior and the aberrations of Herman Melville than he learns of Maugham's view of *Moby Dick*. On the whole, however, his approach in these ten discriminating essays is justified;

one reads *Madame Bovary* with more understanding and pleasure when he has read Maugham's illuminating analysis of Flaubert and account of his life and personality. In the other volumes of essays published in the 1950's he writes about the private lives of the Goncourts, Goethe, and others with enormous gusto. Had he so chosen, he could have been a most entertaining biographer of the Lytton Strachey school.

Maugham is of course sound in his judgment that human behavior is often incalculable. Early in life he became aware of ironic contradictions in character; he learned that human nature is complex, that divided loyalties often make man's motives perplexing or obscure to himself as well as to others. He learned that a kind and devoted son and father can be dishonest in business matters, that a generous person can be egregiously self-centered, even selfish, that extreme piety and cruelty are often present in the same person. He once remarked on the difficulty of using an interesting acquaintance in a novel and making her believable. She was, he said, a liar, a snob, and a quarrelsome bully. She was jealous, vindictive, vulgar, and vain. But she was also charming, tasteful, generous, hospitable, and sympathetic. "She is hateful and lovable, cruel and kind, egotistic and unselfish." He asks, how can a novelist make such a character credible? The reader's demand for credibility sometimes leads the novelist, and even more so the dramatist, to oversimplify human character. Readers and audiences demand clear motivation such as is rarely found in real life. (It is Chekhov's refusal to yield to this demand that adds a fascination and piquancy to his plays and stories.) Everyone has had the experience of being astonished by the actions of someone he thought he knew well; everyone has been puzzled even by his own conduct. Who has not admitted, "I don't know why I did such a thing"? Attempting to analyze himself when he was twenty-one Maugham confessed that he looked over various parts of his character with perplexity, conscious that he was made up of several persons. "But which is the real me? All of them or none?" Somerset Maugham is enigmatic in the same way that all men are imperfectly known. "Every man is a dark forest."

Actually he is one of the least puzzling and enigmatic of all writers. To begin with, his prose style, like Bernard Shaw's, is lucid and unequivocal: a reader may not always agree with what he says, but he understands it. He is not a member of the crossword-puzzle school of writers, who receive the attention of little quarterlies and esoteric scholarly journals. There is little excuse for any reader's being baffled by Maugham's religious beliefs, literary and aesthetic tastes and theories, attitude toward humanity, ethical judgments, concepts of the good life, attitude toward death, belief in a physical basis of personality and character, or his views on the meaning (or meaninglessness) of life; as well as his cynicism, misogyny, and hedonism. He has made himself clear on all these matters, so much so that in comparison we know far less about Dickens, Kipling, and Hawthorne; we know even less about writers like Hugh Walpole, whose public appearances and contributions to popular journalism made him into a minor public figure; or novelist-peachers like Lloyd Douglas, who opened his heart to millions of readers in the 1930's and 1940's. Perhaps the real enigmas are the Norman Vincent Peales and Billy Grahams, whose platitudes convey emotionalism but little precise meaning. Maugham has analyzed his personality and clearly outlined his philosophic, religious, and aesthetic beliefs. As a writer he has freely acknowledged his debt to Dryden, Swift, Voltaire, and Maupassant. When asked directly, he has discussed the origins of most of the characters in his books—Mildred Rogers in *Of Human Bondage* is one notable exception. He has told so much about himself as a dramatist and story-writer that he, like Bernard Shaw, has spoiled the chances for dozens of Ph. D. theses of the *policier* type.

There is no mystery about his religious views. He has been an atheist since boyhood, and the account in *Of Human Bondage* of Philip's sloughing off his religious beliefs is autobiographical. He has never regained these beliefs or regretted losing them. There is nothing ambiguous about the entry he made in his Notebooks when he was twenty-seven: "I'm glad I don't believe in God. When I look at the misery of the world and its bitterness, I think that no belief can be more ignoble." It is inconceivable to him that there can be an after life. When still at St. Thomas's he expressed the hope that death would cover his years with night. He has no capacity for the kind of idealism that enables one to believe a thing is true because he wills it to be true. Whether or not he ever read a certain letter written by Thomas Huxley to Charles Kingsley, he would agree with its sentiments. When Huxley's young son died, Kingsley in an attempt to comfort the scientist wrote to him that he *ought to* believe in immortality. Huxley replied, "My business is to teach my aspirations to conform to the facts, not to try and make facts harmonize with my aspirations."

Idealism, Maugham asserts, can lead only to hypocrisy. For example, he considers that the mainspring of most action is love of self; since this is natural, we can suppose that it is necessary for self-preservation; but by making a vice of self-interest, idealism (or Christianity) has made men into hypocrites. As to the romantic, comforting notion that pain ennobles and strengthens the character, it has been his observation that it more often makes men peevish, self-pitying, and disagreeable. The uses of adversity are not always sweet. Much of our vaporish talk about idealism seems to him to stem from hypocrisy or a cowardly wishful thinking. To a great extent he agrees with Mark Twain, who was a far blacker pessimist than Maugham, that everyone expects a return for his unselfishness, that all our altruistic acts arise from egoistic motives. One wonders, though, about Maugham's own generosity, his aid to young writers, which is more extensive than is generally known, his other benefactions, his many kindnesses to people who cannot repay him. It would be illuminating to have him analyze his own philanthropies and many acts of seemingly disinterested kindness.

He attacks idealism not only because as a man of reason he deplores wishful thinking, but also because, like Ibsen and Bernard Shaw, he believes that it is harmful. In one of Ibsen's plays a character says bitterly, "Don't use that foreign word *ideals*; we have a good native word, *lies*." Maugham agrees with Shaw that many of the ideals with which young people are brought up (he calls them fantasies and fairy tales) unfit them for life. They can never achieve a basic happiness until these illusions are shattered. Who, he asks, is responsible for this well-intentioned but

St. Thomas's Hospital, where Maugham received his medical training.

Somerset Maugham at 32, 1906

Somerset Maugham in 1910

pernicious indoctrination? "Half-educated persons, mother, nurse, masters, who surround the youth with their loving care." In her partly autobiographical novel *The Pursuit of Love* Nancy Mitford has young Fanny comment that the "great advantage of living in a large family is that early lesson of life's essential unfairness." In his old age Maugham made the observation that idealism leads religious people to ascribe to God omnipotence and omniscience, but not common sense and tolerance. "If he is capable of feeling, he must be capable of remorse," he reasons, "and if so, with his omniscience he must see what a hash he has made of things." As to God's omnipotence, Maugham makes the fanciful suggestion, worthy of Thomas Hardy, that perhaps he has used it to destroy himself. Maugham has never found any satisfactory explanation of the compatibility of evil with an all-powerful and all-good God. Perhaps one can be an idealist only if one is able to make such a reconciliation.

He possesses no conventional religious beliefs or faith whatever. As a reader of history he has found that faith is strongest during periods of diminished vitality; he acknowledges that faith to those who have it "solves difficulties which reason finds insoluble." Not all, however, is black negation. There are elements in Maugham's philosophy of life that suggest more than just love of wisdom and a guide to day-by-day living. He praises the bravery of spirit that man can at times exhibit, and man's ability to rebel against fetters that cannot be broken. He exhorts man to keep in his heart the spark of freedom that enables him to continue a hopeless battle, asserting defiantly to the last that pain and suffering, poverty and friendlessness are bad things, not mysterious manifestations of a higher good. Maugham is content to accept the universe as an enigma that the wit of man cannot solve. Finally, like Bertrand Russell, he finds a partial answer to the black pessimism of the Book of Ecclesiastes in the courage and dignity with which man is able to face the irrationality of the world. Although man is a reed, he is not the feeblest in nature, for he is a thinking reed. For all his reputed cynicism and misanthropy Maugham believes in a basic nobility in man depending on neither culture nor breeding, but rooted in man's instincts. That man on occasion can act with splendor of spirit provides some refuge from despair.

He notes that unfortunately man does not often exhibit this nobility of spirit. When a brash nineteen years of age he wrote that most men are such fools that it is no great compliment to say that a certain man is above the average; the older and wiser Maugham would deplore such a cheap generalization. He does not assume that his fellow men will behave altruistically or exhibit what he calls nobility of spirit, and hence when they do, which is more frequently than he expects, he is agreeably surprised. He has never suffered the pessimism of the disappointed idealist, but his disaffirmation, like Mark Twain's, of all altruism we must accept with reservations.

But that is all. When anyone speaks to him of the Higher Good and of the Absolute's being richer for every discord, he answers quietly, without bitterness, "I have seen a child die of meningitis."

If in the ordinary meaning of the words he has no religious faith, he has long had a philosophy that provides him with the *aes triplex* every man needs on his pilgrimage through life. The core of his philosophy is found in the writings of wise men in all ages; in the nineteenth century it received its classic expression in Ralph Waldo Emerson. When Maugham says, "Our business is right living. The problem of right living is complicated by the fact that there is no one code for everybody; one's job is to find out what is right for oneself and then follow it," he might be summarizing in a sentence Emerson's "Self-Reliance." The closing words of *The Summing Up,* actually a quotation from the sixteenth-century mystic and lyric poet Fray Luis de Leon, rephrase the credo: "The beauty of life is nothing but this, that each should act in conformity with his nature and his business." A widely approved moral code, Maugham admits, is useful to the weak-minded, but the strong evolve their own. He found middle age tolerable because he had formed his own code; he had "reached a reconciliation" with himself; he suspected that young people are often unhappy because of "their vehement desire to be like other people."

The attempt to shape a philosophy which would provide him with enough serenity and courage to accept the inevitable was not an easy task. As a boy and young man he was tormented by his failure to find answers to his questions. When he was twenty-two he arrived at the conclusion that everything in life is meaningless, that pain and suffering are futile. "There is no object in life." But this negation afforded him no comfort at that age. Even as late as his fourth year at St. Thomas's he found himself repeatedly asking, What is the meaning of life? What is its object or end? What guide to conduct is there? "In desperation I cried out: I can't understand it! I don't know!" There came a time, however, when he was no longer tortured by his inability to find answers to his questions and a meaning in life. The moving passage in *Of Human Bondage* in which Philip, sitting before the two-thousand-year-old gravestones in the British Museum, realizes exultantly that life has no meaning and that therefore he need no longer suffer in vain attempts to find one is a condensation of a much longer experience. "Thinking of Cronshaw, Philip remembered the Persian rug which he had given him, telling him that it offered an answer to his question upon the meaning of life; and suddenly the answer occurred to him: he chuckled: . . . The answer was obvious. Life had no meaning . . . Philip exulted . . . He felt inclined to leap and sing. He had not been so happy for months."

Maugham himself does not remember having any such experience in the Athenian marbles rooms of the British Museum. Unlike Philip he arrived at a disburdening and consoling unbelief only after much reading of the philosophers and five years of scientific study of a sort. Although the scene in the novel is invented, before he was out of his twenties Maugham had come to the same negative conclusions as those which he ascribes to Philip.

He formed his philosophy of life not only from reading Plato, Spinoza, and Schopenhauer and from his scientific "studies" at St. Thomas's, but also from his realistic scrutiny of people and their behavior, and finally from a deep belief in necessitarianism, or determinism. His study of science, although he declares that it was most primitive and rudimentary in the early 1890's, persuaded him of the inevitability of cause and effect, with no mystical intervention in the relationship. In 1944 he wrote that might, not right, would win the war. He admitted that it was cruel to say such a thing and that our prejudices as well as our idealism lead us to deny it, but it is true. His advice to nations is that they make sure to have the might to defend their own conception of right.

Moreover, he arrived at the scientific, non-religious certainty of the irreparableness of every act; we must not assume that our mistakes are remediable. He would agree with Bernard Shaw and Lady Macbeth that what is done cannot be undone, at least not by such figments as repentance, penance, forgiveness, and absolution. One can be appalled by one's past errors and resolve not to repeat them, but one cannot undo them. ("Go and sin no more," is the simple, uncompromising dictum of Jesus.) "Can they unburn me?" asks Joan of Arc when she appears in the king's dream.

It occurred to him that a man who sits out in the rain for a noble object is just as liable to get rheumatism as the drunkard in the gutter. The rain actually does fall on the just and the unjust alike. He became convinced, like Zola and Dreiser, that what we call character has a physical basis, that its origin goes back to that of the individual organism, and that physical conditions, especially environment, influence it after birth. "It is very hard that a person through no fault of his own should possess a character, perverse and difficult, which condemns him to an unhappy life." He notes that some novelists are evidently unconscious of the importance of physical traits and their effect on character. "The world is an entirely different place to the man of five foot seven from what it is to the man of six foot two."

When he was seventy years old and reviewing his three

score years and ten, he pointed out how accidents of the body can shape one's "soul"—one's consciousness of oneself, the "I in the personality which is me." He declares that his "soul" would have been quite different if he had never stammered and if he had been several inches taller. Had proper attention been given to his teeth when he was a child, the cast of his face would have been different, and consequently so would the reaction of his acquaintances, and hence his disposition and his attitude toward his fellow men. The new physical environment provided by the socialist state so changed the people of Bermondsey that he abandoned his projected novel about them. His travels convinced him that climate, food, and other physical influences help determine character. He has said many times that bodily pain often is brutalizing. (A French engineer, an educated and cultivated man, confessed that he became so hungry in a Nazi labor camp that he attacked his closest friend and tore some moldy potato peelings from his hand.)

He also believes that freedom from physical want and distress can soften and improve a man's disposition, and consequently his character. He has welcomed this mechanistic view of man, not only because it harmonizes with his concept of common sense, but also because it has protected him from the delusions suffered by the idealists. A young British novelist whom Maugham regards as promising is John Braine. In his *Room at the Top* the opportunistic hero notes that charm comes from a gracious living, which is a by-product of an ample income. His landlady's son had charm and a winsome personality because the family could afford to give him the background for it. "It is astonishing how often good hearts and silver spoons in the mouth go together."

The frequent assertion by critics that Maugham writes as a clinician with the detached, systematic habit of observation found in the scientist's laboratory, thus revealing his training in medicine and surgery, is not convincing. Similar pronouncements have been made about Schnitzler and Chekhov. If these three writers were not known to be physicians, critics would probably not hear laboratory echoes in their stories and plays.

Maugham's ethical views derive from his largely materialistic philosophy of life. He believes that the requirements and necessities of day-by-day living form our ideas of right and wrong, which change when these requirements change. He was delighted to find this rarely quoted but unequivocal advice by a respected father of the Church, St. Chrysostom: "Do not ask how these [Old Testament precepts] can be good, now when the need for them has passed: ask how they were good when the period required them." Maugham agrees with Thomas Huxley that man's study of ethics is a part of his study of nature, for, Maugham says, "man must learn his place in the world before he can act rightly and reasonably." He has also made the harsh statement that morality depends partly on the state, for might is right. He accepts with equanimity the fact that many, perhaps most, of man's actions are motivated by selfish reasons, even his "good" actions. He points out that people often feed the hungry so that they can better enjoy their own meal. Unalloyed altruism he believes is rare, a pleasing figment of man's imagination, and one is unwise

to expect it of others. It must be noted again that Maugham
never recovered from his first encounter with La Rochefoucauld, who supports his skepticism concerning man's
morality. The fact that "people will sometimes forgive you
the good you have done them but seldom the harm they
have done you" is a tart observation that serves many times
as a motif in his stories and plays; and it comes straight from
the French aphorist.

Maugham, however, imperturbably denies the common
charge brought against him that his philosophy of life
and his view of man are cynical. He confesses that his native
gifts are not remarkable but that he has common sense to
supplement his deficiencies. "I can see what is in front of my
nose . . . the greatest writers can see through a brick wall.
My vision is not so penetrating. . . . I have been described
as a cynic: I told the truth." He is not an utter misanthrope.
As he has said many times, because he expects little from
man he is more pleased than most people when he en-
counters unselfishness and goodness. Some critics have
gone so far as to tag him as a romantic when he writes about
saints and heroes. It is interesting to note that he finds
Alyosha Karamazov the most delightful character in fiction—an unexpected and disconcerting choice to those who
dismiss Maugham as a cynic. Except for humbugs and
vulgar opportunists among his characters he seldom expresses contempt, more often a sort of pity. His indigna-
tion, when there is any, he directs at Providence, not at
men.

He has found much to like in unpretentious people who
have an eye for things other than the main chance. One
wishes that he had written about his beloved brother

Charles, who has been described by all who knew him as a saint. He always wrote with affection about his unselfish landlady on Vincent Square, Mary Ann of the vicarage, his pathetic, browbeaten aunt, and other unaffected, modest people he has known. No thorough cynic would remark as he did in 1917 when he was engaged in Secret Service work, "The majority of us are fairly decent, doing our best in that state of life in which chance has placed us; and if we believe in a judgment we feel that God has too much wisdom and good sense to bother about failings which we mortals have no difficulty in forgiving our neighbors."

As to the charge of hedonism brought against him he admits its truth and defends himself, declaring that all men choose to do that which is a pleasure to them. He adds that although he is an Epicurean, he is also abstemious when sense demands that he be, for though all pleasure is good, some pleasures have harmful consequences and have to be avoided or enjoyed in moderation. Many caustic things have been said and written about Maugham's luxurious habits, his comfortable and beautiful home and automobiles and servants. Would some critics have handled him less roughly if his books had had a slender sale and he had been forced to live more austerely? He finds that at times it is fashionable to despise, or pretend to despise, material and transient pleasures, and that hypocrisy inevitably follows such pretense. He reminds the religious who live in a certain way in hope of eternal bliss that they are the supreme hedonists. Maugham is a realist and philosopher as well as a hedonist and knows that pleasure, like happiness, is incidental, not an end in itself, that happiness will escape the *bon vivant* who fixes his mind on the search for pleasure. A character in *The Circle* remarks that there is no more lamentable pursuit than a life of pleasure. And pleasure, of course, need not consist only of sensual gratification; Maugham knows, too, the pleasures of the mind.

There is nothing enigmatic about his hedonism, his love and defense of the good life. He says that no sensible person can deny that throughout man's history the sum of unhappiness has been greater than the sum of happiness. Man, then, is justified in whatever harmless pleasures he can wring from a world indifferent to his welfare. Maugham long ago conceived of his life as having a pattern with a design to provide him with a maximum amount of harmony and satisfaction. Because he wove his pattern with intelligence and taste, it has served him well, so well that in old age he has admitted that in spite of his unhappy childhood, his stammer, and "many severe illnesses, tuberculosis, dysentery, malaria, and I know not what," in spite of his having suffered from poverty [he has elsewhere denied that he ever "suffered from poverty"] and the anguish of unrequited love, disappointment, disillusion, "that his has been on the whole a good life, better than most people's."

For one bitter accusation brought against him there is considerable justification, his misogyny. What caused it? His stammering and indifferent health as a youth that made him unattractive to girls? Portraits of him as a schoolboy at King's, as a medical student and as a young man in his twenties and thirties suggest that contrary to what he has said about his early infirmities he was sturdy and handsome. Was it the reaction of a man of sense against the Victorian

...way at Villa Mauresque.

A portion of the interior of Villa Mauresque

*Paul-Louis*

idealization of women, which struck him as hypocritical? He is reticent about his own sexual experiences, although his confession that the dreadful Mildred Rogers in *Of Human Bondage* is a composite portrait, or a "sublimation," may be illuminating. And to resort to disagreeable jargon, his "mother-complex" (Maugham would no doubt say of this phrasemongery what he says of "nymphomaniac"—"a very silly word") may have forced him to set his sights too high. He has admitted that after more than seventy-five years he has never recovered from the hurt caused by his mother's death, and we are reminded how moved he was when he tried to read about the death of Philip's mother in the first chapter of *Of Human Bondage* for a recording. Certainly his unsuccessful marriage did not soften his misogyny.

With only a few exceptions in his fiction and plays he has treated women and the sexual impulse unromantically, one would think with chagrin and annoyance to his millions of women readers. Sally and Norah in *Of Human Bondage* and a few other women characters escape unchivalrous treatment, among them Rosie Driffield (Nan), who came directly from the author's experience and emotion. In spite of her faithlessness and promiscuity he writes of her in the novel always with affection and admiration, though without romantic glorification. But Rosie is his one heroine who came from the heart and not from detached, unemotional observation. His affair with Nan came to an end after a period of eight years when it became obvious that a durable alliance was impossible; but the incomparable experience, although of unrequited love, probably contributed little to his failure to view women romantically. There was never the least tinge of bitterness in his feeling toward Nan.

A witty and sardonic professor of gynecology at St. Thomas's introduced into his lectures devastating remarks about women which no doubt amused the twenty and twenty-one-year-old boys listening to him, of whom Maugham was one. When success in the theatre opened the doors of high society to him, he was not enchanted by the lion-hunting hostesses who specialized in artists and writers. He concluded that no man is quite so cynical as a well-bred woman. He analyzed just why women writers, beginning with Charlotte Brontë and her Rochester, have exalted the strong, silent man. There are, he suggests, three reasons: he offers women protection; strong as he is, when he is submissive to their influence, their innate desire for domination is flattered; and silent men, whether strong or not, give women more opportunity to do the talking. Whatever truth there is in his assertion, made in his twenties, that if it were possible decently to dissolve marriage during the first year, not one in fifty couples would remain united, only experienced sociologists and marriage counselors could estimate. Years later in the Far East the wives of planters and government officials aroused as little admiration in him as did their husbands. Although one finds an occasional Sally, Mrs. Talbret, Mrs. Athelny, or kind landlady in his books, it must be admitted that he regards thoroughly good women as the exception. Most of his women characters fail as wives, mothers, or mistresses.

One generalizes about Maugham's misogyny, but it is surprising to examine the seven important women charac-

ters in his most widely read novel, *Of Human Bondage.*
Two are pathetic and treated with sufficient sympathy:
Aunt Louisa and Fanny Price. A third is fundamentally
pitiable, too, lonely and sexually frustrated as life has
passed her by, a bit ludicrous but not despicable, Miss
Wilkinson. Norah, Sally, and Mrs. Athelny are cheerful,
likable, and unselfish. Only Mildred is obnoxious. To offset
this generous treatment in *Of Human Bondage,* we should
remember the odiousness of the two principal women
characters in *The Moon and Sixpence* (the native women
of the Islands he writes about with respect), and the phari-
saical second Mrs. Driffield and the rapacious Mrs. Barton
Trafford in *Cakes and Ale.*

His views of literature and art, aesthetics in general, are
in no way enigmatic, for he has always expressed himself
freely and clearly concerning fiction and drama, the mis-
chief done to the creative arts by propaganda, his predilection for story-telling. He believes that nothing in fiction
becomes dull and out of date so quickly as the topical and
up to date. Once when H. G. Wells was a guest at Villa
Mauresque he discovered an entire shelf of his own books,
which thirty years before had been cram-full of revolutionary ideas and had blown a million cobwebs out of young
minds. Wells ran his finger along the many volumes, turned
to Maugham and said, "They're all as dead as mutton,
you know."

His early acquaintance with a number of young artists
in London and Paris, his close friendship with one or two
of them, his sojourns in Seville, Toledo, and Florence, his
discovery of El Greco and the French Impressionists all
deepened his interest in painting and helped make him

a gifted amateur critic. Whatever he writes about Velasquez, Zurbaran, Murillo, El Greco, Vermeer, Titian, the
Barbizon School, and the moderns is illuminating. But
when he becomes philosophical about the value of art he is
uncharacteristically vague. His frequent assertion that the
primary value of art lies in its effects, that is, not in the
beauty but in the promotion of right action, he fails to
make persuasive. What evidence is there that more good
action is done by people who daily cross a beautiful bridge
than by those who cross an ugly one, or that guards in the
great museums behave better than guards in factories?
Is there more good action in Venice and Florence than in
Wolverhampton and Akron? One would expect Maugham
to agree at least partially with Emerson (and his brother
Henry Maugham) that beauty is its own excuse for being.
In his essays and digressions in his novels he always asso-
ciates beauty with art, although his own wide tastes and
his private collection reveal a sympathy with modern non-
representational painting of a kind that aims not at "beauty"
but at vitality and a suggestive power sometimes obtained
through distortion and the grotesque, or through superficially simple geometric patterns. Puzzling abstractions
as well as Renoirs and Manets hang on the walls of Villa
Mauresque.

Although he makes no pretense of being a literary critic,
he rarely fails to arouse our interest in this comments on
his wide reading. He never allows the technical phraseology
(or the jargon) of the professional critic to obscure his
remarks. He does not write clever essays on symbolism,
time, and myth in literature, but allows us to share the
experience of an intelligent reader of Balzac, Dickens,

Tolstoy, Goethe, Eliot, Kipling, Yeats, Dostoievsky, Flaubert, Melville and many other writers he has enjoyed. Even though one may be totally unfamiliar with Goethe's novels one finds himself reading Maugham's essay on this unlikely subject with absorbing interest. The clever quarterlies would no more welcome his critiques than they would the delightful gossipy chitchat about writers by Van Wyck Brooks. It was pointed out in 1959 that his final book, *Points of View,* was as old-fashioned as its title, and recalled such bookish tomes as Lowell's *From My Study Windows* of seventy years before. There is justification for such an analogy. James Russell Lowell did for his generation what Maugham to a much lesser extent has done for his: he shared his wide reading experience with others. A lover of great books for seventy years or more, Lowell was a reader to the end. When Oliver Wendell Holmes visited the dying Lowell and asked him how he was feeling, he replied, "I haven't the slightest idea. I am reading *Rob Roy.*" It would be pleasant to think that Somerset Maugham will go into the long sleep with a copy of a book by one of his great favorites, Stendhal or Balzac, open and propped up in front of him, or perhaps his favorite of all novels, *War and Peace.*

# THREE AUTOBIOGRAPHICAL NOVELS

## *Of Human Bondage*

Thousands of readers have enjoyed *Of Human Bondage* without knowing or even caring about its autobiographical nature. They have found it a complete and satisfying novel, and like most readers of fiction have had little interest in authors and the background of books. Many other thousands, however, have been deeply curious about the personal elements in the story. It is probable that no other autobiographical novel, not even *David Copperfield* or *The Way of All Flesh,* has ever aroused more curiosity about similarities in the life and personality of the author and those of the principal character in the book.

*Of Human Bondage* is not an autobiography but a novel. The reader must not take a word of it literally, for Philip Carey's adventures are not an exact transcript of the author's. Maugham admits, however, that in general Philip's backgrounds were his own and that he drew from his own experiences for many episodes in Philip's early life; moreover, he has confessed that the book is largely autobiographical in spirit, that into it he poured the bitterness and frustration of his early life, so completely that the book provided for him a great psychological catharsis. That is why he wrote the long and harrowing story of Philip Carey. Yet the book is not actually depressing, any more than *Antigone, Hamlet,* or *Anna Karenina,* for in art only stupidity and banality are depressing. For all the loneliness, suffering, and unhappiness, the book is not negative in essence, for it traces the hero's evolution from painful uncertainty and bewilderment to maturity and spiritual freedom. Eventually he achieves adjustment and a reasonably satisfying philosophy of life. Although Philip's (and Maugham's) exultant discovery that life has no meaning may seem grimly existential, it is for Philip a positive and liberating discovery that enables him to come to terms with life.

In a brief address when he presented the manuscript of *Of Human Bondage* to the Library of Congress in 1946 Maugham told what he remembered of the origins of the novel, omitting some details that he had included in a preface prepared for an edition published in 1934. After the modest success of *Liza of Lambeth,* at the age of twenty-three he went to Seville and settled down to write an autobiographical novel. Following the ornate fashion of the day, he gave his second book the pompous title, *The Artistic Temperament of Stephen Carey.* "It finished with my hero at the age of twenty-four, which was my own age when I finished it, and it sent him to Rouen, which I knew only from one or two visits, instead of to Heidelberg, which I knew so well; and it made him study music, of which I knew nothing, instead of making him study painting, of which in later years I was to learn at least a little. I have never had the courage to read it again." Fortunately he was unable to get it published on satisfactory financial terms. There was a further difficulty: the publishers feared that Mudie's, which would have been largely responsible for circulating the novel, would object to the episode of Miss Wilkinson. Maugham put the manuscript aside and started writing *The Making of a Saint*. But he could not get "Stephen Carey's" story out of his mind. "I could not forget the people, the incidents and the emotions. . . . The book continued to write itself in my mind and many things that happened to me found their place in it. Certain of my recollections were so insistent that, waking or sleeping, I could not escape from them. My memories would not let me be. They became such a torment that I determined at last [in 1912] to have done with the theatre till I had released myself from them."

He was aware that the novel was too long for popular taste, the long Victorian novel being temporarily out of fashion, but he was writing not to please the public but to free himself from an unbearable obsession. He declared that he achieved the catharsis he aimed at, for neither the incidents nor the people ever tormented him again; in fact they seldom crossed his mind except in casual recollections or in attempts to answer the many questions he has been asked about the novel. "I cannot remember it in detail, but I am sure it has many grave faults. It represents what I was when I wrote it, but I hope I am now wiser, more tolerant, and more amiable. I know now much more about the technique of the novel and I think I write better English." This last admission explains partly why he considers *Cakes and Ale* a better novel than *Of Human Bondage*. He first called it *Beauty from Ashes*, from Isaiah, but learning that another novel bore that title, he made the happy change to *Of Human Bondage*, from Spinoza. He was struck by the philosopher's assertions that we can make experience valuable when by the use of our imagination and reason we turn it into foresight; that thereby we can help shape our future and cease to be slaves of the past; that the submission to passion is human bondage, but the exercise of reason is human liberty.

He corrected the proofs in the autumn of 1914 in a billet near Ypres, by the light of a candle, within sound of the big guns. Some of his fellow workers in his Red Cross unit were mystified by this singular activity of Dr. Maugham. Since its publication he has opened the book only once—in 1945, when he was asked to read the first chapter for a recording for the blind. "I did not make a very good record of it because I was moved, not because the chapter was particularly moving but because it recalled a pain that the passage of more than sixty years has not dispelled." As a matter of fact, when he was reading the chapter in the studio, he broke down and wept and was unable to complete the recording at this time. This touching incident leads one to wonder whether writing *Of Human Bondage* provided a thorough catharsis after all. Maugham is too modest: the first chapter, written simply, unemotionally, almost bleakly, in which a dying mother sees her young son for the last time, is very moving. In Chapter Five the doomed woman has her photograph taken—"She wanted her son to know what she looked like at the end." The incident was from life, and Maugham still has on his bedside table this photograph of his lovely mother taken in 1882.

There is no question about the strong autobiographical nature in all except the closing section of the book. Although it follows the general pattern of such popular English autobiographical novels as *David Copperfield*, *The Way of All Flesh*, *Sinister Street*, and *Clayhanger*, it differs from them in its complete simplicity. The hero is pictured without defense or undue explanation. There is no effort to conceal Philip's faults—his inordinate sensitiveness, his self-pity and egotism, his stubbornness and aloofness, his snobbishness. The author seems so determined not to idealize Philip that at times he makes him almost repellent. He can be masochistic when he feels the need for suffering, a morbid desire to be tortured. He yearns to do Griffiths "a bad turn." He has little self-control, although he seems to have it because he is "indifferent to many of the things that move other people." He admits that he is envious. His treatment of Norah is brutal. He cannot forgive his uncle and cold-bloodedly longs for his death and the legacy he will receive. His passion for Mildred is revolting. He views the members of the firm of accountants and the pathetic staff at Lynn and Sedley's with snobbish condescension. It is remarkable that we are able to harbor much sympathy or affection for Philip. Yet we do, and rejoice when his struggles come to an end and he arrives at a philosophy that enables him to face his days with confidence. It is an unvarnished portrait, for when at the age of thirty-six Maugham started to write *Of Human Bondage*, Philip was the boy and young man he remembered himself to have been.

In the early part of the novel many of the factual differences between Philip's and Maugham's experiences are
minor. Mrs. Maugham died in 1882, Philip's mother in
1885; Mrs. Maugham died in Paris, Mrs. Carey in London;
in the novel the father died first. Whitstable becomes Blackstable, and Canterbury becomes Tercanbury. Maugham's
aunt died when he was in medical school and the vicar
married again soon afterward, three years before his death
in 1897.

The vicarage, built in 1871, hardly a notable period in
domestic architecture, is far more attractive than the novel
suggests, for in the book we see the place through the eyes
of the unhappy boy. It is still called "The Old Vicarage"
although no clergyman has lived there since 1924, when
a new church house was built next door to the church, a
mile away. The spacious stone house stands in beautifully
landscaped grounds of more than an acre, with pleasant
gardens, shrubbery, clumps of trees, stretches of smooth
lawn, a tennis court, and two ornamental pools (by one of
which in the novel Philip rather uncomfortably makes
love to Miss Wilkinson). The house and grounds are much
the same today as they were in 1882, except for modern
plumbing and heating, a garage, and usually an automobile
or two standing in the widened driveway. The heavy drapes
and oppressive Victorian furniture have gone, and the
rooms are bright and cheerful. Since the drawing room
where the vicar had his Sunday afternoon nap, like drawing
rooms in many houses today, is little used and the study is
small, the cozy dining room is still the "sitting room" as it is
in the novel. Willie's little room at the head of the stairs—
the unattractive wood carvings of the Four Evangelists

have been removed from the balusters—looks much the same with its narrow bed, bookshelves, and chair. The large tree is still in front of the bedroom window. Across the road opposite the front gate is "The Limes," mentioned in the novel, and behind it is "The Manor House," the owners of which shared the daily *Times* with the vicar. Life at the vicarage, described in the novel with dry humor, was probably much as Maugham remembered it after thirty years, except that, as he later admitted, he was probably somewhat unfair to his uncle.

Maugham, of course, never had a club foot, but his bad stammer occasioned a mental anguish as painful as that caused by a more noticeable physical deformity. For some people stammering, like toothache or hay fever, has an element of the comic or grotesque, and does not arouse a sense of pathos, but Maugham knew from his days at St. Thomas's how easily such people could feel a warm sympathy for a crippled child. At King's School the boys laughed at his stuttering, and the masters, as it seemed to the unhappy, lonely boy, were impatient and sometimes even brutal, taking a sadistic delight in humiliating him. In Chapter Thirteen we read, "Philip passed from the innocence of childhood to bitter consciousness of himself by the ridicule which his club-foot [stammer] had excited." The analyses in the early chapter of Philip's religious experiences are essentially factual. The touching incident of Philip's prayer to be healed of his club foot is taken directly from Maugham's own experience: when his stammer did not disappear in spite of his complete and passionate faith, he suffered his first religious disillusion.

The account of Philip's exhilarating year at Heidelberg

is almost completely autobiographical. For Maugham it was an exciting year of growing up. Here as he gazed down at the Rhine valley he was moved by its beauty, and it was borne upon him what art might offer to the spirit of man. From Heidelberg he made his first journeys, throughout Germany and into Italy, and learned the delights of change and travel. In the lively municipal theatre he made his first acquaintance with the revolutionary new drama of the early 1890's. For the first time he had intelligent, brash, and disputatious companions, and largely through them his conventional views of religion, truth, and ethics were challenged. In Chapter Twenty-nine is a moving account of the start of the author's long quest for a philosophy of life.

Like Philip, Maugham was uncertain as to a profession when he returned from Germany in 1892. With his uncle's approval he, too, underwent a brief period of training to become a chartered accountant. He entered medical school the same year at the age of eighteen, much younger than Philip. During his first two years at St. Thomas's he spent much time in general reading and filling notebooks with ideas for stories and plays, for like Philip he was not much interested in the preliminary courses and lectures of the college. Although not a brilliant student, he never failed as does Philip; he successfully completed his course in five years and was qualified at the early age of twenty-three.

Miss Wilkinson is founded on an Alsatian friend of his uncle, a governess in France, who spent one or two holidays at the vicarage. Fanny Price was drawn largely from a pathetic and talentless girl Maugham knew in Paris in 1904. The most teasing question concerning *Of Human Bondage* is, of course, who was Mildred in real life?

This odious creature we can be sure is not altogether a product of Maugham's inventive imagination. The few literary detectives who fancy that they have found an answer to the question seem content to keep their secret and accept the author's partial answer: he had no one protracted and tormenting love affair like Philip; the Mildred episode is only remotely similar to an experience in his youth—he calls it a "sublimation" of this experience. Maugham confesses that all the excruciating details of the graceless and humiliating affair with Mildred are largely fictional except one, and this, ironically, is the most incredible of all. Seized by "a devil of self-torture," Maugham actually gave his rival five pounds as Philip finances Griffiths' jaunt to Oxford with Mildred. So far as the novel is concerned, to what extent Mildred is drawn from life is of little or no importance. She is a completely realized human being, unforgettable, one of the most hateful, disagreeable female characters in fiction. Readers have confessed to hissing when she appears on a page. Maugham's skill as a story-teller is never more manifest than in his making her a living, believable woman, and in convincing us that Philip, fastidious as he is and thoroughly aware of her vulgarity, hard lack of sympathy, and appalling unfaithfulness, still loves her with all his heart.

Unlike Philip, Maugham never studied painting in Paris, although he lived there for some time at the beginning of the century. His Paris friend Gerald Kelly served partly as the model for Griffiths in *Of Human Bondage*, and later checked this novel and *The Moon and Sixpence* for accuracy in matters of painting. An acquaintance, Gilbert Clark, who in a bleak period of financial distress had been employed at Swan and Edgar's on Piccadilly Circus, gave Maugham the material for the melancholy chapters describing Philip's near-slavery at Lynn and Sedley's on Oxford Street; for the purposes of fiction the novelist exaggerated the hardships of the shop assistant. Maugham, of course, never suffered such excruciating poverty. The character of Cronshaw was suggested by Aleister Crowley, an eccentric poet and dabbler in the black arts who was notorious in his day and whom Maugham, along with the whole crowd of English expatriate writers, had known in Paris in 1904. Crowley was at times a most entertaining rogue, at other times a sinister but tedious charlatan, who in violent reaction against the crudities of his parents' Plymouth Brotherhood was pleased to nominate himself as the "wickedest man in the world." Crowley, who had a dynamic but chaotic intellect, great erudition, and no common sense, was less attractive than Cronshaw.

Up to the end of the book many incidents are taken from Maugham's life. The details of hospital activities and Philip's adventures in the Out-Patients' Department are almost transcripts of actual experiences. Philip dreams of journeying to the Far East—Malaya, Siam, China, India— faraway places which Maugham saw himself visiting if he should abandon his ambition to become a writer and take a post as a ship's doctor. But at the end the novel veers sharply from Maugham's life. He did not marry until nearly twenty years after he qualified, when he was a well-known dramatist; and he did not marry a naive, uneducated girl like Sally, but a career woman, the sophisticated daughter of a celebrated physician and philanthropist. He was still unmarried when he wrote *Of Human Bondage*.

The first sentences of the novel are, "The day broke gray and dull. The clouds hung heavily, and there was a rawness in the air that suggested snow." The final sentences are, "He smiled and took her hand and pressed it. . . . They stood for a moment at the balustrade and looked at Trafalgar Square. Cabs and omnibuses hurried to and fro, and crowds passed, hastening in every direction, and the sun was shining." This cinema-like ending seems somewhat disingenuous and fabricated. Many readers have found it banal and unconvincing, or at least have objected that it is "conventional" to bring the novel to a close with Philip's supposedly happy marriage to an uncultivated, uneducated girl whom he does not even love. They cannot believe that Philip would choose a wife so commonplace. Maugham admits that the ending was an exercise in "wish-fulfillment" at a time when it seemed to him that a writer or artist should have a wife who would give him comfort, kindness, and peace; she need not, perhaps should not, share his intellectual interests, and certainly should exert "no spiritual influence"—whatever that may be. Such a wife as Sally would seem dull and stupid to worldly-wise outsiders, but Maugham says, "Becky Sharpe may be great fun, but give us the tender Amelia to live with." When he was completing the novel, he was growing tired of the rhinestone glitter of London society, the monotonous round of fashionable "entertainment," and perhaps tired, too, of the smart, knowing, conventional women he sat next to at a hundred dinner parties.

It has often been suggested that this long novel could very well end with Philip's gaining his freedom from Mildred, for many readers feel that this sordid love story constitutes the novel's main concern. Actually the book's central theme is Philip's quest for a philosophy that will free him from intellectual and emotional bondage—that will enable him to meet life with equanimity, courage, and humor. The climax of the novel, one of the most moving scenes in modern fiction, in which Mildred plays a minor part, is the episode in the British Museum, when Philip finds the answer to his agonizing question as to the meaning of life. He rejoices in his new-found freedom from bondage to established beliefs that have offended his intelligence and to the bondage of his degrading passion for Mildred. His humiliating experience with her is only one of many experiences that have enabled him to know himself.

The book had only a very modest success when it appeared in 1915. Readers in the second year of a war that was bringing sorrow or tragedy into nearly every English home were in no mood for a long, largely dolorous novel. The review in the influential *Times Literary Supplement* was not propitious. Without knowing the impulse back of the writing of the book, the reviewer complained that Maugham got his effects by straining. "It is partly the fault of the day, when novelists in general are tainted with the notion that only the miserable things are worth writing about." The critic especially resented having to spend so much time with such a repulsive female as Mildred. "Love and happiness are no less 'life' than lust and misery and quite as good material for fiction, if our novelists would see it." Along with such banalities the reviewer calls attention to the Persian rug allegory, shrewdly pointing out that there is a definite significance in the design of a Persian rug, for every figure in it has a symbolical meaning. The acceptance of *Of Human Bondage* as a novel of unusual merit might have been delayed for years had not Theodore Dreiser's laudatory and persuasive review appeared in the New York *Nation*. It was followed within a few weeks by other favorable notices in American journals, for in 1915 Dreiser was an authoritative critic among the intellectuals. Even with the novel's modest transatlantic success, it was not widely read until the best-selling *The Moon and Sixpence* four years later drew attention to the earlier novel. Since then *Of Human Bondage* has been a great favorite. Like *The Razor's Edge*, it has an especial appeal to young men and is widely used in English courses in the schools. Maugham viewed this dignification of his novel with misgiving: "It has now gained the doubtful honor of being required reading in many educational institutions. If I call it a doubtful honor, it is because I am not sure you can read with pleasure a book you have to read as a task. I had to read *The Cloister and the Hearth,* and there are few books for which I have a more hearty dislike." Many an American high-school student could heartily substitute *The Tatler and Spectator Papers* or *Silas Marner* for *The Cloister and the Hearth*.

He wrote *Of Human Bondage* after a long period of playwriting, the influence of which is discernible in the dialogue as well as in the general economy and precision. Here he follows more scrupulously his own advice, "Stick to the point," than he does in *The Moon and Sixpence* and *Cakes and Ale*. The dialogue is spare and stark like that in prewar plays by Barker, Hankin, and Galsworthy. The style of the novel is not exactly mannered, but the attempt, like that of Hemingway a few years later, to make plain

drawing room at Villa Mauresque.

Maugham in his study.

Ed.

statements of fact with few adjectives results for occasional readers in monotony. They feel such a style cannot give proper expression to deeply felt emotions and lyrical feeling. They assert that Maugham in going so far to avoid richness and the jeweled phrase has not always escaped dryness and flatness. Some readers have wished that he would "let himself go." A reader of fiction interested in the disparate uses of the English language could profiitably examine any page from a novel by Joseph Conrad or Thomas Wolfe and compare its style with that of *Of Human Bondage*. Maugham believed that the subject matter of his novel did not warrant the use of a relaxed and urbane colloquial style, which he was to handle with success later in *Cakes and Ale*. Most readers are certain that the novel often gains in strength and reality because of its severity and plainness; narrative passages such as those in the first four chapters are moving and powerful because they are stripped and bare.

On one topic, however, he allows himself the luxury of relaxing from his determination to stick to the point, and that is when he writes of art. These digressions in *Of Human Bondage* can be only partly defended by Philip's (and Maugham's) deep interest in painting; they contribute little to the main theme of the novel. But they are so interesting in themselves that even few Philistines skip them. These tangential discussions of Velasquez, Manet, Degas, and El Greco are instructive and free of the jargon of conventional art criticism. Thousands of readers of Maugham were first made acquainted with El Greco through *Of Human Bondage* and *Don Fernando,* parts of which could serve as corollary guides to Toledo and the Prado Museum in Madrid; in a similar way a generation earlier gallery-goers were prepared by Browning not only to look at Andrea del Sarto's Madonnas but to see them (and Lucrezia) as well.

The complaint that the novel is too stark and unrelieved —it has been called one of the "best read" rather than "best loved" novels of the century—that it is too bleak and cheerless is understandable. One of the author's oldest and best friends, a great reader himself, confesses that he has never been able to read it, although he knew the models for some of the characters and was familiar with much of the background. The novel is not without humor, but much of it is astringent if not downright bitter. The portraiture is sometimes salty, but there is nothing in it of what Goldsmith calls laughing humor. The delineation of the lazy, pampered vicar, the simpering Miss Wilkinson, the literary parasite, Upjohn—even the priggish and puritanical young Philip—is not even bittersweet. There are some dryly humorous episodes: the little boy being seated on the Bible and Prayer Book at the dining table; the substantial tea enjoyed by the vicar immediately after Aunt Louisa's death; the selection of the inscription for the tombstone; Mildred's displays of phony gentility. Such briny humor, however, is not enough for those who demand relief from a naturalism they find almost painful.

This complaint, from the novelist's point of view, is unreasonable. Maugham wrote the kind of book he was impelled to write in 1912, and wrote it with complete honesty. We must believe him when he declares that he wrote it to rid himself of an intolerable obsession, not to please readers. Such candor and honesty, however, do not in themselves produce a great novel. It is easy to agree with Maugham's judgment that *Cakes and Ale* is a more satisfying example of the novelist's art. Ironically, however, with the unpredictability, if not the perversity, of the reading public, *Of Human Bondage,* which he wrote for himself to have done once and for all with painful memories of the past, indifferent to the supposed tastes of readers of fiction, has had twenty times as many readers as the gay and cheerful *Cakes and Ale,* which was written in high spirits with great ingenuity and artistry.

In a letter written in 1954 to the author of this book Mr. Maugham gives his explicit attitude toward a "life": "There are in the United States and England eleven people [the number has since more than doubled] altogether who are anxious to write my biography. Several have applied to me for sanction. I have invariably refused to have anything to do with any such scheme. In my Will I have instructed my executors to refuse permission for the publication of any of my letters. I know quite well that I cannot prevent anyone from writing a biography, but as he will never have any more than such data as he can acquire from my books and from the reminiscences of people who have known me, why should I care? I am all against the writing of a biography for a variety of reasons. I would not in the least mind the whole truth being written about me, but it would be gravely embarrassing to other persons." In a letter written three years later he writes: "I know quite well that three or four people in the United States and the same number in England are impatiently waiting my demise in order to write books about me. Of course I cannot prevent anyone from writing about me that wants to, but in my Will I have inserted a clause instructing my executors not to assist in any way persons who wish to write about my life. In any case, no one knows the facts except myself." And on his eighty-fifth birthday he wrote: "You know how little I like to read about myself, but was forced to read . . . . . . . . . . . .'s book. It is full of inaccuracies . . . and he has an unfortunate knack for so repeating a sentence of mine as to kill the point."

His insistence that no "life" of him be written has only partial justification in his assertion that he has come much closer to telling the truth about himself in *Of Human Bondage, The Moon and Sixpence,* and *Cakes and Ale,* the travel books, his many prefaces, *The Summing Up,* and the *Notebooks* than could any biographer writing from the outside. No biography or autobiography is final; there is no such thing as a definitive biography. Biographies of great figures of the past have to be rewritten for every generation. Even the most complete and exact life is only partially true. One would have thought eighty-five years ago that Nicolay and Hay's gargantuan *Life of Lincoln,* written by two men who knew him more intimately than any man in public life or any member of his family, and who had access to government documents and private papers, would suffice for generations; but who besides Lincoln scholars reads it now? Who wants to read lives of Napoleon written in the 1820's? Through the medium of his fiction and to a lesser extent in his notebooks and critical writing we possibly do learn more about Maugham than from factual accounts of his life. Nevertheless he is only partially justified in discouraging a biography. Thoreau wrote about himself for more than twenty years, but how unfathomable an original he would be if Emerson and Canby had not also written about him. Maugham's further argument that no one knows the complete story of his life is indisputable, but it is true of every one. It is probable, however, that we learn more about Maugham from his books (especially the novels) than we learn of most authors from their own writings, and we shall some day have the autobiography, or autobiographical fragment, he is now writing for publication after his death. Until a detailed, documented life of Somerset Maugham appears, and a few years hence there will be a number of biographies, *Of Human Bondage* will provide a satisfactory account of Maugham as a young boy and as a medical student.

## The Moon and Sixpence

Although generally acclaimed as a minor masterpiece of twentieth-century fiction, *The Moon and Sixpence* is inferior to *Of Human Bondage* if judged by one of Maugham's own criteria of the good novel—that the story must take precedence over all other elements. It is above all, like much of Maugham's fiction, a study in paradox; it is a long illustration and analysis of one of his favorite convictions, the half-truth that runs through most of his fiction and plays like a leitmotiv, that human nature is unpredictable, that the secret places of man's heart and mind are rarely penetrated. In spite of the excellent characterization and some dramatic episodes, *The Moon and Sixpence* is slightly essayish in flavor; it is full of digressions and comments on art, philosophy, and man's quixotic conduct.

Though the narrative was suggested to Maugham by the

life of the French-Tahitian painter Paul Gauguin, there are strong autobiographical elements as well, and for long stretches Strickland's adventures are of subordinate interest. On rereading *The Moon and Sixpence*, one is surprised to find that almost half of the book is devoted to the story of Dick and Blanche Stroeve, the Dutch painter and his unfaithful wife. Their sordid and barely credible tragedy clearly illustrates Strickland's sardonic inhumanity, but one wonders whether the novelist may have distended their dreary misadventures because Strickland's own story is hardly sufficient for a full-sized novel. There are other digressions, such as the long account of Captain Nichols' career and the essay on beachcombers, and the unlikely story of Dr. Abraham. Although these excursions violate one of the author's own principles—"stick to the point"— they do not annoy the reader, for they do not violate an even more basic precept of good fiction: that it must hold the reader's interest. Nor does *The Moon and Sixpence* for the most part lack the qualities of a good novel listed by Maugham: "It should have a coherent and plausible story, a variety of probable incidents, characters that are living and freshly observed, and natural dialogue."

The plausibility of the narrative derives mainly from its having been suggested by the strange life of the stockbroker turned painter, Paul Gauguin. "Suggested" is the proper term, for *The Moon and Sixpence* is not a biographical novel. When Gauguin's widow read *The Moon and Sixpence*, she declared that she saw no resemblance between Strickland and her husband, and, happily, she saw none between Mrs. Strickland and herself, for she was not offended. When the novel first appeared, it was not at once associated with Gauguin. There is no mention of the painter in the earliest reviews. Maugham had heard of Gauguin and seen some of his paintings at the turn of the century when he was intimate with a group of young painters in Paris, who had been excited and even disturbed by the few boldly colored canvases on occasional exhibition. When the story of Gauguin's Tahitian adventures and his harrowing last illness and death in 1903 became known and when his exquisite *Noa Noa* was published, the novelist was struck by the dramatic possibilities in a story based on the painter's life. On a secret mission before the end of the First World War, Maugham went to the South Pacific, and while there he took advantage of the opportunity to talk with natives and Europeans who had known the artist.

Among those willing to talk about the mysterious Frenchman was Lovina Chapman, a half-caste (Tiaré Johnson in the novel), the monstrously obese proprietress of the Hotel Tiaré. In both *The Moon and Sixpence* and the *Notebooks* Maugham writes of her with admiration and tenderness. She was well known to travelers in the South Seas and to readers the world over, for nearly every book about the South Pacific written in the first two decades of the century has an account of her and her hotel; Rupert Brooke and Elinor Mordaunt were two of the many writers who had paid tribute to her benevolence and hospitality as well as to her dignity and common sense. She had befriended Gauguin when he was in need, with no thought of recompense and no gossipy curiosity about his past. She hung her "drawing room" walls with signed photographs and her own banal flower paintings, not unlike Dick Stroeve's in quality. The good woman died a victim of the world-wide influenza epidemic in 1919. Another local figure, Dr. Paul Vernié, who attended Gauguin in his last illness and wrote an account of the painter's last days, appears in the novel as Dr. Coutras.

When a native chieftainess, who lived about thirty-five miles from Papeete, told Maugham that there were pictures by Gauguin in a house not far away, he at once hired a car and drove to the dilapidated frame dwelling. The large native family living there were friendly and invited him to come in—and the first thing he saw was an unmistakable Gauguin painting on the upper glass panel of a door. Then he discovered remains of similar paintings on the other two doors of the room, but these unfortunately had been ruined by the children, who had scratched off most of the paint. The head of the family told Maugham that a strange French artist had painted the doors as a gesture of gratitude to the father of the present owner for kindness to him during an illness. When Maugham learned that the son took no interest in the remaining picture and was willing to sell it, he paid him two hundred francs (twice the price demanded) for the door, took it off its hinges, sawed off the lower half, and took the panel to France. Years later, when he acquired Villa Mauresque, he had it installed in a window opening in his writing room on the roof of the house. After a few years he had the opening bricked up at the back because the strong Mediterranean sun was fading its colors. It is probably one of the most valuable modern paintings in the world.

More people know, or think they know, about Gauguin's life and the character of his paintings through *The Moon and Sixpence* than through all the non-fiction studies of the painter, of which there have been many. For details of his early life and a shrewd analysis of Madame Gauguin perhaps the most valuable is *My Father, Paul Gauguin,* although Pola saw his father only once to remember him, when the boy was seven years old. A reading of the various biographies and of the recently discovered accounts-book and other documents in an abandoned house in Hivaoa shows that *The Moon and Sixpence* is far from a biography; it is for the most part pure fiction. Both Paul Gauguin and Charles Strickland left their businesses and families to devote themselves to painting; both went finally, alone, to the South Seas, where in the few years before their death they painted highly original pictures with strange, haunting colors; both had tremendous vitality and a rage to paint; both were egotistical, cynical, at times violent, often savagely misanthropic, and on occasion brutally inconsiderate of others. Both took native "wives."

But the differences are far more numerous. Madame Gauguin, unlike Mrs. Strickland, was long aware of her husband's love of painting, but she considered him a contented, successful businessman and regarded him as a "Sunday painter." She was bewildered when he abandoned his profession, but they did not at once separate; she lived with him in Rouen for eight months when he felt impelled to get away from Paris. After that experience she concluded that she could not accompany him in his wanderings and possibly bear more children (there were five already), so she returned to her parents' home in Denmark. Gauguin and his wife never ceased to write to each other, and he visited her in Copenhagen. He even took a commercial position in Denmark for a short time to try to convince his bitter in-laws that he was not a feckless vagabond. But he found that no compromise was possible, and again he fled from respectability and obligations to devote himself to painting. Madame Gauguin said of her husband that he was a strong man in his disposition and actions, with no malice or suspicions (his behavior did not always conform to this agreeable estimate); that he acted according to his own convictions, but calmly, without fanaticism. After many years she admitted that he had a right to act as he did.

She of course knew before his defection of his friendship with Schuffenecker and Pissarro, both of whom encouraged him to turn to painting, and she knew, too, of his exhibiting at the Salon and of the high praise he received from Manet and Huysmans. Before he left for Tahiti, a school of young painters had formed about him in Brittany and Paris, and he had stayed with Van Gogh in Arles. He knew Verlaine, Morice, Rodin, Carrière, and Mallarmé. He was not content in France, and the dream of roving grew in his mind, perhaps nourished by reading Loti, who wrote the first novel of the South Seas. Before he left for Tahiti to assume an official but unpaid post under the Director of Arts of the French government, the Café Voltaire Circle gave him a farewell party. He wrote a most affectionate letter to his wife, and he never ceased to write to her.

After over two years of strenuous activity in Tahiti he brought his new pictures and some wood carvings to Paris to exhibit. Critics withheld judgment, bewildered and perturbed by the exoticism and audacious use of color. After an unsatisfactory sojourn in Paris, Brittany, and Denmark he said farewell to his family and returned to Tahiti. He was in ill health when he disembarked and was never really well again. He was a frequent patient in the Papeete Hospital before he moved on to the Marquesas, which he fancied would be less civilized than Tahiti. Like Strickland, he resolved to paint a masterpiece at the end of his life. For a whole month he worked many hours a day and with tremendous passion and energy, and declared that he put into the picture all his vital force and "passionate pain, and a vision so clear that it needed no correction." The painting is the great and enigmatical masterpiece, "Where do we come from? Who are we? Whither are we going?" Unlike Strickland he did not ask that his crowning achievement as a painter be destroyed after his death.

In the Marquesas he was constantly ill, and his physical suffering, like Strickland's, was often excruciating. He was frequently at odds with the Catholic bishop and the local government. It is now known, however, that he was neither hungry nor friendless in his last months. A recently discovered accounts-book shows that his expenses during fifteen months of 1901 and 1902 amounted to nearly 12,000 francs, the equivalent of almost 3,000,000 francs in 1959. Moreover, he had a number of European and Marquesan friends, who were his intimates to the end. He did not die of leprosy: the cause of his death was a simple syncope of the heart. There was a final stroke of irony immediately after his death that should have appealed to Maugham's sense of humor, but the novelist made no use of it: the bishop, whom the agnostic painter had detested and ridiculed, claimed his body, and Gauguin was buried with full rites of the church. As a further irony and anti-climax, the painter's grave was unmarked and no one has been able to locate it.

Fifty years after Gauguin's death Willard Price, while gathering material for *Adventures in Paradise,* asked a weather-beaten old native who was picking up coconuts whether he knew where Gauguin's hut was, explaining carefully that Gauguin was a famous French artist who had died in the Islands. The old man, Emil Tail, replied that the hut was gone, but that he knew about the artist.

"I am his son."

Emil Tail, the brown-skinned son of Gauguin and his native wife, Tehura, had none of his father's talents or interests; he was illiterate and content to be a laborer and gardener. When 300 school children in Tahiti sent paintings to Paris in 1953 for exhibition in the Pedagogical Museum, those of Tail's six children created great interest, and some French critics spoke knowingly and feelingly of hereditary talent. In the ironic and amusing final chapter of *The Moon and Sixpence* we meet Mrs. Strickland again and find her basking in the posthumous fame of dear Charlie. The Strickland son, who is present when Ashenden, the narrator, calls, is an aggressively hearty and virile clergyman who declares piously but cheerfully that war brings out the best qualities of a man. His sister is also present, and as Ashenden had predicted, she is a soldier's wife. While he watches the pompous young Strickland, Ashenden remembers what he had heard of Strickland's half-caste son— merry, lighthearted, fond of the sea and adventure. Emil Tail was a far less romantic figure.

Although the novel's popularity and reputation rested

and still rest largely on its exotic Tahitian section—most people think of *The Moon and Sixpence* as a novel of the South Seas—less than one-fourth of the book is devoted to Strickland's adventures in the Islands; most of it deals with his life in London, Paris, and Marseilles. An opera, based on the novel, composed by John Gardner with a libretto by Patrick Terry, Manager of the Covent Garden Opera Company, was produced at Sadlers Wells in London in 1958. It was at first only moderately successful, perhaps because the harsh, atonal, music must be listened to more than once before it can be enjoyed. Those who heard the opera a second time were less disturbed by the dissonance, and were persuaded that the drama and music are integrated and not merely a running commentary on each other. In a retrospective prologue to the opera Mrs. Strickland looks back on her dead husband's career, which she considers a failure. The three acts deal almost entirely with the painter's life in the South Seas.

*The Moon and Sixpence* was published in 1919, the Herman Melville centennial year. In America there appeared a great many critical and biographical articles about the almost forgotten great nineteenth-century novelist, and there was a revival of interest in *Omoo* and *Typee* as well as in *Moby Dick*. These romantic tales of the South Seas were read again and perhaps increased interest in the new novel by Maugham.

The actual popularity of *The Moon and Sixpence* probably owes little to the author's frequent cynical preachments, which give a sardonic flavor to the book. Few novel-readers are likely to be amused by the wry observations that clergymen have an amazing gift of explaining un-

pleasant things away; that it is distressing when right lacks
might to back it up; or by Maugham's too often repeated
assertion that suffering does not ennoble but makes men
petty and vindictive; that women are cruel to men who
love them but whom they do not love; that a woman can
forgive a man for the harm he does her but not for the
sacrifices he makes for her; that love plays an insignificant
part in the life of an average man; that man is not what he
wants to be but what he must be; that nice women are
ashamed of working for a living—for a lady it is decent to
live only on other people's earnings; and so on. The average
reader probably skips over these tart observations as he
would skip the forbidding paragraphs of description in
the novels of Sir Walter Scott or James Fenimore Cooper.

The autobiographical element in *The Moon and Sixpence* is only slightly less substantial than in *Cakes and Ale*.
Maugham, the narrator, refers to his uncle's home in "Blackstable," to his own lodgings in London, and to his travels.
Of course the story of Charles Strickland and that of the
Stroeves had no relation to his own experiences, and many
of the styptic remarks are the author's asides. But it is safe
to assume that Strickland's violent tirades against women
are an expression of Maugham's misogyny. Strickland has
much to say also about aesthetics in general, and painters
and paintings in particular. All readers of Maugham are
aware that these are his own views. Ashenden (Maugham)
speaks of his rooms near Victoria Station and his eventual
breaking into literary circles; he refers to his medical school,
to Uncle Henry, the vicar, and to his artist acquaintances in
Paris; there are discussions of the art of the novelist and
Ashenden's confession of self-doubt; and finally there is

an account of his journey to Tahiti and the Marquesas and an accurate description of Lovina Chapman and other local residents.

Maugham has admitted many times that he has had to get his characters and events from life, and that his own imaginative powers are not remarkable. He has admitted, too, that the model he has most often used for his characters is Somerset Maugham. *The Moon and Sixpence* gives further insight into the author's own personality and life. As in *Of Human Bondage* we find a man who is very sensitive to the undeserved suffering and meaningless cruelty in the world sheltering himself behind skepticism, lacking the armor of sentimentalism that offers most men a measure of protection. The cynic or skeptic is usually more impressionable and thin-skinned than the thorough optimist, whose predilection for easy answers dulls his capacity for feeling as well as his powers of accurate observation.

The teasing title of the novel Maugham says he took from the review of *Of Human Bondage* in the London *Times* (although he maintains that he never reads reviews of his books). Speaking of Philip Carey, the reviewer remarks, "Like so many young men he was so busy yearning for the moon that he never saw the sixpence at his feet." Maugham liked the phrase and thought it an admirable title for his new novel. Every year since 1919 he has received letters asking about the meaning of the title and its application to Strickland's story. When he was eighty he admitted, "I really don't know any more. I did at one time but I don't now."

In a sale at Christie's in London in 1955 the original manuscript of *The Moon and Sixpence* was sold for £2,800.

## Cakes and Ale

In *Of Human Bondage* the author's youthful loneliness and frustration are recollected, if not in tranquillity, at least in a period of professional success and adjustment. *Cakes and Ale,* however, is the record of a long (much shortened in the novel) but abortive romance, recollected with warmth and pleasure; for the element of pain that often accompanies and follows a deep love had disappeared by 1929 when he wrote the book. For all its cynical asides and devastating satirical portraiture it is a warm and happy book written in the highest spirits. The fact that the author's enchanting affair with "Rosie" came to an end adds no note of frustration or heartbreak, for Maugham believes that a pleasure is no less a pleasure because it does not last forever. In a television interview in 1959 with A. S. Frere, chairman of Heinemann's, his publishers, Maugham said that *Cakes and Ale* is still his favorite among his novels. Astute critics everywhere except in France regard it as his best. The French critics like precision. They have always been annoyed by the formlessness of much English fiction, and they object to the sprawl and tangential excursions in *Cakes and Ale.* They think more highly of such firmly constructed novels as *The Narrow Corner* and *The Painted Veil.*

The central character, "the skeleton in the closet," is Rosie, the original of whom (Nan) Maugham knew and loved,  as did too many of his acquaintances and friends. His uncle and aunt, the vicarage, the sea front, shops, and public houses of Whitstable, its Joy Lane and High Street, the curate, the vicarage servants, his rooms and landlady in London while he was a medical student, and other places and people are real; they quicken the novel and persuade the reader of its factuality. Although his uncle and aunt and Mary Ann as well as Whitstable and Vincent Square are accurately transplanted from life, many traits of personality of the principal characters and their backgrounds are violently altered. The most successful transformation is that of Rosie herself. The essential Rosie is in the novel—her warm animality, her mischievous smile, her uncalculated goodness and kindness, her imperturbability, her great beauty, especially her gold-and-silver skin, her expertness at cards, her amorality and promiscuity. Yet when *Cakes and Ale* was published in 1930 and became at once a *succès de scandale* because of the two novel-writing characters, no one pretended to identify Rosie.

Maugham was quietly amused by the uproar about Thomas Hardy and Hugh Walpole, to the author minor characters in the book, while, except in Whitstable, there was no speculation about Rosie, the memory of whom impelled him to write the novel. While keeping her essentially as he knew her, he carefully made certain that no one could identify her. In real life she was not a barmaid in a provincial town, but the daughter of a prominent figure in public life, celebrated in London social circles for her great beauty. One of her sisters was for a time Lady in Waiting to Queen Mary. When the novel appeared, Rosie was still living and only about forty years of age. She was married twice, first to a theatrical producer, then to the younger son of a well-known nobleman; because of an extraordinary sequence of births and deaths Rosie barely missed becoming a peeress. Her second husband later became a distinguished political figure. She is transcribed from real life far more directly than either Alroy Kear or Edward Driffield. A lifelong friend of Somerset Maugham and of the original of Rosie has declared that Maugham in 1929 still felt for her so much affection that he made enough changes to conceal her identity completely. Because of the author's affectionate memory of Rosie, *Cakes and Ale* achieves at times a warmth and glow quite foreign to Maugham's usual unadorned and temperate style.

Although in an author's preface to a later edition of *Cakes and Ale* he speaks frankly about Thomas Hardy and Hugh Walpole, he carefully says nothing to lead one to identify Rosie. He merely states that in his youth he had been "closely connected" with the young woman called Rosie, who had grave lapses of morals; "but she was beautiful and not withstanding her incontinence, good." "Incontinence" is almost a euphemism to apply to her amoral behavior. Like Browning's Last Duchess, she directed her smiles everywhere, but unlike Her Grace she dispensed far more than her smiles. In *The Summing Up* Maugham mentions his suffering unrequited love. It was not that Rosie did not love him, but that she loved a dozen or so other men equally well. The relationship between them came to an end after a number of years. Maugham's friends declare that her promiscuity made marriage unthinkable; members of her family still maintain that she jilted him. The memory of Rosie lingered for years, and he knew that eventually he would put her into a work of fiction. To some critics who feel a compulsion to seek out symbolism in everything worth reading, Rosie is an obvious symbol: this ex-barmaid

stands for Life as opposed to Literature. But to the author
as well as to readers, Rosie is specific, whatever her meta-
phorical or symbolic meaning. Maugham's bent and gift
for the specific have discomposed a whole body of modern
critics who value highly the indirect and the allusive,
especially myth and symbol.

The first suggestion for *Cakes and Ale* is to be found
in his *Notebooks*; in this early note Rosie is not in the
novelist's vague plan: ". . . my reminiscences of a famous
novelist, living at Whitstable with a common wife very
unfaithful to him. While married to her he writes his great
books. Later he marries his secretary, who cossets him and
makes him into a great figure." Maugham suspects that in
old age the novelist at times grew restive at being made
into a monument and recalled with nostalgia the unrefine-
ment of his early years with his jolly companions and cheerful hours in the village pub. Maugham first planned to use
the material for a short story; then when it occurred to him
that he could make Rosie the first wife, he decided that its
proper use would require a brief novel or tale; but finally
he discovered that Rosie was too much of a character for
anything less than a long novel.

*Cakes and Ale* is superbly written, ingenious in construction, with well drawn characters and expert use of the
colloquial style, so unlike the austere manner of *Of Human
Bondage*. But the reason it is the author's favorite among
his novels is that he is satisfied with his portrait of Rosie.
Maugham's long affair with Nan, the Rosie of *Cakes and
Ale*, had come to an end more than fifteen years before he
wrote the novel, but the memory of her beauty, kindness,
warmth, and amorality was still undimmed. She was an

educated woman but not an intellectual. She was intelligent, and her shrewd comments on people and events Maugham found worth listening to. He was attracted by her warmth of heart, her invariable good humor, her good sense, her expertness at bridge—Maugham agrees with Poe that skill at whist is possible only for those with acute analytical powers—and her great beauty. Compared with most of the professional hostesses of Mayfair and Belgravia who sought the company of the successful young author, Nan was simple, artless, generous in her affection. She had what Barrie's Maggie Shand defines as charm: "a sort of bloom on a woman."

He says of her in his preface: "She is the most engaging heroine I have ever created . . . she could never have recognized herself in my novel, since by the time I wrote it she was dead." On the contrary she was living when he wrote it and did not die until eighteen years later. Members of her own family failed to recognize her but she most certainly could have identified herself by the detailed account of her portrait in the white dress, an exquisite painting which is still in existence—in the painter's studio but not on public view. In *Cakes and Ale* it is accurately described: the white dress, the bow of ribbon in the hair, the golden-silver skin, the facial expression of tenderness and innocence, for the usual mischievous smile is missing. It is to be hoped that some day this striking portrait will be uncurtained and available to all the admirers of *Cakes and Ale* and of Rosie.

Among other reasons for concealing her identity was the fact that her second husband was still alive. "He is a very nice man," says Maugham, using the present tense, for he is still living (1960). He is of course in no way like Lord George Kemp, and he did not emigrate to America. Rosie lived in her last years in a beautiful English country house, where she died soon after the end of the Second World War.

Some minor characters are also taken directly from life: Mary Ann, the sharp-tongued, warm-hearted servant at the vicarage, the novelist's uncle and aunt, and his landlady on Vincent Square in London. In Chapter 24 occurs an amusing incident also taken directly from life. While strolling down High Street toward the vicarage, Ashenden (as Maugham calls himself) meets an old school friend, whom he describes as shabbily dressed and unkempt and driving a ramshackle car. In the novel he is identified as a Whitstable general practitioner in obviously straitened circumstances. The model for this character was a Whitstable physician; he and Maugham had been boyhood companions and schoolmates, but had drifted apart when they attended different medical schools. When the Reverend Henry Maugham died, this boyhood friend went to Maugham and accompanied him to the funeral. The other nephews did not attend: Charlie was busy in Paris, and Henry and Frederick so detested their uncle that they refused to go to Whitstable for the services. When *Cakes and Ale* appeared, the Whitstable physician (a kinsman of Lord Nelson) was not offended by the unflattering description, for he recalled with amusement that when he had returned home after meeting his old schoolmate he had announced to his family, "I just saw Willie Maugham on High Street. I wonder why anyone with all his money dresses so shabbily." The doctor felt that their disparaging remarks canceled each other. He and Maugham still see each other at intervals. They are two of the three surviving Old Boys of Maugham's class at King's School; Maugham is the youngest of the trio.

As a *roman à clef* in 1930, however, *Cakes and Ale* aroused tremendous excitement in literary circles because Edward Driffield was seized upon as an uncharitable if not malicious portrait of Thomas Hardy, and Alroy Kear as a venomous caricature of Hugh Walpole. Maugham at once denied that he had used Hardy as a model, declaring that he did not have him in mind any more than George Meredith, Anatole France, or any other writer of advanced age. He never much cared for Hardy's books and did not think his English very good. He had met the Wessex novelist only once, at a large dinner party at Lady St. Helier's. Actually Maugham drew the character of Driffield largely from an obscure writer and impecunious journalist who settled in Whitstable with his family in the 1880's and whose name he does not remember. When a boy Maugham would ignore his snobbish uncle's warning and slip away to visit the somewhat disreputable but amiable writer, whose ungenteel conversation fascinated the schoolboy. One day, much to the vicar's righteous satisfaction, the writer and his family disappeared leaving numerous debts to Whitstable tradesmen unpaid.

Maugham confessed that he knew little of Hardy, only that both he and Driffield were "born in humble circumstances and both had two wives." Actually Thomas Hardy came not "from humble circumstances" but was of good yeoman stock, as the substantial house in which he was born is evidence. Although many admirers of Hardy choose not to believe Maugham, he has always declared that in 1929 he knew scarcely anything of Hardy's life, for the widow had not yet published her two-volume biography, and the critical studies of Hardy published before 1929 had not attracted his interest and attention. Hardy served his time as an architect and was particularly interested in the restoration of old churches. He also designed Max Gate, his attractive but modest, villa-like home near Dorchester. Neither of his wives was remotely like either of the two Mrs. Driffields. Both were highly cultivated women and both were themselves writers. Florence, the second wife, who was probably a distant relative of Hardy, was born in 1879, the daughter of the headmaster of a London school, and grew up, like the first Mrs. Hardy, in an educated atmosphere. She often visited at Max Gate and voluntarily helped the aging writer with secretarial work; she was never paid. He came to depend on her quiet efficiency. When his wife died, he telegraphed to Florence, who came to Max Gate, made all the necessary arrangements for the burial, and then slipped away. They later married when she was thirty-five and Hardy was seventy-three. Until his death at the age of eighty-eight she was a devoted wife and companion, but she did not cosset him and try to make him into a monument as does the second Mrs. Driffield.

It is easy to see how ill-informed readers might conclude that Hardy served as the model for Driffield. *Cakes and Ale* was written the year following Hardy's death, when many articles about the Grand Old Man of English Letters were appearing in the critical journals and weeklies. Driffield, too, is termed the Grand Old Man of English Letters and like Hardy is the recipient of the Order of Merit. Both impart an Elizabethan quality and rough humor to their lower-class characters. Driffield is "rather keen on architecture." Both late in life wrote two painfully realistic novels that shocked their readers. The impact of Hardy's *Jude the Obscure* on the late-Victorian reading public was like that of Driffield's *Cup of Life*. Except for Driffield's beard, they were physically similar.

But that is all. In most ways, perhaps intentionally, although Maugham does not remember doing so, he stresses dissimilarities. Hardy never lived in or near Whitstable, but in the southwest of England. He never ran away to sea; he was never a sailor, cab driver, or booking clerk. None of his novels have Kent as a locale. Florence Hardy was not a hospital nurse but a writer of children's books and magazine articles. The first Mrs. Hardy was a lady with a flawless reputation. It is preposterous to think of Hardy playing the banjo and singing vulgar music-hall songs. He did not haunt public houses. No Mrs. Barton Trafford was responsible for inflating his reputation in his old age. Max Gate was homely, tastefully furnished, comfortable, lived in, and not a collection of set pieces like the rooms at Ferne Court. Perhaps the greatest dissimilarity is that Hardy was the most notable poet of his day. In more than one critical article at the time of his death in 1928 he was acclaimed as the most distinguished English poet since the Romantics, a greater poet than Browning, Arnold, or Tennyson. Driffield writes only fiction.

The reading public was outraged by what it considered a vicious attack on a great novelist and poet recently dead, but it was titillated and amused by the character of

Alroy Kear, whose supposed counterpart, Hugh Walpole, was very much alive and successful but not universally loved. Walpole read *Cakes and Ale* "cold." Knowing nothing of the story or the characters, one evening he picked up the novel idly and started reading. Before he had finished the first chapter he realized that he was Alroy Kear. He later confessed that he read on with growing horror, absolutely certain that the acid portrait was his own. He was so shaken that he never slept all night, and the next morning he rang up J. B. Priestley, who tried to comfort him with Maugham's denial that Walpole was the model for Kear, for immediately on publication of *Cakes and Ale* the gossip began. Walpole wrote a letter of protest, which Maugham answered in a most friendly and urbane manner, insisting that Kear was a composite picture of Frankau, Drinkwater, Benson, Cannan, McKenna, Walpole, Somerset Maugham, and others. The suave letter did not placate the offended Walpole, who wrote in his diary that it was far clearer to him than to anyone else that he had been used as the model for Kear. He found some consolation in persuading himself that Maugham was cynical and unhappy, deeply sentimental, but so revolted by his sentimentality that he turned on anyone else whom he thought sentimental. Seven years later more than one American and British actress felt herself caricatured in *Theatre,* and again Maugham protested that Julia was a composite portrait of dozens of women of the theatre he had known during his thirty years of playwiting. He admitted that Ethel Barrymore, for example, had provided him with a trait or two, but to say that she served as the model for Maugham's unrepentant slut is absurd.

Hugh Walpole was ten years younger than Maugham and equally popular as a novelist in 1930. But the thorn in his flesh was that the first-rate critics, with the exception of Virginia Woolf (one is puzzled by her enthusiasm for his fiction), ignored him or dismissed his novels as inconsequential. He yearned for a serious critical recognition he never received. He was helpful to young writers but jealous of established authors of his own age. He was the darling of women's clubs and the most popular author-lecturer in America and Britain for years. He moved in fashionable social circles, belonged to the best clubs, was painted by Sickert and Kelly, made more money than he could spend although he spent thousands annually on paintings and *objets d'art,* and was knighted by the King; but the important critics denied him the nod of approval he longed for.

If Alroy Kear is Walpole, Maugham is no more acrid than some other contemporaries. One well-known portrait painter who knew Walpole intimately and painted him three times describes him as insincere and egotistical. Margaret Steen suggests that God is the leading character in all his novels, and mentions his ecclesiastical manner and pomposity. George Doran accused him of meanness and jealousy. Walpole's biographer, Rupert Hart-Davies, describes him as a social climber, terrified of missing anything, unable to refuse an invitation. Could Maugham have had Walpole in mind when he created the character of Elliott in *The Razor's Edge*? In Walpole's diary there is a surprising entry made shortly before his death: "My talents are small and my character is middling." In the London *Times* at the time of his death there appeared an unflattering account of his life in which the expression "sentimental egotist" occurs. His journal reveals that he firmly believed every unfavorable review of his books to be based on personal dislike. James Agate and St. John Ervine, for example, he regarded as personal enemies because of their failure to admire his novels.

*Cakes and Ale* contains frequent references to Kear's shattering heartiness, his aggressive virility, his opportunism, his flattery and wheedling of reviewers, his marketable talent untouched by genius, his appalling egotism, and his shameless courting of popularity. Maugham blandly pointed out that such flaws were not peculiar to Walpole but were found in most writers. Moreover, he makes Kear an expert golfer and fervid fox hunter, and Walpole was neither. Walpole met Hardy only once, briefly at a tea in 1910. Florence Hardy he came to know well near the end of her life; she saw the Jubilee procession in 1935 from the balcony of his flat in Piccadilly. He never wrote about Hardy. Nevertheless there is no doubt that Maugham used him primarily as the model for Kear, although he borrowed traits from a few other Georgian novelists, Gilbert Cannan in particular. The portrait is all the more stinging because of the apparent friendliness with which it is painted, for Maugham knows that angry satire defeats itself. Ashenden, the "I" of *Cakes and Ale,* speaks of Kear's friendliness and kindness, his affectionate nature, his jollity, his occasional modesty, with the result that the novelist repeatedly cuts off Kear's head with a golden axe.

The use or misuse in fiction of living celebrities or the illustrious dead is of course nothing new. Smollett and Sterne both attacked personal enemies through spiteful caricatures easily identified by their readers. Disraeli's novels are full of unflattering portraits of contemporaries, and early readers of *Bleak House* recognized two living important figures in public life. More recently H. G. Wells, Aldous Huxley, Hemingway (who modeled a character on Sherwood Anderson), Thomas Wolfe (who used Sinclair Lewis and many other contemporaries), and many other novelists have made use of such caricature. Their portraits range from the slyly humorous to the savage. The practice is also common on the stage. Bernard Shaw, for example pummeled living drama critics in *Fanny's First Play*, and well-known political figures in *Geneva* and in *Back to Methuselah*. The fact that such near-libel is common does not, of course, justify its use or settle the question of literary ethics involved. As time passes, however, such gossipy interest fades, and soon *Cakes and Ale* will be read and enjoyed, like *Bleak House*, without any curiosity whatever concerning life models of the characters. Thirty years after its publication few readers of Maugham's still widely read novel have much interest in Thomas Hardy and Hugh Walpole.

*Cakes and Ale* aroused anger and shock in Whitstable. The Ganns, numerous and severely respectable—it is said that they owned half of Whitstable in 1930—were especially outraged because Maugham named his strumpet of a heroine Rosie Gann. A Gann family still lives in the villa next door to the Old Vicarage. The Kemps were also numerous, prominent in business and the church, and active on school boards and in civic groups. Many townspeople fancied (with some it was wishful fancy) that they had been lampooned; one local citizen made and circulated a list of characters in the novel with a corresponding list of townspeople to identify them. Whitstable has never forgiven Maugham for *Cakes and Ale*. As late as 1951, when he made a sentimental journey to his boyhood home, the local paper grudgingly reported in a brief note on an inside page, "Well known novelist visits Whitstable." While there he was interviewed by London reporters, and detailed accounts of his visit appeared in the metropolitan press. Reporters sought out the former proprietress of the Bear and Key, who had long resented the references in the novel to the sordid inn and its draggletailed staff.

"Mrs. Appleton should not be upset," Maugham told the reporters. "The proprietress was a woman I knew in the 1890's, long before her time. I'm sorry she should think I made her my Mrs. Brentford, because that is not so. And Rosie Gann was not a Whitstable girl. I found her somewhere else and imported her into the story." These mollifying remarks were not published in the Whitstable paper.

Willie Ashenden, the narrator, is Somerset Maugham. Ashenden expresses the novelist's views of life and aesthetics. Maugham describes young Ashenden as he fancied himself as a boy, especially his shyness and snobbishness; and describes himself further as a young man and then finally as a writer of some success. There are caustic asides cencerning literary rivalry and English reverence for longevity; there are numerous echoes of La Rochefoucauld ("It is not difficult for them [the English] to maintain their principles at the cost of discomfort to others"). Most factual and unimagined of all is the narrator's attitude toward his uncle and aunt, Mary Ann, Rosie, and his London landlady. It might be noted here that Maugham's reputed cynicism is never directed toward simple, unpretentious people. His treatment of Mary Ann, Mrs. Hudson [Foresman], and the Driffields is invariably warm and sympathetic. Even the rascally Lord George Kemp is described with a measure of humorous respect. Maugham is at his most scathing when he writes of the professional, arty hostess, the literary opportunist, the female who fawns on artists and writers, the poseur. There is no doubt that his novels contain too many such humbugs and too few sincere and artless characters for the taste of some readers.

The literary gossip engendered by the publication of *Cakes and Ale* was still circulating when in 1931 Elinor Mordaunt's *Gin and Bitters* was published in the United States. It was a vicious, unmistakable attack on Maugham through the character of Laurence Hurle, a novelist who travels through Malaya and elsewhere in the Far East, unscrupulously using his hosts and others who were kind to him as characters in his fiction, and incorporating into his stories gossip heard about them. *Gin and Bitters* might have been a delightful satire if it were not so angrily yet feebly written, and if the author had not gone to such ridiculous extremes in picturing Hurle as senile, platitudinous, boorish, ungrateful, arrogant, and vain; and if she had not stressed his hatred of England, his eventual complete loss of popularity as a writer, and his dying friendless and bitter. There are obvious allusions to Thomas Hardy and Hugh Walpole in the novel.

Some readers at first credited Walpole with the authorship, but he was sincerely shocked by the poisonous attack, and when requested by Heinemann's to appeal to

Maugham to try to prevent its publication in England, he did so. It was pleasantly ironical that in less than a year after he had felt himself pilloried in *Cakes and Ale,* he appealed to Maugham "to see reason" and stop the publication of *Gin and Bitters* in England. "The book simply bristles with hate. I figure as Mr. Polehue. When will all this end?" There was speculation in literary circles about Walpole's coming to Maugham's defense, and not surprisingly many attributed to his intervention a discreditable motive: that if he spoke out in Maugham's behalf he would be less identified with Alroy Kear. As a matter of fact, Hugh Walpole had considerable natural goodness. There were never fewer than three sons of friends being educated at his expense. (It is hard to understand why George Doran accused him of meanness.) In his papers after his death dozens of letters were found testifying to his help and kindness, letters from the Sitwells, Betjeman, Joyce Cary, Graham Greene, Charles Morgan, Dylan Thomas, Thomas Wolfe, and others. It is quite probable that Walpole acted from an unselfish motive in supporting Maugham's publishers.

In spite of Heinemann's efforts, however, the book was published in England, by Martin Secker, Ltd., under the title *Full Circle.* Almost immediately Maugham's solicitors issued a writ for alleged libel against Elinor Mordaunt, and a month after publication *Full Circle* was withdrawn from circulation, for Secker's did not care to run the risk of a libel suit. What happened to Maugham's celebrated sense of humor that he would consent to such legal measures? The book was so egregiously feeble that it would soon have been forgotten. Some years later a somewhat preposterous book about Maugham appeared, full, he declared, of inaccuracies, near-slanderous remarks, and nonsense, but when he was urged to have his solicitors prevent its publication in England, he laughed at the suggestion.

It is amusing to note that in 1936, in *John Cornelius,* Walpole introduces a novelist, Archie Bertrand, clearly based on Maugham, "a cynic, a pessimist, a realist who sees things exactly as they are." Both *John Cornelius* and *Gin and Bitters* gather dust on library shelves while *Cakes and Ale* remains a classic example of the story-teller's art. The rich characterization, the humorous asides, the skillful shuttling between past and present, the warmth and cheerfulness of the story, the deceptively simple, colloquial style have established it among the masterpieces of modern fiction. Best of all, there is Rosie. *Cakes and Ale* is worth reading if only to permit the reader to savor the rich humor of her hilarious and natural remark which brings the book to an end.

Although *Of Human Bondage* and *Cakes and Ale* are Maugham's most notable autobiographical novels, there are strong autobiographical elements in much of his other fiction. There is, for example, much of Maugham himself in *The Narrow Corner* and *The Razor's Edge,* and the "I" in his short stories is nearly always more than just a writer's device to limit scope and afford a plausible means of interpreting event and character. Many of his stories are seasoned with his own philosophy of life and his views of unexpected contradiction of character; in fact, the chief interest in many stories lies in this characteristic irony, rather than in the narrative itself, as for example in "Before the Party," "The Fall of Edward Barnard," "Mackintosh," and all the stories in *First Person Singular*. In *The Razor's Edge* he boldly names a minor character "Somerset Maugham" and uses him to observe and comment.

## IV

## O T H E R   F I C T I O N

I N ADDITION to the three novels discussed in the preceding chapter Maugham wrote seventeen other novels between 1897 and 1948, when he resolutely brought to a close his career as a writer of fiction. Of the seventeen, six have enough merit to interest a discriminating reader today; the others are without any great distinction, and they sometimes violate the wise counsel of Maugham's favorite novelist, Balzac, from whom Maugham likes to quote: "The first requirement of a novel is that it interest. Well, to arouse this interest it is necessary to persuade the reader that the story being recounted actually happened." Although like most critical generalizations this is only a partial truth, it must be admitted that eleven of Maugham's novels lack both the interest and conviction that intelligent readers of fiction demand.

His first novel was written in 1896 and published in 1897, just before he left St. Thomas's properly qualified as physician and surgeon. Earlier the young medical stu-

dent had submitted two long stories to the publisher Fisher
Unwin, whose letter of rejection made the aspiring writer
deliriously happy: he asked Maugham to submit a full-
length novel if he had one. Of course he had none but he
began *A Lambeth Idyl* at once, although he was at the
busiest period of his medical studies and duties as an
interne. He worked at the hospital all day and wrote in his
room in the evenings. Fortunately his material was at hand:
he needed to do no research or reading. He drew directly
and relentlessly on his hospital experience for the story and
characters of *Liza of Lambeth*, as it was later called. In
his final year in medical school he spent his required
periods in medical, surgical, and obstetric work. For the
obstetric certificate the student had to attend twenty
confinements; Maugham attended sixty-three in three
weeks, during which time he rented a room near St.
Thomas's. He tells of being awakened late at night by
a hospital messenger (the telephone had not yet reached
Lambeth), who led him through the dark and silent streets,
up stinking alleys and into sinister courts. He was taken
to squalid, crowded tenements, in some of which large
families lived in a single room, and shown into a stuffy
chamber where two or three women stood about the bed
on which the patient lay. He talked with these people, most
of whom did not appear rebellious or particularly unhappy
in their poverty and dirty clutter, but accepted their lot
with resignation. The experiences of these crowded weeks
found their way into *Liza of Lambeth* and were drawn upon
again eighteen years later when he wrote *Of Human Bondage*. His first novel is little short of a transcript of real life.

Admittedly under the influence of Maupassant, and indirectly of Flaubert, he imitated the French story-tellers' methods, grateful that he had as an example those who "had so great a gift for telling a story clearly, straightforwardly, and effectively." He admits that in the novel he described without addition or exaggeration the people he had treated, and the incidents that had struck him on his visits to out-patients in the slums. He had no need to draw upon imagination, and very little gift for it; he has made the questionable observation that the young actually have little creative imagination, which comes with maturity. Written in the impersonal method of Flaubert, *Liza of Lambeth* is somewhat dry and cold, but it is an excellent first novel and deserves the acclaim it at once received from a few eminent critics and the place it holds in the affections of its author. It is baldly objective, a brilliant work of reportage, free of superfluous detail and comment; it is an unvarnished account of the last year in the life of a young factory worker, her emergence from girl to woman, her brief but happy love affair, her pathetic death. It is a period piece with the current grotesque slang of the cockney, the amazing costume and coiffure of Liza, the innocent vulgarities of a Bank Holiday in the eighteen nineties. It is as vital as a drawing by Hogarth. The phonograph, radio, television and films, the motorcycle and second-hand cars (and many new ones, too), as well as sanitary corporation flats and universal education for the young, with daily orange juice and milk provided free in the schools, and adult education centers have made Liza's East End as remote as Moll Flanders' and Oliver Twist's. But it is a real world in the novel, and its people live and breathe; for the slum doctor knew Liza, her gin-loving mother, and

Jim, their street, their homes, their interests, their language and manners, their human weaknesses.

Not all the notices were flattering, and like all young authors Maugham was more discomposed by the unfavorable reviews (he admits to some sleepless nights) than encouraged by the favorable ones. In these last years of the Victorian period the naturalistic novel in England received little critical support. George Moore was anathema to the respectable; Arthur Morrison and George Gissing were all but ignored; at almost the same moment that *Liza of Lambeth* appeared, Thomas Hardy was so discouraged by the outcry against *Jude the Obscure* that he abandoned novel-writing altogether. A typical review and one that was particularly upsetting to Maugham was that of the influential *Athenaeum*, which admonished that "readers who prefer not to be brought into contact with some of the ugliest words and phrases in the language should be warned that Mr. Maugham's book is not for them . . . [it] is emphatically unpleasant as literature." One of these offensive words (a reader discovers them with difficulty today) was "belly," which was changed by the publisher to "stomach" in the second impression.

The book was not so downright shocking and harrowing as the French prototypes and *Jude the Obscure*, but vaguely disquieting. It was the first English novel of consequence to treat the slums realistically and objectively. Readers preferred a sentimental attitude toward poverty: writers should fix the blame, provide a scapegoat, and condemn or approve their characters' conduct. In *Liza of Lambeth* there is none of this. The slums and grinding poverty are the background, but do not constitute the villain as in the work of social propagandists. The half dozen characters are presented with clarity and precision, and we are not asked to condone or condemn. None are completely odious, none very admirable. The lack of affection between mother and daughter pained many Victorian readers. These slum-dwellers are more primitive and naive than their fellow townsmen of the West End, and obey their instincts more easily; at the same time they are involved in a complicated set of petty taboos and codes of honor like the bourgeoisie. But the novelist, like Flaubert and Maupassant, is content to report; he does not judge.

Some of the reviews were most favorable, and the young internist was enraptured when the eminent French critic Auguste Filon wrote a warm appreciation for *Le Journal des Débats*. His proudest moment came when his beloved landlady, Mrs. Foresman, heard Wilberforce make it the subject of a sermon one Sunday evening at Westminster Abbey. When a week or two later Unwin Fisher, his publisher, informed him that a second edition was to the published at once, he determined to abandon medicine as a career as soon as he received his degree, and to become a writer.

The book was successful enough to lead Fisher to ask Maugham for another story of the slums, but the young doctor had in mind a more colorful subject, in addition to a projected autobiographical novel. For two or three years he had been reading about the Italian Renaissance, and he had spent an enchanting holiday in Italy. Moreover, he took to heart Andrew Lang's dubious advice that a young writer should not attempt to write about his own time and the life about him: a beginner should try his hand at a historical novel. All the time he could spare from the hospital Maugham spent at the British Museum, reading and making notes on Italy in the fifteenth century. When summer holiday came, he went at once to Seville and wrote his autobiographical novel, but when he failed to get it published he took his Italian notes to Capri and spent a happy summer writing *The Making of a Saint*. The book received a frigid treatment by the critics, found very few readers, and is properly omitted from the collected edition of the novels. Historical romance is not the type of thing he was best suited to write. He already had a keen sense of critical humor and a respect for fact. In *The Making of a Saint* his cynical and youthfully brash observations on "the people," the mob, the rulers, and the general frailty of mankind were violently out of place in the romantic historical novel of the time. Equally exceptionable was the bitter ending, dark with disillusion and pessimism.

His third published novel, *The Hero* (1901), suggested by the Boer War, is equally undistinguished and has never been reissued. It has some interest for students of Maugham's works, for they find there the shocking observations, wry humor, and the protoypes of characters he was to handle with skill when his art matured. The story, however, is rather absurd, and the ending, in which the hero commits suicide in order to escape marriage with the pious Mary, is grotesque.

His excellent fourth novel, *Mrs. Craddock* (1902), which placed him among the important novelists of his day, was published only after it had been turned down by every London publisher of consequence; they were apprehensive of its frank treatment of sex, its bold study of a passionate, intellectual woman in love with a cold, selfish, stupid boor who has an overpowering physical attraction for her. Finally William Heinemann reconsidered and consented to publish the novel if the author would remove certain offensive passages. When Maugham revised the novel in 1928, he examined the original manuscript and confessed, "On reading it over, I cannot for the life of me imagine what they [the shocking passages] are. . . . On the contrary the propriety of the book is almost painful." He eliminated some absurdities from this early novel, but left others which although embarrassing belonged to the period. He felt that the value of the book lay in the picture of life in England just before the end of the nineteenth century, when British complacency had not been shaken by the Boer war, and the landed gentry, "narrow, stupid, and intolerant . . . prudish, formal, and punctilious," were about to yield much of their power and prerogatives to the new moneyed class.

The value of *Mrs. Craddock* does not lie, of course, in its social picture: it lies in its candid study of a marriage trying to succeed on a physical basis, the equally candid study of a woman with strong physical desires shamelessly pursuing the male who attracts her. Victorian notions of modesty and the ritual of courtship were thrown to the winds. Here is Maugham's most searching analysis of a marriage. He makes credible the initial attraction of Bertha and Edward to each other, and like Strindberg skillfully traces the transformation of love into hate. Bertha is intellectual, restless, and sensitive, but so strongly sexed that she debases herself before a cloddish man of property. Edward is a completely realized character, who just misses being a caricature of the middle-class Anglo-Saxon—unimaginative, narrowly patriotic, energetically a good fellow, conservative, virtuous. He is a stupid and a happy man. He has no doubts, no struggles, no self-criticism. With a touch of dry humor, Maugham makes him a product of his own school in Canterbury. Long before Edward is killed in an accident, Bertha has lost all love for him. After she sees his body before the flattering ministrations of the embalmer, she jubilantly feels herself free. With composure she picks up the book she had been reading when her dead husband was brought home, and begins reading again. Both husband and wife are intolerant and inelastic; both are detestable. As a result the novel lacks warmth and charm, although it possesses vigor and reality. It is one of Maugham's best novels.

A delightful minor character is Miss Ley, treated by the novelist with warmth and affection. Drawn from life, she reappears in a biographical sketch in Maugham's preface to *What a Life!* by Doris Arthur-Jones, and in *Conversations with Max* [Beerbohm] by S. N. Behrman. Both Maugham and Max describe her, Mrs. George Steevens, as generous, hospitable, frank of speech and fond of shocking the prude and the narrow-minded. Maugham makes her a flywheel of common sense in the tumultuous lives of her friends, expressing the novelist's comments like the ancient chorus, or the *raisonneur* in an Edwardian problem play. Her temperate philosophy of live and let live is refreshing in the midst of so much Victorian busybodiness and do-goodism. Her comment on a Miss Glover, whose zealous, implacable philanthropy is often embarrassing, is typical: Miss Glover, she says, is fit only for heaven "with her colorless hair hanging down her back, wings and a golden harp, singing hymns in a squeaky voice, morning, noon, and night." Such a character as Miss Ley was made-ready for Maugham, who used her again in *The Merry-Go-Round* and *The Bishop's Apron.*

The next four novels are among his worst. The *Merry-Go-Round* is interesting as the source book for some of the author's other work. It is a hodgepodge of four narratives, two of which furnished the plots of *A Man of Honour* and *Grace.* Much of the philosophy reappears in *Of Human Bondage* and many comments and epigrams are used in later plays. (Like Oscar Wilde, Maugham is fond of quoting from himself.) *The Bishop's Apron* (1906), his most successful book up to that time, has long been out of print, but it is readable and lively. Except for *Cakes and Ale* and *Theatre* and possibly *Catalina,* it is his only humorous novel. It is cheerful and sprightly, but as we would expect, the humor is styptic. The bishop is worldly, pompous, and ambitious, but not detestable. His sister, while she knits, lets fall not words of canny wisdom like Maggie Shand, but darts of truth and iconoclasm which graze but do not puncture the bishop's monumental egotism. Her favorite comment after an outpouring of the oracular or pompous is "Fiddlesticks!" The next two novels, *The Explorer* (1907) dedicated to "My Dear Mrs. G. W. Steevens," and *The Magician* (1908), we can charitably forget as the novelist asks us to do.

Six years passed between the publication of *The Moon and Sixpence* and his next novel, *The Painted Veil.* In the interval he had been occupied with short stories, Chinese sketches, and a half dozen plays. *The Painted Veil* was an immediate product of a long journey through China. Maugham had a sharp eye for the strange and beautiful in China, and with imperfect detachment he observed the British colonials, many of whom he found to be less engaging figures in the Far East than they were by their own firesides or in their own gardens back home. He listened, too, with interest to the stories he heard in trains, ships, clubrooms, and homes of colonial officials.

This is no place to discuss the ethics of the novelist's craft, but it is alleged that certain people and events in "The Letter," *The Painted Veil,* and other stories caused no little embarrassment, and furious anger, in some Chinese or Malaysian communities. Maugham's tart comment, "if the shoe fits, wear it!" is sufficient reply for the average reader, but it is not always enough before the rigorous law of libel. *The Painted Veil* was first published serially in *Nash's Magazine* and in *Hearst's International.* The scene was laid in Hong Kong, and other actual place names such as Canton, Happy Valley, and The Peak were used. The bacteriologist and wife were called Walter and Kitty Lane, and while the novel was still being serialized, a couple by the same name living in China threatened to sue for libel. The action was settled out of court, and Maugham renamed his characters Walter and Kitty Fane. Then a colonial government official protested against the use of Hong Kong as the setting for the novel, and the publishers took action. Eight thousand copies of the book had been printed, and half of them had been delivered to booksellers. These copies were recalled and all but seventy-four were returned. Changing Hong Kong to Tching-yen required considerable work for the printers and binders, and other complications resulted in there being six editions. No novel is more interesting bibliographically than *The Painted Veil*. Maugham notes with characteristic amusement that the astute reviewers who "neglected" to return their first copies had in their possession a collector's item. In a prefatory note to the new edition Maugham declares that he gets the names of his characters from the obituary column of *The Times*, that no writer would be such a fool as to libel a total stranger.

Elsewhere he asserts that the roots of *The Painted Veil* go back to his student days at St. Thomas's. While reading Dante during a holiday in Florence, the would-be novelist was much struck by this passage:

> *Siena mi fe; disfecemi Maremma:*
> *Sulsi colui, che, innanella pria*
> *Disposando m'avea con la sua gemma.*

"Siena made me, Maremma unmade me: this he knows who after betrothal espoused me with his ring." His instructor in Italian, his landlady's daughter, had her own interpretation of the lines: a gentlewoman of Siena, Pia, was suspected of adultery by her husband, who exposed her to the noxious vapors of his castle in the Maremma. She did not die, however, and he finally had her killed. This grim tale stuck in Maugham's mind, and he often repeated the line *Siena mi fe: disfecemi Maremma*. It was not until his journey decades later that he hit upon the modern, exotic setting and circumstances which would make the story plausible today. He confesses that *The Painted Veil* is his only novel in which he started with a story rather than from a character. The title derives from a sonnet by Shelley: "Lift not the painted veil which those who live call life."

Perhaps because in *The Painted Veil* the novelist is more concerned with story than with character, it strikes the reader as inferior to *Of Human Bondage, The Moon and Sixpence,* and *Cakes and Ale,* all of which have flesh-and-blood people whom we can believe in. The characters in *The Painted Veil* are trivial and dull; their adventures of marital infidelity (Maugham himself has said that adultery can now serve only as a theme for comedy) and self-sacrifice are shopworn and banal. It is a matter of indifference to the reader whether Kitty commits adultery or not, whether her husband shoots her or not, whether they all die of the plague or not. Kitty's father is a cipher. Her mother is rapacious, scheming, and unprincipled. Her sister is frivolous and self-centered. Her husband is without charm, elegance, or humor. Her lover is stupid, selfish, and vain.

Never has Maugham needed his gifts of story-telling so desperately, and in the first three-fourths of the novel they do not fail him. The opening scene is exciting, and narrative interest is sustained until the death of the husband. The rest of the story is feeble. Maugham's often repeated declaration that a story must have a beginning, middle, and end finds no brilliant illustration here. *The Painted Veil* sputters out, the dialogue of the last pages sounds like early Pinero, and the final sentence of the novel is as shocking and irrelevant as the closing line of Galsworthy's *Justice.*

The novel has merits of course, but its laudation by French reviewers as a masterpiece shakes one's faith in French criticism. The story is sometimes exciting, the style is clear and liquid (except near the end), and there are brief passages of beauty, particularly descriptions of the

Chinese countryside. Moreover there is the usual *raison-neur* or chorus found in many of Maugham's stories, Waddington, a customs officer, who is bald and ugly enough to preclude any "affair" with Kitty, and who probably speaks for the author. He is a free-thinker, a man of the world, a kindly cynic with much of the novelist's philosophy. Speaking of the nuns he remarks, "I wonder if it matters that what they have aimed at is illusion. Their lives are in themselves beautiful. I have an idea that the only thing which makes it possible to regard this world we live in without disgust is the beauty which now and then men create out of the chaos, the pictures they paint, the music they compose, the books they write, and the lives they lead. Of all these the richest in beauty is the beautiful life. That is the perfect work of art." Sometimes he speaks like Cronshaw in *Of Human Bondage*: "Some of us look for the Way in opium and some in God, some of us in whiskey and some in love. It is all the same way and it leads nowhither." He says of his religion, "I describe myself as a member of the Church of England, which I suppose is an inoffensive way of saying that you don't believe in anything very much;" and of the colonial official, "So long as Charlie Townsend's got her to depend on he's pretty safe never to do a foolish thing, and that's the first thing necessary for a man to get on in Government service. They don't want clever men; clever men have ideas and ideas cause trouble; they want men who have charm and tact and who can be counted on never to make a blunder."

*The Narrow Corner* (1932)—"Short therefore is man's life, and narrow is the corner wherein he dwells"—is one of Maugham's most enjoyable novels. There is not a dull page in it, but its reception by many critics in the early 1930's, when only novels and plays of social significance seemed important, was lukewarm. The average notice was patronizing. Reviewers admitted that the story was unfolded in a masterly fashion and that it was impossible to put the book down once it was begun; but their praise was temperate, for here was a novel unconcerned with any problems except those dealing with human character and man's unpredictable behavior. *The Narrow Corner* was simply entertaining.

Of the five principal characters one appears in *The Moon and Sixpence* and another in *On a Chinese Screen*. Captain Nichols of *The Moon and Sixpence* is the beachcomber who helps Strickland secure passage from Marseilles to the South Pacific. In *On a Chinese Screen* Dr. Saunders annoys a missionary who had fled from the steaming Chinese city to the cool of the hills. Both men are pictured just as we find them in *The Narrow Corner*. Maugham has said that these two preliminary sketches did not dismiss the two attractive scamps from his mind, and that eventually their stories had to be written. The other three characters are more heterogeneous. Fred Blake is a commonplace young fellow with three claims to eminence: his skill at dancing and at cribbage, and his extraordinary good looks. Ironically these advantages bring about his tragic end. Erik is a Scandinavian giant, gentle and idealistic. His idealism brings about his tragedy. Louise Frith is a Nordic jewel set in the silver South Sea, free of inhibitions and coldly determined not to permit herself to be possessed. When the lives of these five people touch, tragedy comes not to those without morals but to those without philosophy.

*The Narrow Corner* is Maugham's most underrated novel. Nowhere else has he more successfully combined wit, philosophy, mystery, humor, and careful scrutiny of behavior and motive. The central character is Dr. Saunders, whose shady activities in his profession have caused his removal from the Register; he then settles in China, lives happily in the native quarter of a large city, and succeeds in his practice. He has acquired an ironical philosophy, a deep sense of humor, and a complete indifference to other people's conduct. He is shrewd and skeptical. It is characteristic of Maugham to make a man without conventional morals or faith or human ties derive a great deal of pleasure from life. He is a hedonist, but in addition to good food, drink, and comfort, he enjoys watching the spectacle of human life and is diverted by the phenomena of human behavior. His philosophy of life is something like that arrived at eventually by Philip Carey, and that expressed by Maugham in *The Summing Up*. The novelist puts so much of himself into Dr. Saunders that *The Narrow Corner* might well be considered with the autobiographical novels. He regards illusions and sincere idealism as menaces to happiness, and fraudulent idealism as a revolting vice. He rejects asceticism and has learned to regret nothing. "Life is short, nature is hostile, and man is ridiculous; but oddly enough most misfortunes have their compensations, and with a certain humor and a good deal of horse-sense one can make a fairly good job of what is after all a matter of very small consequence." He is quick to detect uncalculated goodness, and that exquisite phrase "the beauty of holiness" has a meaning for him. He has acquired resignation "by the help of an unfailing sense of the ridiculous."

At the end of the novel he looks toward the future with cheerfulness, sure of his spiritual independence and free of human bondage. Is it an example of Somerset Maugham's sense of humor that he should give to a minor rogue so much of his own philosophy of life?

Captain Nichols is less complex. He is a rascal of the first order, and does not flinch even at murder when it is to his advantage. He illustrates Maugham's contention that man is "not of a piece," for Nichols has a sense of humor and is almost without fear. His courageous behavior during a terrifying storm would well become a saint. Dishonest, shifty, untrustworthy, he nevertheless possesses courage, which deserts him only when his wife, prim, calm, and determined, appears on the scene and reduces him at once to cringing subjection.

Louise Frith is the most striking character in *The Narrow Corner*. Although Maugham's estimation of women in his plays and fiction is often harsh and unflattering, he writes with cold admiration of Louise. She is intelligent and not without culture and sophistication (she is aware of the Freudian element in Erik's love for her), but she is at the same time an amoral primitive. She lives by instinct, but uses her intelligence to guard her independence, which thoughtless submission to her instincts would destroy. She knows neither inhibitions nor remorse. When her infidelity (she spends a night with Fred) drives Erik to suicide, she takes the sharp edge off the tragedy by her cold-blooded analysis. She is sorry he is dead, but holds herself blameless. He didn't really love her, but her mother (now dead), and the daughter had fallen short of the ideal he had made of her. If he had really loved her, he would have forgiven her, but he loved his ideal, in which he wanted to imprison her. Now that both Fred and Erik are out of her life, she feels relieved: ". . . at the back of my mind I know it has given me freedom."

From the point of view of Louise and Saunders this novel, too, might well have been called *Of Human Bondage*. Although on the surface it is a story of mystery, murders, and suicide, it is leavened with philosophy and lifted far above the average novel of adventure by its penetrating study of character. Maugham at his best is not only a good story-teller: he knows people, knows that man is neither good nor bad and that thinking will not make him so. There are brief descriptive passages of beauty, and comedy, too; especially memorable in its grim humor is the burial at sea of the Japanese diver. The author does not fall into the Dickensian trap of hyperbolizing the eccentricities of the Friths or the hypochondria of Nichols. *The Narrow Corner* has proportion, restraint, suavity, tolerance, understanding, and a praiseworthy brevity. It is a wise book and makes no sentimental concessions to either the romantic setting or the dramatic theme of the story.

Only a few years after he wrote *The Narrow Corner* he established his permanent home in the south of France and ceased making long voyages to the Far East; the setting of all his novels after 1925 is in Europe, except for a few American scenes in *The Razor's Edge*.

*Theatre* (1937) with a London setting, was his first novel after *The Narrow Corner*. It is a trivial work that did not demand to be written: it did not rid his soul of plaguing obsessions. He wrote it for his amusement and succeeded in pleasing a vast number of book-buyers, but it disappointed those who expected a worthy successor to *Mrs. Craddock, Of Human Bondage,* and *Cakes and Ale.* Its theme and characters are of no consequence, it has neither depth nor sweep, it is often shoddy. It is as artificial and unsubstantial as its title suggests, for its world is the weird microcosm of the theatre, a world Maugham knew intimately: for years he had supplied it with plays; he was acquainted with its managers and the fantastic economy of the most capricious of all business enterprises; he knew most of the famous British and American actresses from 1908 on. When he wrote *Theatre* he entertained no romantic notions concerning the significance or glamor of the theatre.

"I have sought to worm myself into a woman's heart and see life through her eyes and feel emotion through her sensibilities. No one but a woman can tell if I have succeeded." What a monstrous blurb from Somerset Maugham! The world through Julia Lambert's eyes is a stage; her every action is a performance, every remark a "line," every emotion designed and in character. In moments of crisis when her soul, that is, her egregious vanity, is touched, she quotes apt lines from her plays. Her husband, her son, her lovers and her acquaintances (she neither has nor desires friends) are merely more intimate members of her vast audience. She becomes incapable of honest emotion, and like Lady Kitty's, her soul is as thickly rouged as her face. When she is affronted or insulted, it is the actress, not the woman, who is resentful. It finally occurs to Julia that the real woman is on the stage, that she is a shadow when away from it. When her son excoriates her for her exhibitionism and hollow life, she can hardly understand what he means, and considers him a prig. One of his remarks, however, comes so close to penetrating her incrustation of sham and make-believe that for a moment she is uneasy: "When I've seen you go into an empty room I've sometimes wanted to open the door suddenly, but I've been afraid to in case I found nobody there."

The other characters are equally disagreeable, ranging from a caddish gigolo to a gross Lesbian. But the story is executed with a graceful theatricality, it is sometimes witty, and, one feels, honest in its way. These trivial people are not worth writing about and perhaps not worth reading about, but Maugham lavishes his great technical gifts on their inane experiences, and many have found the novel entertaining. One wonders how many readers, if any, ever began *Theatre* without reading it through to the delightful last scene in the Berkeley, in which Julia celebrates her spectacular multiple triumph over her rival, husband, and lover: she treats herself to a supper of beer, steak, and onions.

*Christmas Holiday* (1939) has much more substance than *Theatre* and is written with equal skill. It is second-best Maugham, which means that although it lacks the warmth and smooth execution of *Cakes and Ale* and anything comparable to the sincerity, power, and sweep of *Of Human Bondage*, it conforms to Maugham's own conception of a good novel: it has an absorbing story, an agreeable style free of irritating eccentricities, a group of living and diversified characters who are interesting in themselves, and dialogue proper to the characters and pace of the narrative. Moreover, the novel is quietly stamped with the author's private view of the universe. Although he has repeatedly asserted that a novel should not deal with issues and problems but only with human beings and their behavior and should aim only to entertain, no one, not even Somerset Maugham, can write in a vacuum. Written in the uneasy year of 1938 when totalitarian forces in Europe were obviously and brutally menacing constitutional government and human freedom, *Christmas Holiday* reflects the novelist's awareness of the nature of dictators and dictatorship, and of threatened, if not inevitable, economic and social revolutions in this brave or cowardly new world. He shows, too, a shrewd understanding of the cultural forces of his day. But these matters, ominous as far as politics is concerned, are a part of the climate of the novel and the background; Maugham's emphasis is almost entirely on men and women, on the dark places of the soul, on the complexity of human nature. Under Maugham's suave and restrained treatment the portrait of the embryonic dictator, Simon, becomes as chilling as anything in Koestler or Kafka.

But Simon is a minor character. The narrative is concerned with young Charley Mason's five-day holiday in Paris, beginning on Christmas Eve. The callow, virginal Charley, coming from a home of elegance and culture, is thrust into sordid and harrowing adventure which upsets all his nicely collocated values of the arts and of morality, and destroys his complacent satisfaction in his own enviable, well-ordered existence. We see first his well-to-do parents—their artiness, their self-conscious culture and magnanimity, their glitter and shallowness, their smug confidence in the permanence of their world. When after five days Charley returns to sedate Porchester Close, W. 2, to his parents' impeccable house with the right Impressionist paintings on the walls and expensively modern but not daring furnishings, to a world of the *Times* and the *Financial Times,* of dressing for dinner and toying with walnuts over the port, Charley is changed. Actually he had *done* nothing. But he had discovered a new world—that of a murderer, a prostitute, a fanatical revolutionary. The story of the murder and the atonement is gripping. Charley sleeps with the Russian prostitute and remains a virgin, much to the astonishment of Maugham's readers. From his adventures on the periphery of violence involving theft, murder, prostitution, revolutionary intrigue, police courts, the underworld, he comes away superficially unchanged. The novel ends, ". . . only one thing had happened to him, it was rather curious when you came to think of it, and he didn't just then quite know what to do about it: the bottom had fallen out of his world."

*Up at the Villa* (1941) the author describes as "a little story to pass an idle hour." The story is certainly a little one and a reader would have to be idle indeed to spend an hour on it. Why did Maugham waste his time on such trumpery? This dull story about very dull people is written with the deceptively simple, easy, and direct style that is the author's hallmark, but it is very small beer. Was Maugham after his safe arrival in America, following his dramatic escape from France in 1940 and sojourn in London during the height of the bombing, moved to occupy himself with a brief project far removed from the horror of war and the human suffering he had only recently witnessed?

During the war Maugham was asked by the British Min-

Winston Churchill and Somerset Maugham.

istry of Information to write a novel showing the effect of the war on a typical British family. Maugham detested the assignment, for he declared that he could not write with satisfaction under government orders. *The Hour Before the Dawn* was serialized in the *Redbook* and then published in New York in 1942. It has not been published in England and will not be if the author's wish is followed.

The Hendersons are not at all a typical British family. They are "military" and "county," typical only of the small landed class whose way of life is quite unlike that of most Britons. When Maugham reached England after his escape from France, he lived at the Dorchester on Park Lane; probably most of the fellow residents of this luxury hotel were well-to-do refugees from the bombings. They were as atypical of the British in war time as lodgers at the St. Regis would be of Americans. Maugham might have done better if he had chosen a lower middle-class family like the Sunburys in "The Kite," or the low-class Kents in *Liza of Lambeth*. There were hundreds of thousands of such families living and working on the front line, which was Britain during the bombings. The conscientious objector in *The Hour Before the Dawn*, Jim Henderson, was probably suggested by a young relative of Maugham who was a leader of the widely publicized "We will not fight for King or Country" group in the 1930's. Most members of this celebrated group of pacifists signed up soon after war was declared, Maugham's relative among them, but some, like Henderson, never wavered from their unpopular position.

In the meantime, comfortably established in his little house on the Doubleday plantation in South Carolina, and with *The Hour Before the Dawn* out of the way, he had the time and freedom from interruption to write a novel the idea of which had haunted him since his memorable visit to India in 1938. The war prevented his return to India in 1939 to complete gathering his material, and so *The Razor's Edge* is not at all the novel he had intended to write, but it afforded him a vehicle in which to set forth his impressions of Indian mysticism and mystics and to restate many observations on religion, evil, God, punishment, and and spiritual exaltation which he had been entering in his notebooks during the preceding fifty years. He even attributes to Larry the delicious minor article of faith that Maugham learned when he was twenty-four from Augustus Hare, who inked out many lines from the Prayer Book from which he read to his family and domestic staff daily. "I've crossed out all the passages in glorification of God. God is certainly a gentleman, and no gentleman cares to be praised to his face. It is tactless, impertinent, and vulgar. I think all that fulsome adulation must be highly offensive to him." Actually the Indian mystical element in *The Razor's Edge* is minor and not very persuasive. It could hardly be otherwise. Maugham was fascinated by the effect of such strange and powerful metaphysics on the lives of millions, and nowhere writes of it except with sympathetic respect if not with understanding, but it no more touched him personally than it would have stirred Voltaire and Anatole France.

The novel is concerned principally with a young Chicago war veteran, Larry Darrell, who returns from the war determined, like Thoreau and Maxwell Anderson's Van Dorn, to live his life as he pleases, to avoid the American stereotypes of success, to find a faith he can respect and live by, to seek answers for the eternal questions concerning life, soul, and death. To his friends and the girl who loves him he is a quitter without ambition or responsibility to society or to anyone but himself; to some cynical readers he may seem to be the victim of a glandular deficiency. What a hero for Maugham to create and treat seriously—a seeker of the Absolute, an unworldly searcher for a life of the spirit and humble selflessness! According to the novel his quest is successful. He easily puts behind him all worldly temptations, achieves a mystical illumination in the perfect peace and abnegation of an ashrama, disposes forever of his annual income of $3,000, and returns to America to be a mechanic or a taxi driver. He achieves however a Thoreauvian fortune: for a man is rich in proportion to the number of things he can let alone. He still has his faith. In the first pages of the novel Maugham wards off criticism by declaring that he writes about Larry simply because his story interests him, although he met him only a few times and he cannot pretend to follow him in his transcendental flights. He is merely an observer, and in the novel appears as a character, a novelist named Somerset Maugham.

*The Razor's Edge* ("The sharp edge of a razor is difficult to pass over; thus the wise say the path to Salvation is hard"—*Katha-Upanishad*) was enormously popular, partly because of the deft execution of the narrative, and partly because Larry's indifference to what seemed important to ninety-nine per cent of young Americans piqued their curiosity. It caused them to question their own set of values, made them uncomfortably suspicious that the ideal pattern of college, business success, and the showy suburbanite or exurbanite way of life might be hollow and dull. Mention has already been made of the thousands of letters the author received from servicemen, whose lives had already been turned upside down by the war, and who were prompted by Larry to question the value of the "good life" they had longed to return to or achieve.

Maugham himself has remarked that literary works change with the years, and he likes to point out that the great odes of John Keats are different poems from what they were a century and a half ago. *David Copperfield* is not the same novel in 1960 as it was in 1850, when readers were captivated by David, Dora, and Agnes; today we hurry by them to the passages in which Micawber and Uriah Heep appear. The secondary characters in *Great Expectations*, not Pip, now absorb most of our interest in that superb novel. Something like that has happened to *The Razor's Edge* in less than twenty years. We still find Larry agreeable, ingratiating, and all but saintly, but he is more often a bore than he was in 1944. His sweet smile we now sometimes interpret as an expression of spiritual smugness, which can be offensive. His exercises in faith-healing we find embarrassing. We feel like congratulating the young women who failed to snare him as a husband. He has by no means become objectionable in such a brief lapse of years, but he is often tiresome, like many who have "found the truth." On the other hand, Elliott Templeton strikes us as a more interesting and more substantial characterization when we reread the novel. At first he seems merely a ludicrous snob, a wealthy expatriate who finds America vulgar and strident, and who chooses assiduous activity in aristocratic London and Paris "society" as his profession. But he is not a caricature. He is not only snobbish, demasculinized, and exquisite, gossipy and trivial; he is kind, loyal to his family and friends, and generous, and underneath the sophistication is an engaging innocence and naïveté. In the death scene Maugham is at his best, both witty and sincere, aware of both the comedy and the pathos. Elliott Templeton is a composite picture of dozens of expatriate social climbers and snobs, male and female, whom Maugham had known over a period of half a century in European "society," and whom he had pilloried nearly thirty years before in *Our Betters*. There probably is a touch of Henry James in the portrait, which for all the absurdities and trivialities is not unattractive.

*The Razor's Edge* is so good we wish it were better and equal in merit to his three great novels. It is full of good things: the knowledgeable picture of western Europe between the wars; the novelist's success, in spite of his modesty and qualms, with American characters; the sharp portaits of Elliott, Isabel (who suffers from no glandular deficiency), Gray, Suzanne, Gray's father, Mrs. Bradley; the humor; the perceptive comment of the *raisonneur;* the clever structure of the novel, the story told in the first person with Maugham rarely on hand to participate in the crises of the narrative; the lucid, smooth, and adult prose style. But the novel misses real greatness largely because one feels that Maugham regards the saintly Larry as a phenomenon rather than a real person; the reader can believe in him no further than does his creator. The novel does not actually sprawl, but it could be tightened, like *Cakes and Ale;* for example, the sordid story of Sophie Macdonald could be omitted, for the turbulence of her adventures and death is too violent, perhaps frantic, for its function in rounding out the spiritual education of Larry.

Nevertheless *The Razor's Edge* is almost vintage Maugham, and one is able to read it and even reread it with pleasure and interest in these people and their adventures. It has been translated into a dozen languages and next to *Of Human Bondage* and *The Moon and Sixpence* has done most to consolidate Maugham's reputation among a vast number of intelligent readers of fiction.

Just as he determined in the late 1920's to write only four more plays, which were "pigeon-holed in my fancy all ready to be written and I knew myself well enough to be aware that they would pester me till I wrote them," though he felt they would add nothing to his reputation or popularity, so in the middle 1940's he had plaguing ideas for three final novels which he felt a compulsion to write. He knew that no one of them would command even a small fraction of the millions of readers of *The Razor's Edge,* but he was unconcerned with their fate after he had finished writing them. His prognosis was correct: the two he was able to write were not so popular as most of his novels had been and were damned with faint praise in most reviews.

*Then and Now* (1946) is a not very exciting historical novel of politics and amorous intrigue, derived straight from "literature": he translates the powerful play *Mandragola* by Machiavelli into a novel, ingeniously making the novel serve as the genesis of the drama. Maugham enjoyed rereading sixteenth-century Italian history and reacquainting himself with Machiavelli and *The Prince.*

His last novel—and he meant what he said when he termed it his last—*Catalina* (1948), which he calls a romance, is a charming end-piece to his shelf of novels beginning with *Liza of Lambeth* fifty years before. It is a Spanish story, and Maugham writes with understanding and affection of the country where he first knew the delights of his chosen profession. The action of *Catalina* takes place during the Inquisition. It is the tale of a crippled but beautiful and sensible girl who sees a vision of the Virgin Mary in an age when it seemed easier to cross the frontiers of the natural, and who is told that she will be miraculously cured of her lameness by one of three brothers. Although Maugham treats the faith healing simply and without cynicism, he characteristically assigns the healing power not to the eminent and powerful bishop, or to his brother the successful soldier, but to their humble brother, an insignificant baker. Maugham writes with humor of the intrigues of church and state, but the reader's interest lies in the career of Catalina after her lameness disappears. She with difficulty escapes a religious career, wins back and marries her lover, bears him six children, and has a flattering success on the Spanish stage over a long period of years. *Calatina* has a warmth and lighthearted charm that lead one to believe that Maugham wrote his last novel with real pleasure and with affection for his characters. Though essentially a romance, it is agreeably salty and wise.

V

## THE SHORT STORIES

SOMERSET MAUGHAM is more widely known as a writer of short stories than as a dramatist, novelist, or critic, for through the medium of the magazine, radio, film, and television—particularly the popular magazine—his short stories reached hundreds of thousands, perhaps millions, who never attend the theatre and seldom read a book. Moreover, the numerous collections of his stories have been widely read. Many serious critics take little notice of his stories, preferring the relative formlessness of Chekhov and the sometimes blurry indirection of Katherine Mansfield, which they praise as subtlety. Stories by distinguished writers in recent years have been largely in the Chekhov manner, for the definiteness of form in Maupassant and Maugham strikes them as artificial and contrived. Cyril Connolly, however, in the somewhat high-brow *New Statesman* describes Maugham as "the greatest living short-story writer," and without any qualification "a great writer."

Maugham himself has written at length about the stories

of Maupassant and Chekhov, perhaps the greatest of all writers of the short story and the most important in defining its literary form and exemplifying its method. Maupassant, who frequented Mrs. Maugham's salon in Paris, and whom Maugham as a boy may have seen there, set the fashion for the tightly constructed, crisp story, bare of inconsequential detail, with a well-defined beginning and a series of closely connected incidents leading to a sudden and, if possible, unexpected ending. Maugham says of the French writer's stories: "They do not wander along an uncertain line, so that you cannot see where they are leading, but follow without hesitation, from exposition to climax, a bold and vigorous curve." The characters are clearly presented, but they are not complex or subtle. The chief interest is in the anecdote and its irony; brief but adequate descriptions of places and people serve only to advance the story. There is no byplay or witty observation to relieve the tension as we read; few narratives deserve more justly the abused adjective "gripping." Chekhov's stories are of a pattern so different that often they seem to have no pattern at all. They are as casual as the men and women in his four long plays. Irrelevant and sometimes wrong things are said, inconsequential things are done, crises are approached and shunned, climaxes are averted; the stories often end in the air. Despite the differences, the stories of the great Frenchman and the great Russian are equally readable and moving. Chekhov gives a mood, or a sense of the fluidity, perplexity, and mystery of life, or a subtle characterization, or a glance at life in perspective rather than a "slice of life." He has told us that he aims at creating a sense of reality rather than realism, which after all, he implies, is a literary device; Maupassant strives directly not so much for realism or violent naturalism in itself, as for the dramatization of his anecdote.

The first literary influence on Maugham was Maupassant, whose stories he read and reread as a boy and very young man in Paris on visits to his brother Charles and his family. When at eighteen he began writing, he naturally used Maupassant as his model; "naturally" not only because of his acquaintance with the French stories but also because of a similarity of temperament and philosophy. He has admitted that very probably there was from the beginning a definite French influence on his work. He early read French fairy stories and when a schoolboy, Maupassant; at Heidelberg he discovered the maxims of La Rochefoucauld, and later Anatole France, Loti, Racine ("From him I think I learned restraint and composure"); and finally Stendhal, Balzac, Flaubert, and Voltaire. In spite of the French influence Maugham is a thoroughly British writer of fiction, far more in the tradition of Thackeray, Butler, Gissing, Moore, Bennett, and Kipling (Maugham was only fourteen when *Plain Tales from the Hills* was published) than of French novelists and short-story writers of the past century; and as a dramatist he belongs in the theatre of Wilde, Houghton, Hankin, Pinero, and Rattigan. But the French infuence was great. He admits a preference for the type of story Maupassant wrote, but there is a more fundamental reason why Maugham's stories recall Maupassant's rather than Chekhov's: he says flatly that it is the only kind of story he can write. One must "write as he can and as he must, because he is a certain sort of man." Each writer has his own natural endowments

J. Arthur Rank Organization, from "Encore"

Maugham and his dog on the terrace at Villa Mauresque.

Recent portrait study of Somerset Maugham.

Allan G. Chappelow, M.A., F.I

and his own idiosyncrasies, and as a result he sees things in a manner peculiar to himself, and "he gives his vision the form that is forced on him by his nature."

Maugham likes a plot. He declares that it is a "natural desire in a reader to want to know what happens to the people in whom his interest has been aroused, and the plot is the means by which you gratify that desire." He likes the kind of story one can tell at the club or dinner table. For all the excellence of Chekhov, one would have difficulty in relating in an intelligible manner one of his plots, either of a story or a play. The fact that before 1951 Maugham's stories were more popular, or at least more seriously considered, in France than in England and that the French critics have never damned them as "competent" has for the author this explanation: "The French, with their classical sense and their orderly minds, demand a precise form and are exasperated by a work in which the ends are left lying about, themes are propounded and not resolved, and a climax is foreseen and then eluded. This precision on the other hand has always been slightly anti-pathetic to the English. Our great novels have been shape-less. . . . This is the life they know, they have thought, with its arbitrariness and inconsequence. . . . If I am right in this surmise, I can do nothing about it and must resign myself to being competent for the rest of my life. My preposses-sions in the arts are on the side of law and order." In 1951, however, the *Complete Short Stories* in three volumes were published in London and for the first time he enjoyed an enormous popularity in England as a short-story writer.

In 1960 Maugham became the first British author to motivate a major television series. The Associated-Rediffusion dramatized one story weekly, after having secured rights for sixty-three of the hundred stories, and hoped to contract for more.

Maugham defines a short story as "A piece of fiction, of any length you choose, which deals with a single situation, but this situation may be a mood, a character, or an event." This definition he arrived at over twenty years ago after he had read hundreds of short stories in preparing an anthology. He read all of Chekhov, Henry James, Poe, and Kipling; he read widely in the works of Hawthorne, Katherine Mansfield, Franz Werfel, Stephen Crane, Huxley, Conrad, Ring Lardner, and dozens of other writers. He read definitions of the short story form by Poe, Chekhov, and others. His own definition is necessarily wide to include them all. Although most readers prefer stories of incident, the current predilection of readers and critics among the upper levels of the intellectuals is for the plotless story, perhaps only delineating a mood, and consequently there has been much exaltation of Chekhov and his "school" at the expense of Maupassant and his "school." It is quite improbable that Somerset Maugham today could place even one of his best stories (under a nom de plume) in *The New Yorker* or any of the literary quarterlies. He accepts with composure his disrepute among most of the intellectuals and asserts that it is the fashion of the time, that the delineation of character or incident need not be of less consequence than the delineation of a mood. He has read with interest various textbooks on short-story writing, as Barrie is said to have perused books on playwriting, for he enjoys theory and criticism, but he does not find these guides helpful. He has written many pages outlining his own theories of fiction, particularly of the short story, but an aspiring writer would likewise not find them very helpful.

His stories, however, speak for themselves. They are distinguished by their lucidity, simplicity (Shakespeare reminds us that "an honest tale speeds best being plainly told"), and liveliness. The fact that they are "readable" is sufficient proof of their *competence*: readability is the first of merits, and probably accounts for the fact that he is the most widely read story-writer of the century. Desmond MacCarthy points out that some literary reputations spread outward from a narrow circle of admirers, whereas others spread inward from a wide circumference of readers; some authors and artists first impress the discriminating few and gradually achieve popular success, whereas others first win popular success and then impress the intellectuals. For the most part reputations such as Dickens's, Mark Twain's, Charlie Chaplin's, and Balzac's, which spread inward from without, are more sure. Maugham belongs to that happy group whose books please the many and at least enough of the discriminating few to draw serious attention to his work. He first enjoyed a wide audience because of comedies, and years later multiplied the number of his admirers with his exotic stories of the East. Serious criticism and appreciation of such masterpieces as *The Circle* and *Cakes and Ale* formed more slowly but have grown steadily with the passing years.

He wrote his first stories when in medical school, and by 1899 had a volume ready, *Orientations*. The six stories in the collection have no great distinction: they are "orientations, to find one's literary self," as the young author explains (rather pompously, in French) after the Table of Contents. They are interesting only as the youthful work of one who later tried seriously to improve his style. The prose has little of the simplicity, suppleness, and rhythm of his later work, but it is evident that his lively sense of humor and irony were acquired early in life—qualities he does not give to Philip in *Of Human Bondage*. The very first story in *Orientations*, "The Punctiliousness of Don Sebastian," is a reminder of his first, happy trip to Spain, and is "immoral" like the play *Schiffbrüchig* which he wrote at eighteen and *A Man of Honour* a few years later. It is the humorous account of a Spanish don who, after his wife's death, discovers that she had long been the mistress of his own brother, an archbishop. He thereupon murders his brother, becomes a court favorite, and makes a successful second marriage. He suffers no twinges of conscience.

"A Bad Example" is the story that he was to dramatize thirty years later as *Sheppey*. A city clerk who tries to apply Christianity literally to daily life is certified as insane. It its not well written. Maugham later made a serious study of English prose style and would never in his maturity write such a sentence violent with adverbs as this: "She walked tempestuously down to Fleet Street, jumped fiercely on a bus, frantically caught the train to Camberwell, and having reached her house on the Adonis Road, flung herself furiously down on a chair." The satire has a sharp sting; the wife regards serious Bible readings as a symptom of abnormality; the clergyman is irritated by the proposal to interpret literally the Sermon on the Mount; the physician's notions of sanity are far from scientific.

Of the other stories only "Daisy" has any merit. Here for the first time he uses Blackstable (Whitstable) as the scene, and his characters are small-town gossips and snobs. The story lacks fairness—the virtuous people have all the disagreeable qualities and the sinners have too much charm and generosity, but it has the vigor and slashing humor of *Main Street*, which it somewhat anticipates. Like Dreiser's *Sister Carrie* and W. L. George's *Bed of Roses,* "Daisy" has a shocking ending: a former prostitute, unrepentant, is left wealthy and not particularly unhappy. This was a bold ending in nineteenth-century fiction. The stories in *Orientations* presage the author's unconventionality, if not the excellence of his prose style. He would not permit the inclusion of these stories in the one-volume collection published in London in 1934 under the title *Altogether* and in America as *East and West,* or in *The Complete Short Stories* published in 1951.

Until the First World War Maugham's chief interest was in the drama and novel, and he wrote no more short stories for nearly twenty years. It was not until his war-time journey to the South Seas furnished him with themes which he thought more suitable for the brief narrative than for the novel or drama that he resumed short-story writing. Ignoring *Orientations,* he says, "It was as a beginner of forty that I wrote the story that is now called 'Rain.' " He wrote these stories, practically all of which were first published in magazines, as a relief from other work which was growing irksome. By this time he was financially free of worry and could afford to write as he chose. On this journey he took notes on what he observed and listened to other men's stories. When he had written six somewhat long tales, he published them under the title *The Trembling of a Leaf* (1921). The title is from Sainte-Beuve: *L'extrême félicité à peine séparée par une feuille tremblante de l'extrême désespoir, n'est-ce pas la vie?* The characters are Europeans in the South Seas, in an alien environment to which they adjust themselves with difficulty and often with loss of balance and tranquillity. The title suggests that they are of an unsettled nature, equally susceptible of happiness or despair—which are separated only by the trembling of a leaf. This book made Maugham's fame as a writer of short stories as great as his fame as a dramatist and novelist.

The first story is "Mackintosh," a powerful psychological study of an island administrator and his assistant, who are completely unlike in temperament, tastes, education, personal habits, and ethics. The administrator, Walker, Pickwickian in appearance, is gross, sensual, boorish, thick-skinned and unscrupulous; but in his uncouth way he is competent and underneath his drive and harshness he has an affection for the islanders, whom he regards as children. His assistant, Mackintosh, gaunt and ascetic, is scholarly, tidy, refined, educated. He grows to loathe his vulgar superior, who never suspects that he is the object of hate and who drives Mackintosh to exasperation by his crudeness. The assistant makes it possible for a disgruntled native to kill Walker, and then Mackintosh, seized by an agonizing remorse, kills himself. There is a fierce irony in the catastrophe: although he is not guilty of murder, his puritan conscience does not relax in this land of easy morals, and he destroys himself because of the death of a man he hated savagely. The story is told objectively, and we feel pity and horror for both; Maugham uncharacteristically observes the old law of poetic justice.

Travel agencies and steamship companies were, possibly still are, indebted to "The Fall of Edward Barnard," a cheerful story in which life in the South Seas is painted in its most alluring colors. It, too, is a story of environment, but this time the effects are not disastrous. One gathers that some of the author's views are expressed by Edward Barnard, who, having been sent to the South Seas on a business mission, succumbs to its spell, renounces his American fiancée, a successful future, and the various amenities of civilized existence in Chicago. He remains in Papeete, shorn of ambition but happy, maintaining that he has lost the whole world but has secured his soul. His good friend who comes to take him back to America, the personification of success and decorum, is shocked by the languid, torpid life on the island, and a bit nettled that wants can be satisfied with so little expenditure of energy. He attempts to persuade Edwards to return to Chicago, and in their debate the author states sympathetically the views of Edward, whereas his friend, in high stiff collar, is a caricature of civilized man. The initial situation is not unlike that of Strether and Chad Newsome in *The Ambassadors*, although the short story has little of Henry James's subtle analysis of character and environmental influence. Few can read "The Fall of Edward Barnard" without craving to set sail (or fly) to the South Pacific, and many readers fancy that they would be content to "fall" as well.

According to his own criteria of the good story, Maugham

is justified in considering "Red" the best of his hundred stories. Its technique is flawless. Every detail serves to make the final irony shattering; a plausible unity of time is secured through a natural and clever revelation in dialogue of antecedent events. The story begins with a rapturous idyl, an account of the great and beautiful love of a white sailor and a native girl. Both are of extraordinary beauty. One day Red, the sailor, disappears and the girl is inconsolable. After some years she is persuaded to marry another white man, but her worship of Red does not abate. When she is old and fat, Red accidentally meets her and her husband. Red is obese, bald, and vulgar. She does not recognize him but her husband does. "Was that the man who had prevented him from being happy? Was that the man whom Sally had loved all these years and for whom she had waited so desperately? It was grotesque. . . . He had been cheated. They had seen each other at last and had not known it. . . . The gods had played him a trick and he was old now. He wondered what she would say if he told her now that the fat old man sitting in the chair was the lover whom she remembered still with the passionate abandonment of youth." No crueler love story has ever been written. Paolo and Francesca, Romeo and Juliet die in love and beauty, but Red and Sally live to be obscene in appearance and shabby of soul. Maugham makes the beginning lovely and idyllic to intensify the bitterness at the end; the result is that "Red" is haunting and tragic. If the style were more austere, a little less rich and elegant, it might well pass as an ironic and savage story by Maupassant.

"The Pool" is also tragic but not so moving. It is a sordid

story of the degeneration of a Scotsman who, ignorant of native psychology, naïvely trusting in the saw that human nature is the same the world over, marries a lovely native girl and treats her as a white man would treat a white woman. The marriage fails but his infatuation survives. Miserable, jealous, almost constantly drunk, he sinks under public scorn and self-loathing and commits suicide. A favorite touch of Maugham irony is here: if the Scotsman had been less decent and taken the native girl as a mistress, tragedy might have been averted. European notions of honor are sometimes disastrous at home (as in *A Man of Honour*) but they must be practiced with even more wariness in the East. The story is not without beauty and poetry; especially exquisite are the descriptions of the pool, which becomes a mysterious symbol. But life in the South Seas is far less alluring here than in "The Fall of Edward Barnard."

"Honolulu" is a fantastic but rather dull story of unexplained animal magnetism and voodooism, a piece of folklore about which the character to whom the story is told is properly skeptical.

The final story in *The Trembling of a Leaf* is "Miss Thompson," later known as "Rain," and Maugham's best-known tale. It had its beginning in a brief entry in the author's notebook. While traveling from Honolulu to Pago Pago, he jotted down impressions of passengers who attracted his attention. Of Miss Thompson he wrote: "Plump, pretty in a coarse fashion, perhaps not more than twenty-seven . . . a white dress and a large white hat, long white boots from which the calves bulged in cotton stockings." Of the missionary he wrote, "He was a tall, thin man with long limbs loosely jointed . . . hollow cheeks and high cheek-bones, his fine large dark eyes were deep in their sockets, he had full sensuous lips, he wore his hair rather long. He had a cadaverous air and a look of suppressed fire." And of the missionary's wife: "She was a little woman . . . New England . . . not prominent blue eyes behind gold-rimmed pince-nez, her face long like a sheep's. . . . She had the quick movements of a bird . . . her voice high, metallic, and without inflection. . . . She was dressed in black and wore round her neck a gold chain from which hung a small cross." Maugham talked with the couple but once and with Miss Thompson not at all. Here is his note for the story: "A prostitute flying from Honolulu after a raid, lands at Pago-Pago. There lands there also a missionary and his wife. Also the narrator. All are obliged to stay there owing to an outbreak of measles. The missionary finding out her profession persecutes her. He reduces her to misery, shame, and repentance. . . . He induces the governor to order her return to Honolulu. One morning he is found with his throat cut by his own hand and she is once more radiant and self-possessed. She looks at men scornfully, exclaims: 'Dirty pigs!' "

"Rain" is a little masterpiece which the tense, melo-dramatic stage, cinema, and musical versions, with their lurid advertising, have not damaged. Its power comes from its restraint and fairness. The missionary is not merely a narrow-minded fanatic; he is courageous and sincere. Sadie is friendly and generous, but nauseatingly gross. Dr. Macphail, the *raisonneur* and chorus of good sense, is in-effectual, and the thin piping of his rationalism is all but unheard amid the blasts of Davidson's fanaticism. The maddening effect of persistent rain is cleverly suggested by a minimum of weather talk. The Freudian undertones of Davidson's tragedy are heard only once—in his "hills of Nebraska" dream. Practically none of the conversations between Sadie and the minister are reproduced; the most dramatic scenes, Davidson's attempts to make love to the prostitute and his suicide, are not described at all. The ending is swift; the final lines, Sadie's outburst of disgust— "You men! You filthy, dirty pigs! You're all the same, all of you. Pigs! Pigs!" reveals the whole truth. The qualities of "Rain," however, are not all negative. The characters are as sharply delineated as one can expect in a brief tale; Pago Pago is unforgettably painted; the everlasting rain at first depresses the reader, but its effect is cumulative and becomes almost distracting. The story, taut in construction and simply told, is bold and exciting. The implications of unhealthy asceticism and sex repression make "Rain" a notable pioneer in Freudian fiction.

From the church's point of view it no doubt has had a damaging effect on the popular image of the foreign missionary, for many thousands of readers and theatre and cinema-goers think of a missionary only in terms of Mr. Davidson. Graham Greene asserts that Maugham has done more than anyone else to stamp the idea of the repressed, strait-laced clergyman on the popular imagination. Greene quotes the famous remarks by Mr. Davidson which reveal his religious sincerity but at the same time repel the reader and impair or destroy any sympathy he may have for the labors of the missionary: "When we went there they had no sense of sin at all. They broke the commandments one after the other and never knew they were doing wrong.

And I think that was the most difficult part of my work, to instill into the natives the sense of sin."

"Miss Thompson" was rejected by a half dozen magazines before it was finally accepted by Mencken and Nathan for *The Smart Set,* a sprightly periodical with a small circulation. One wonders idly whether Maugham's ship companions, especially the missionary and his wife, ever read "Miss Thompson." It is most unlikely that they ever saw a copy of *The Smart Set.*

Maugham's third collection of stories, *The Casuarina Tree,* appeared in 1926 and repeated the success of *The Trembling of a Leaf.* The author explains the meaning of the title: the casuarina is a grey, rugged tree found on tropic coasts, a bit grim beside the lush vegetation about it. It suggests the exiled Europeans who in temperament and stamina are often ill equipped for life in the tropics. (There is a casuarina tree in Mr. Maugham's somewhat lush garden at Cap Ferrat.) The stories had already been published in magazines, for by 1926 the competition among editors for Maugham's stories was keen—and profitable for the author.

Although again all six tales deal with the British in the Far East, the setting of the first, and best, story is in England. "Before the Party" is an ironical comedy unusual in technique. Nothing happens in the story. A middle-class country family consisting of two young women and their parents are about to leave for a garden party at the vicar's. While they draw on their gloves and await their car, the widowed daughter tells the truth about her husband's death in Borneo. The interest lies not so much in her sordid narrative as in the reception of the shocking story by her formal, decorous, pious family. The reader knows as little as the family and shares their surprise when they learn that their son-in-law had been a hopeless drunkard and that their daughter had murdered him. Upset as they are and involved in a hideous moral dilemma, they leave for the tea party, given in honor of a visiting bishop, which they must attend. The technique is like that of *Rosmersholm*: it is nearly all exposition. Whereas Maupassant and O. Henry use an unexpected twist of event to surprise or shock the reader on the last page, Maugham in a number of stories startles or jolts the reader by an unconventional ethical point of view. The surprise at the end of "Before the Party" comes from calm statement of the murderess, who is free of remorse. "You'll get used to it, you know," she said quietly. "At first I thought of it all the time, but now I forget it for two or three days altogether. It's not as if there were any danger." "Footprints in the Jungle," "The Back of Beyond," "Winter Cruise," "A Marriage of Convenience," "The Ant and the Grasshopper," "The Facts of Life," "The Mother," "A String of Beads" all end with a flouting of what is called poetic justice. Sometimes, says Maugham, man can eat his cake and have it, too.

"P. & O." is a rather flat story of the strange death at sea of an Irishman whose native mistress has put him under a spell. A shipboard acquaintance returning to England to divorce her husband is so moved by the Irishman's death that she becomes less self-centered, sheds her vanity and hardness, becomes Christianly forgiving, and unchristianly tolerant of wrongdoing. This sudden regeneration seems as improbable as the voodooism.

"The Outstation," however, is Maugham the short-story

writer at his best. It is a study of snobbishness, more ludicrous than detestable. The situation is similar to that in "Mackintosh": two officials thrown together in an out-of-the-way post come to despise each other. Warburton is a gentleman and as snobbish as Elliott Templeton. He dresses for dinner (on the edge of the jungle), at breakfast carefully unfolds and reads *The Times*, six weeks late to the day, corresponds regularly with Lord This and Lady That back in England. He is a good administrator, and just. Cooper, his assistant, is a man of the people, vulgar in tastes and manners, careless in dress and language, and disdainful of class distinctions. He is tactless with the natives. Neither character monopolizes our sympathy, and their thickening animosity becomes very dramatic. Finally Cooper is killed by an outraged native. Although Warburton suspects his assistant's danger and takes no step to prevent the murder, he is not driven to suicide like Mackintosh, but feels a great relief. He resumes with satisfaction his formal, stuffy routine, which had been rudely upset by the barbarian Cooper. "The Outstation" is a simple but powerful study of antipathy that grows into intense hate when two people of very different backgrounds and temperaments are thrown closely together in a lonely place.

"The Force of Circumstance," which treats of the white woman's attitude toward miscegenation, is equally simple, and free as it is of irony, it is closer to the pathetic than most of Maugham's stories. What seems to be an ideal marriage is shattered when a young wife discovers that her husband had once had an alliance with a native woman, who had borne him several children. Her reason assures her that the affair is over, that her husband loves her devotedly, but her instincts (or prejudices) override her reason. She tortures herself by picturing the Malay woman's black arms around Guy's neck; she recalls with horror that his dark children were born in her bed. She goes back to England, and Guy, crushed and lonely, permits the Malay woman to return to his house. The revelation of antecedent action comes slowly and dramatically as in "Before the Party." The story is presented with complete objectiveness. The French critic Paul Dottin points out that Guy is the victim of two weaknesses: his naïve belief that the past does not exist, and his equally naïve belief that woman is a creature of reason, whereas she really follows her impulses and what she considers her instincts.

The other two stories in *The Casuarina Tree* are of little significance. "The Yellow Streak" has an autobiographical interest in that Maugham, like its hero, almost lost his life in a bore (a sudden tidal flow). But the story is weakened by a touch of snobbery: why does the author make the coward a half-caste? Would a hundred percent Englishman never fail to be valorous? "The Letter" has an exciting detective-story interest (Maugham himself later dramatized it successfully), but the characters are too broadly sketched, and there is no psychological study of jealousy, remorse or fear, which the situation might afford. The basic anecdote was told to Maugham in the East, and it may be that in order to prevent identification he handles his characters too loosely and gingerly; as it was, the story caused no little scandalous gossip among certain colonials. Leslie, who murders her lover and barely escapes the gallows, is a monster, almost the only character in Maugham's fiction with no redeeming traits.

In a postscript the author foresees that colonial readers will attempt to identify certain characters in *The Casuarina Tree* with real people. With some asperity he attacks these gossipy readers in advance, and defends the author's right to take *characteristics* from living people. "A work of fiction . . . is an arrangement which the author makes of the facts of his experience with the idiosyncrasies of his own personality. It is an unlikely, and unimportant, accident if it happens to be a copy of life. . . . Facts are but a canvas on which the artist draws a significant pattern. I venture therefore to claim that the persons of these stories are imaginary. . . ." The story of "The Letter" and other incidents were told to him—"I had nothing to do but make them probable, coherent, and dramatic." The snobbish official in "The Outstation" was suggested by a British consul in Spain he had known years before. The germ of "Before the Party" is a fragmentary entry in his notebook concerning a Resident who took a bottle of whiskey to bed with him every night. He has declared that only three of his Far East stories were told to him: "The Letter," "Footprints in the Jungle," and "The Book-Bag." "The rest were invented as I have shown 'Rain' was, by the accident of my happening upon persons here and there, who in themselves or from something I heard about them, suggested a theme that seemed suitable for a short story."

Sometimes the lapse of time between the incident in real life and his use of it in a story made its use safe and inoffensive. For example when he was twenty-seven he made this entry in his notebook: "They were talking about V. F. whom they'd all known. She published a volume of passionate love poems, obviously not addressed to her husband. It made them laugh to think that she'd carried on a long affair under his nose, and they'd have given anything to know what he felt when at last he read them." Many years later he appended to this entry, in italics, *"This note gave me the idea for a story which I wrote forty years later. It is called 'The Colonel's Lady.'"*

Does Maugham protest too much that his characters are largely imaginary? The fact remains that few other modern writers have been so widely suspected of using actual people as models for disagreeable characters in their fiction.

Somerset Maugham waited for ten years after the armistice in 1918 to write his war book, and he wrote it as fiction, using practically none of the material in the published portion of his notebooks. He chose to write not on what he had witnessed in the early part of the war in the Ambulance Corps, but of his adventures later in the Intelligence Department. Obviously he could not give a factual account of these experiences, partly because they were of a secret nature, and partly because they were mostly dull and monotonous. He notes with characteristic dry humor, however, that *Ashenden, or the British Agent* is not much more fictional in character than most war books that pretend to be truthful memoirs.

*Ashenden* is a collection of six long stories and a few brief war-time anecdotes. They are written in the first person. The stories have their settings in Switzerland, France, Russia, and Italy. The author's attitude toward his material is unusual. It is slightly deprecatory; he is somewhat embarrassed by the hackneyed melodrama coloring his duties, and takes refuge in humor and in an austerity that often hardens into callousness. He was aware that in countless novels and plays the experiences of a secret agent had been reproduced or fancied with such raciness that the real thing seemed an anticlimax. It occurred to him that reality seemed more artificial and less sensational than fiction. Switzerland, where he was stationed, had a picture-post-card showiness— ". . . the lake was absurd, the water was too blue, and its beauty, hitting you in the face, exasperated rather than thrilled." Some of the tasks assigned to him seemed to have been suggested to his superiors by their reading of lurid spy-thrillers. But because of understate-ment, humor, and detachment the stories in *Ashenden* achieve a power and verisimilitude they would have lacked had the author exploited more vigorously the melodrama of his experiences.

As would be expected, his principal interest is the obser-vation of people under the peculiar stresses of war. In "Miss King," the story of an old governess who dies before she is able to make a statement of seeming importance, is a sharp picture of Geneva in the second year of the war. "The Hairless Mexican" is a thrilling spy story enlivened by rich humor; its ending, swift and shocking, is both un-expected and plausible. "Giulia Lazarri" is equally exciting and contains opportunities for pathos which the author resolutely shuns. The ending is characteristically ironical in its unexpected revelation of character. "The Traitor" is a harrowing account of the trapping of a German spy. "His Excellency" has a very tenuous connection with the war. An ambassador tells Ashenden of an ignominious love affair which is of particular interest to readers of *Of Human Bondage,* as the vulgar object of the ambassador's passion years before had been another Mildred Rogers. (Why was this odious creature still in Maugham's memory?) "Mr. Harrington's Washing" draws incidentally a picture of St. Petersburg during the early days of the Revolution that is far more memorable than the portrait of Ashenden's astonishing and ingenuous traveling companion.

These stories are realistic but quite unlike the First-World-War fiction of Barbusse, Remarque, Dos Passos, and other realists in that Maugham is content to report without comment. In all of *Ashenden* there is no expression of pacifism or political bias of any kind, no intimation that England and her allies are in any way more virtuous than the enemy, or that the German spies are more perfidious than the British. Why did Goebbels find this book so objectionable that because of it he singled out Maugham for arrest and punishment in 1940? As a matter of fact *Ashenden* is so unconcerned with political and national prejudices that it could very well annoy flag-waving patriots and pacifists who would emphasize the horror or absurdity of war.

Maugham made his reputation as a short-story writer with his exotic tales of the Far East, but he writes with equal felicity about the Englishman in his native land and on the Continent. *First Person Singular* (1931) contains six stories, all of which have a European setting and which are equal in merit to the stories in *The Trembling of a Leaf* and *The Casuarina Tree*. Two of the tales have to do with extremely eccentric behavior, two are humorous, one is a pathetic story of artistic failure, and one is an ironical study in ethics—"The wages of virtue is death." The author's skepticism and critical powers, what his detractors call his cynicism, and his fascination by unpredictable behavior are more manifest than ever. The French and Spanish titles of this collection, demurely called *First Person Singular* in English, are deliciously Latin: *Amours Singulières* and *Amores Raras*. The author is a minor character in each story, a slight catalytic agent in the plot, and a chorus commenting with dry humor. There is a foreword in which the author, to no one's surprise, repeats his views about drawing characters from life.

"Virtue" is as ironical as its title. A middle-aged woman falls in love with a young man and leaves her husband, who adores her. Her husband is driven to suicide and her young lover finally deserts her. The plot is old, but the choral observation is almost fresh: if she had been content to have a discreet affair with young Morton, the husband would never have known and "would be alive today. It's her damned virtue that caused the whole trouble. I prefer a loose woman to a selfish one and a wanton to a fool." "The Round Dozen" is a highly implausible but entertaining story of a bigamist and his twelfth conquest. Mortimer Ellis had his original in real life, a notorious bigamist who had died long before this story was written. The fantastic career of the rogue caught Maugham's fancy, and the "criminal" is allowed to state his own case. He does so with considerable success, and not without conviction and charm. There is an excellent description of a dull English seaside resort in the off season, and of an antiquated family that takes its holiday there in dreadful Victorian formality. "The Human Element" is a trivial story of a wealthy woman who had had for years her handsome chauffeur as her lover.

Much better is "The Alien Corn," a suave and wise account of a Jewish family trying desperately to smother their racial characteristics and become entirely Gentile-English. It is told with sympathy and quite without irony; the pathetic failure of their unconforming and not very gifted son to become a great pianist moves us to pity. The remaining two stories are humorous. "Jane" is a comic version of the ugly duckling theme: a middle-aged woman, dowdy, old-fashioned, and plain, marries a young man deeply in love with her. The strange marriage is a great success until Jane, bored with the inane conversation of youth (moreover, her handsome young husband is obviously quite undersexed), deserts him for an older man of parts. "The Creative Impulse" is a diverting, unbelievable yarn peppered with Maugham's contempt for humorless phony intellectuals and the Chelsea-Bloomsbury literati. Satire is here in plenty, but its sting is hardly felt in the mumbo-jumbo of literary conversation, and in the common humanity of Mrs. Forrester's low-brow husband. The climax comes when Forrester deserts this cathedral of the intelligentsia and elopes with the cook, who shares his taste for penny dreadfuls. The house of the Forresters is as far from reality as the House of Usher, but the author takes advantage of exaggeration, burlesque, and high improbability to create a delightful piece of satirical humor.

In 1933 was published *Ah King*, six stories of the Malay States. They are prefaced by a brief description of the Chinese boy who acted as the author's servant during a six months' journey through Borneo, Indo-China, and Siam. Ah King was the perfect servant, accomplished, cheerful, dependable, clean. When the journey ended, Maugham was amazed to find Ah King in tears. "It had never occurred to me for an instant that he looked upon me as anything but an odd, rather silly person who paid his wages. That he had any feeling for me never entered my head. I was embarrassed. . . . He wept because he was leaving me. It is for these tears that I now give his name to this collection of stories." Perhaps Maugham's purblindness here is significant: there may be more simple, unselfish affection in heaven and earth than are dreamed of in his philosophy. The book might well have been named *The Unaccountability of Man*, for these six stories have the familiar Maugham theme: men under emotional stress do not behave predictably like chemicals in a test tube, but often in unanticipated and startling fashion. Maugham rejects the notion of an orderly moral universe, implying that no two people are the same and that absolute truth does not exist.

In "Footprints in the Jungle," one of Maugham's best stories, the perpetrators of a heinous crime, after a number of years, when it becomes certain that their guilt will never be discovered, cease to suffer remorse and lead a reasonably happy life. "The Book-Bag" with great delicacy reveals the incestuous love of a girl for her brother. Upon his marriage this Electra kills herself; her suicide is a selfish deed that wrecks her brother's marriage. "The Vessel of Wrath" is a droll, almost farcical version of "Rain," with the sex of the principals reversed. Miss Jones is a grim missionary who resolutely looks on the bright side of things. "With the ferocity of an avenging angel she sought out the good in her fellowmen." Spinsterish and aging, she not only reforms a drunken ruffian but marries him. Agitated by an irresistible sex attraction the scamp has for her, she leads him to the nuptial couch persuading herself that she is concerned only with his spiritual salvation. The story is genuinely amusing from the third page to the exquisite last line. "The Door of Opportunity" is the story of a colonial officer who makes the unforgivable mistake of appearing cowardly before the natives. In spite of his many good qualities his white friends turn from him, and his wife leaves him in disgust. "The Back of Beyond" is a fairly stereotyped story of adultery with the unconventional conclusion that cuckoldry is sometimes better than loneliness. In "Neil Macadam," Maugham's most erotic story, an uninhibited nymphomaniac has designs upon a puritanical young Scotsman, who succeeds in repulsing her. Insanely following him into the jungle, she becomes lost and perishes. There is no spirit of burlesque as in *Joseph Andrews,* no cynical laughs at Neil's virginity. Maugham must have smiled at the ending—virtue triumphs and the wages of sin is death.

Ray Long, a famous, somewhat spectacular publisher of the 1920's, who considered "The Book-Bag" the best short story he ever read, won Maugham's consent to write a number of stories for the *Cosmopolitan* brief enough to be printed on two opposite pages of the magazine, with some space surrendered to an illustration. Long had read *On a Chinese Screen* and was certain of Maugham's ability to say much in little, and for once save the reader from the vexation of hunting for the ending of a story among the advertisements in the back pages of the magazine—a vexation one is spared in reading the invertebrate stories in *The New Yorker.* Maugham enjoyed his assignment and discovered how verbose he had always been. He could not afford to waste a word and by necessity followed Mark

Twain's advice, "As to the adjective: when in doubt, strike it out." Since he had always had more plots than he could use, he went to his notebooks and found more than enough material for the twenty-nine stories. After more than two years "my natural verbosity got the better of me and I found myself no longer able to keep stories in the limits imposed upon me. Then I had to stop."

*Cosmopolitans* moved Christopher Morley to nominate Somerset Maugham as the most readable author of his time. All the stories except one have the "design" which the author feels should be imposed on any piece of fiction, and few of them, if any, fail to entertain. Some of the stories are humorous: that of the banker whom the author mistakes for a card-sharper; the cockney woman running a hotel in Asia Minor; the woman who eats only one thing for lunch— and impoverishes the narrator by eating one by one a dozen expensive dishes at Foyot's (a brilliant story); the unhappy husband-to-be who cleverly forces his fiancée to break their engagement; the two madams in a Latin American city who protest (with success) to the authorities against unfair competition by amateurs from the United States— temporary residents seeking an easy divorce; the American woman who achieves a great success in London society by inventing a rugged husband and past—she had already appeared in American folklore and in *Our Betters*. Some have a biting humor: in "The Judgment Seat" three rigidly moral people, whose morality has brought them only misery, are sentenced by God neither to heaven nor to hell, but to oblivion. After the Almighty blows lightly and annihilates them, he says smugly to a philosopher who had been arguing with him, "You cannot but allow that on this occasion I have happily combined my All-Power with my All-Goodness." Another grimly humorous story is "Louise," which describes the worst of tyrants, the selfish weakling who dominates the strong. Louise is a tiresome, formidable "invalid" whose final despicable act is to die of a heart attack on her daughter's wedding day. Some are simple sketches of human goodness. One is in reality a familiar essay on poker. Some are starkly tragic: the story of the four fat Dutchmen whose great friendship is brought to a catastrophic end by jealousy; the artist who becomes a beggar in Vera Cruz; the Hollander who is followed all over the East by an offended native and finally murdered; the Russian who murders his wife. These are nearly all adroit and telling stories, too adult to hold children from play, but lively enough to hold old men from the chimney corner.

His next-to-last volume of stories bears a title derived from medical jargon, *The Mixture as Before*. To detractors of Maugham this title is a confession that he is knowingly a formula writer, content to provide a grateful and rewarding public with what they think they like. In his preface Maugham defends his choice of title and his professionalism. The London *Times* review of *Cosmopolitans* was headed "The Mixture as Before," meant, the author declares, in a depreciatory sense. But he did not take it as such, and boldly used the phrase as the title for his new collection. In his preface he says with a soupçon of tartness, "After pursuing the art of fiction for over forty years I have a notion that I know a good deal more about it than most people [including the *Times* reviewer]." In these forty years, he continues, he has seen the star of many a writer burn brilliantly for a time, then fade out completely, whereas his own fiction has shown no falling off in public approbation. Why shouldn't the professional do better work than the amateur? So, why not the mixture as before?

Although none of the ten stories are dull, only two have the brilliance one expects of Maugham at his best. Perhaps he has overused the upside-down trick. In "The Lion's Skin" a phony aristocrat loses his life behaving almost ostentatiously like a gentleman; three fat women avenge themselves on a skinny acquaintance, who can safely eat anything, by gorging themselves; a convict suffers no remorse for having murdered his wife, but his conscience is tormented by a shabby lie he once told about his best friend; the private life of a celebrated opera singer is vulgar and revolting. The best stories are "An Official Position," the chilling story of a convict-camp executioner preparing for his first guillotining, and "The Facts of Life," a charming, unbelievable story of a boy who violates each of his father's precepts and comes out all the better because of his misconduct. Even more incredible is "The Treasure," suitable for a smoking-car or locker-room yarn. The idea for "Lord Mountdrago" had been in his mind for years, but Maugham is not at his best in using unexplained occultism as a theme.

His last volume of stories, *Creatures of Circumstance* (1947)—a title adequate for most of his fiction—is again the mixture as before. In his Preface he again defends the neatly constructed "magazine story" with a beginning, a middle, and an end. Again he deplores the fact that many young writers are influenced by Chekhov but have an imperfect acquaintance with the Russian genius and his peculiar, quiet skill. In everything Maugham has written about the short story, and he has written a great deal, he deplores the influence of Chekhov. Again, does Maugham protest too much? Is he inclined to be somewhat contentious in defending the kind of story he himself writes? What he says of Chekhov is equally true of him: "The simple fact is that Chekhov believed what writers, being human, are very apt to believe, namely that what he was best able to do was the best thing to do." The closing passage in the Preface to his final volume of stories is not actually peevish, but it is salty: "It has amused me to tell stories and I have told a great many. It is a misfortune for me that the telling of a story just for the sake of the story is not an activity that is in favor with the intelligentsia. I endeavor to bear my misfortune with fortitude."

Four of the stories are excellent, the others readable but somewhat routine and repetitive of earlier themes. Unforgettable, however, is "The Unconquered," Maugham's only piece of fiction with the Second World War as a setting. It is a powerful story of a French girl who is raped by a Nazi soldier. He afterward comes to love her and wishes to marry her, but her fierce hatred of the Germans leads her to drown their child the day it is born. Three of the tales have all the elements needed for a full-length novel. In "The Colonel's Lady," a delightful story of a mousy wife of an almost dictatorial male, it transpires that she had a long and passionate love affair under the unseeing eyes of her smug husband. "The Kite" is one of Maugham's best stories, Freudian in nature, precise in details, tracing the break-up of a marriage. And the fourth story, "Sanitorium," which came directly from Maugham's experience in a Scottish sanitorium in 1919, has all the ingredients for a good novel: there is a group of diversified characters with a common, gnawing interest—their ill health; it has pathos, humor, and compassion; the drama of human lives is played in a setting the author is well able to reproduce. "Sanitorium" does not conform to Maugham's definition of a good short story, for it has various threads of interest and a complexity he would deny a short narrative. But it has what many of his stories lack, an additional dimension of compassion and understanding.

It is possible that a few other stories written by Maugham near the turn of the century have not appeared in any collection. In *Ellery Queen's Mystery Magazine* for February 1959, for example, was published "A Point of Law," which had first appeared in the October 1903 issue of *The Strand Magazine* and had not since been reprinted. The same issue contained A. Conan Doyle's "The Adventure of the Empty House," the first story in *The Return of Sherlock Holmes.* "A Point of Law," written when Maugham was in his twenties, has the same general pattern as many of his later stories: the narrator retells a striking yarn told to him, this time a solicitor's account of a strange will. Maugham's narrative style of nearly sixty years ago already had a characteristic clarity and smoothness, although the colloquial flavor seems forced and artificial.

Where is, or will be, Somerset Maugham's position among writers of fiction? Whose is the more reasoned judgment, that by Cyril Connolly, who considers him a very great novelist, or that of Edmund Wilson, who believes he has no artistic talent? Or Maugham's own judgment, "I know just where I stand: in the very front row of the second-raters"? The author's contention that first of all a novel should "entertain" is far too vague and untrustworthy to serve as a criterion and must be rejected. A reader of just-within-the-law pornographical magazines would find *Madame Bovary* reserved and dull—even prudish. Mark Twain was far from entertained by Jane Austen and Sir Walter Scott, both of whom infuriated him; there are intelligent and discriminating readers who are annoyed by *The Magic Mountain* and *The Sound and the Fury*. One uninformed about and uninterested in the Georgian literary scene might not finish *Cakes and Ale;* and there are fastidious readers of fiction who find *Up at the Villa* and *Theatre* a waste of the author's talents and their time.

Maugham is probably correct in his own judgment of his position among writers of fiction. Although at his best he is an incomparable story-teller and he writes with the lucidity, simplicity, and euphony he strives for, he is not a really great stylist; and although he has written much about style, he has never claimed to have mastered a great style himself. His clever, controlled use of the colloquial, his almost ostentatious simplicity and distaste for excess, the infrequent use of figures of speech—the deliberate avoidance of "fine writing"—result often in a dryness and directness useful in propelling the narrative, but precluding the extra dimensions of the rich and vivid lyricism of Lawrence (if Maugham never wrote a novel as richly poetic and elemental as *Sons and Lovers,* he never wrote one as meaningless and dull as *Kangaroo*), the deep plunges into the inner consciousness of man in Proust and Dostoievski, the wild and wonderful worlds of Dickens and Balzac, the deep-rooted humanity and compassion of Tolstoy. One writes as he can and as he must, and Maugham's rigid and intelligent control over his words and material has enabled him to be the "story-teller" he aimed to be, but it has imposed limitations. Too often he has been content to illustrate the unaccountability of man's behavior when we wish that like Gide or Lawrence or even Sherwood Anderson he would *endeavor* to account for it. His determination to "stick to the point" has imposed further limitations, for the great plays and novels and life itself have many "points." It has led him to undervalue subtlety and the occasional value of the indirect, to avoid the irrelevant, which Chekhov knows is often only seemingly irrelevant, and can be artfully significant, and to oversimplify human psychology or just shrug his shoulders at man's surprising behavior. Have his passion for art, his clinical interest in his fellow men, his love of travel, his warm response to human goodness whenever he finds it, his own generosity and kindness been insufficient to prevent the *sec* quality of his fiction when something warmer and deeper is called for than mere ironical reportage?

Yet "second-rater" should not be an opprobrious term in literary criticism. Few would cavil at Maugham's selection of Balzac, Dickens, Dostoievski, and Tolstoy as the four greatest novelists, and Proust's *Remembrance of Things Past* as the greatest novel of the twentieth century. If these masters of the novel belong in the first class, Maugham finds himself in distinguished company in the second class. And although no two would agree on such finical (and rather absurd) categorization, many would be content to place Maugham alongside Thackeray, Gide, Hardy, Romains, Galsworthy, Bennett, and Conrad. It is discreet here to omit consideration of those writers who have become for the moment the focuses and sometimes victims of cults: Joyce, Kafka, Faulkner, James, Camus, Sartre, Beckett, and Virginia Woolf. It would be even more perilous, and fatuously pedantic, to rank these writers lower than Maugham and Conrad.

The fact remains that Maugham's fiction has been for more than sixty years, and still is, enjoyed by intelligent, if not the most intellectual, readers the world over. In an era of growing anxiety over man's survival the novel will probably decline in importance as a literary form, but one can feel certain that for many years to come enlightened readers of fiction will relish *Of Human Bondage, The Moon and Sixpence,* and *Cakes and Ale.* Whether Philip Carey, Mildred Rogers, Strickland, and Rosie will join the immortal company of Tom Jones, Micawber, and Becky Sharp, only time can tell. While scholars of the future (and the present as well) wrangle over Joyce, Kafka, Faulkner, Sartre, and Proust, ordinary intelligent readers will turn with satisfaction to the lucid and nearly always entertaining pages of Somerset Maugham, who was ashamed of obscurity and dullness, never of readability and competence.

## VI

# THE THEATRE OF
## SOMERSET MAUGHAM

N O LIVING dramatist is so easy to see whole as Somerset
Maugham, for he completed his "theatre" more than
twenty-five years ago and since 1933 has steadfastly refused
to return to playwriting. We can see his work with useful
perspective, like that of Galsworthy and Barrie and even
Bernard Shaw. A few new plays in recent years, such as
*Theatre* and *Jane,* have somewhat deceptively carried his
name tag in large print, for an obvious reason, but he did not
write them. In fine print one reads that they derive from
Maugham's fiction, as did *Rain* in 1922. Maugham has
often remarked that the play of his which made the most
money for him (and is still bringing in royalties) is one
he did not write. When he finished writing "Miss Thompson" he had no more interest in the story, and at the
request of John Colton and Clemence Randolph he turned
over dramatization rights to them, cannily retaining a
percentage of any future royalties. It is estimated that he

has collected over $300,000 from *Rain* as a drama, musical, and film, and from its radio and television adapatations. Although not nearly so successful, *Jane* has had a similar history. Upon completing the short story he sensed its stage possibilities and arranged for a percentage of any dramatic royalties. It was eventually made into a play by Sam Behrman.

Unlike Henry Arthur Jones, Sir Arthur Wing Pinero, Sir James Barrie, Gerhart Hauptmann, and even Bernard Shaw, Maugham knew when the time came to quit writing plays and he stopped; as indifferent as he thought himself to public taste, he disliked the prospect of outliving his popularity in the theatre. In the Preface to the sixth and final volume of the published plays (1934) he writes: "I am conscious that I am no longer in touch with the public that patronize the theatre. . . . It is high time to retire. I do so with relief." He saw that tastes were changing, that the demand for a "good story" was growing less insistent, that the not-well-made play pleased a new generation impatient with literary contrivance, that what he considered good workmanship was yielding to what he considered sprawl, that his crispness, "sticking to the point," and directness of attack were becoming unfashionable.

As a dramatist his reputation in America, and to a less extent in Britain, is now at a low ebb. A dozen of his plays are often performed by repertory and civic theatre groups and occasionally by American "little" theatres, but Broadway and off-Broadway playhouses, the experimental and college theatres pay little attention to him. The new critics all but ignore him. Eric Bentley in *The Playwright as Thinker* devotes half a line to Maugham. (Obviously to

Bentley, Maugham does not think.) Francis Fergusson in *The Idea of a Theatre* does not mention him at all. Only in France, where his plays are frequently produced, does he receive serious attention from eminent critics; perhaps it is partly the traditional French respect for form and symmetry. Although he abandoned playwriting when the relative failure of *Sheppey* convinced him of changing tastes in the theatre (it should be mentioned, however, that four years before he wrote *Sheppey* he had planned to make it his last play), he has never been hostile to the new drama. He continued to see the new plays regularly in London and Paris, and occasionally in Vienna and Rome; he reads the "New Criticism" with relish; many young European playwrights are his friends and come to Villa Mauresque; and American playwrights come too, especially his good friends Sam Behrman, Moss Hart, and Christopher Isherwood.

One must hasten to add that the "low ebb" of Maugham's reputation refers only to the commercial New York and London theatre and to English and American critics of the drama. Actually his plays are constantly being performed all over the world, in Japan, Italy, Spain, Turkey, South America, and behind the iron curtain in Poland and Czechoslovakia. In the mid 1950's a new version of *Theatre* was prepared for the French stage by Sauvajon, an adaptation Maugham considers superior to Guy Bolton's, which was used in England and the United States. *Theatre* enjoyed a run in Paris of nearly three years, almost without precedent in a country where long runs are rare, followed by a triumphant tour of the provincial cities.

It is doubtful that he foresaw the critical, if not always

popular, triumph of the indirect and sometimes fuzzy, the ascendancy of the sitting-room and scullery drama over the elegant drawing-room variety (back to Zola and the early Hauptmann), the literary cleverness and sometimes archness in treatment of ancient myths, the survival of the religious theme—more often pretentious religiosity—, the obsession in a confused and jittery age with neurotic and agonized soul-searching. Whatever his vision, he grew tired of playwriting, perceived the change in taste and fashion, and realized with relief that he had no more plays to write. Unlike Halvard Solness he heard with composure the new generation knocking on the door, and turned gladly to his fiction and essays.

His first play was written in 1892, his last one in 1933. Of his thirty-two plays three are adaptations: *The Noble Spaniard*, from the French of Grenet-Daucourt—this preposterous Victorian farce delighted London audiences when it was revived in 1954 and it is still performed by repertory companies; *The Perfect Gentleman* from Molière's *Le Bourgeois Gentilhomme*—the adaptation formed the prelude to a complete performance of Richard Strauss's opera *Ariadne in Naxos;* and *The Mask and the Face*, from the popular Italian comedy by Luigi Chiarelli. Two are of one act and forgotten: *Schiffbrüchig (Shipwrecked)* written in German and actually performed in a Café-Konzert in Berlin; and *Mademoiselle Zampa*. In forty-one years, then, he wrote twenty-seven original plays, which seems a modest total until we recall his vast output of novels, short stories, books of travel, critical prefaces, and essays during this period. He chose only eighteen of his plays to be preserved in his *Collected Plays*.

Maugham's guardian, his narrow clergyman uncle, with whom the boy lived from the age of ten to eighteen, viewed the theatre with the professional horror proper in the 1880's. Not until the boy at eighteen went to Heidelberg for a year did he see a play. Then he was suddenly introduced to the new drama of Ibsen, Hauptmann, Becque, and other early naturalists. Night after night he went to the grubby, ill-lighted local theatre and afterwards in a *Bierstube* debated solemnly with his young companions the merit and meaning of the revolutionary new plays. It is interesting to note that in spite of this initiation into the new continental drama of the early 1890's, Maugham never wrote the kind of insurgent social-idea plays that excited these boys and young men in Heidelberg in 1892.

He frankly admits that he turned his attention seriously to playwriting early in the new century when he knew he had abandoned medicine as a career and suspected that the rewards of fiction would never provide him with the financial independence he longed for. "I wanted to write plays that would be seen not only by a handful of people. I wanted money and I wanted fame." His outspoken preference for financial success and his freedom from cant concerning the material pleasures of life have from the beginning of his career as a professional writer alienated many critics, who have assumed that as a playwright he has been more concerned with the size of audiences than with literary excellence. When Maugham started playwriting, a half dozen established public favorites, including Pinero, Sutro, Jones, and Chambers, had a strangle hold on the London theatre; managers knew that these prolific and popular playmakers could fill the theatres, and were indifferent to young or untried writers. Aware of the difficulties encountered by Shaw, Barker, Hobson, Hankin, and other "originals" in gaining entree into the commercial theatre, Maugham concluded that if he were to get a foothold at all, his plays must first please a manager, or better still, an actor-manager.

It is a fact, however, that since his forthright attempts from 1904 to 1908 to achieve a popular success on the stage, he has written only as he pleases and what he pleases —with two rare exceptions, and then by request of the British government. Otherwise, he says, "I have always written with pleasure . . . and my pleasure was independent of the result." Almost all of his popular plays from 1909 to 1933 show an indifference to, sometimes a contempt for, popular mores and views.

His first play, *Schiffbrüchig*, written when he was eighteen, has a bold theme that would have made its performance in England in the 1890's impossible: a charming man about town marries a former mistress of a wealthy man who will continue to send her a monthly check. The pair will live on this shady income, and they look forward to a happy marriage free of financial worry. Written a year before *The Second Mrs. Tanqueray*, *Schiffbrüchig* has a bold, new type of heroine, a Paula Tanqueray who cheerfully adjusts herself—or is certain that she will be able to do so—to life in a hostile society. His second play, *A Man of Honour*, suggests that honorable conduct is not only unwise at times, but even disastrous in its consequences. His next play, *Lady Frederick*, required the leading actress to appear on the stage without make-up or beauty aids and before the audience to go through a long, tedious process of transforming herself into a beautiful woman. No well-known actress would consider appearing on the stage under such unflattering circumstances. *Smith,* an attack on the caste system of England, not amusingly satirical but harsh and painful, aroused noisy protestation from the shocked opening-night audience. Both *Smith* and *The Land of Promise* treat the matter of class distinction unsentimentally. *Our Betters* is more scorching than the title implies, and flays both the British and Americans. Superficially a gay farce, *Home and Beauty* is peopled by selfish, unscrupulous women, war profiteers, and misogamists, and the ending is wry and cynical. *The Circle* drew hisses and catcalls on its opening night because of the ending—after it had handled two human triangles unromantically. *The Unknown* in 1920 offended the religious sensibilities of nine-tenths of its audiences, and brought back the distress and heartbreak of the recent war; there were outcries of "No! No!" from the gallery. *The Constant Wife* (1926) cheerfully suggests that marital infidelity need not wreck a marriage. *The Letter* had to be purified for the tender sensibilities of film-goers by the addition of a second murder: the strange moral arithmetic of Hollywood. *The Sacred Flame* condones the murder of a young man by his mother on flimsier grounds than might excuse Mrs. Alving's murder of her son Oswald. *For Services Rendered* is a savage attack on romantic patriotism and glorification of war; and here again we find one of Maugham's favorite theses, that suffering and self-sacrifice are more liable to degrade human nature than to elevate it. His last play, *Sheppey,* is a sardonic comedy which mocks our snobbishness, popular forms of hyposcrisy, and phony Christianity. We must believe Maugham when he says that he wrote to please himself.

Yet the charge that his plays are callously cynical is not altogether deserved. He is almost never churlish or surly (at moments in *Smith*, perhaps), but is inclined to accept life and people as they are. And although he admits to a strain of misanthropy in his nature and an indisposition to believe deeply in altruism or disinterested goodness, he is sensitive to the beauty of good action and says that he is moved when he finds it. Such characters as Smith, Mrs. Ardsley (*For Services Rendered*), Sir Arthur (*Caesar's Wife*), Mrs. Talbret (*The Sacred Flame*), and Sheppey are kindly and unpretentious, and the dramatist treats them with respect and sympathy. He has been called a cynical playwright for suggesting that sexual love does not last forever, that the infidelity of one's mate is more likely to hurt one's pride than one's heart, that people fall out of love as well as in love, that philosophically evil is unexplainable, that literal Christianity is impracticable, or dangerous to one who tries to practice it, that vice is not always punished and virtue rewarded in ways that strict moralists would prefer, that we dislike those whom we injure, that the moderately immoral seem to live about as happily as the rigidly conventional. Most of all, he refuses to attach any great importance to what is popularly considered virtue, or to be revolted by what is generally considered vice. Perhaps just one or two of these heterodox views would arouse little disaffection among his readers and audiences, but the sum total helped fasten the tag of cynic on him.

The flavor of his pages and dialogue has the tartness best described by "dry," "astringent," "styptic"; it is never vinegary.

His first long play to reach the stage was *A Man of Honour,* produced for two performances in 1903 by the high-brow Stage Society. It won some welcome critical acclaim from the ultra-liberal press (with small circulation), but its shocking, perverse theme—that tragedy resulted when the hero behaved according to generally accepted notions of honor—barred it from the sentimental commercial theatre of the day. The conservative periodicals denounced the play, and one daily paper devoted a leading article to it. In 1908 he met unexpected and extravagant success when four plays were running concurrently in London's West End. He became famous overnight, was interviewed repeatedly, and depicted in cartoons as Shakespeare's rival. Of the four plays, only *Lady Frederick* has any merit. It is a pleasant period piece, a mildly amusing example of artificial Edwardian comedy. It is snapping with witticisms and is agreeably nonsensical in story and characters; it is superior to most drawing-room comedies of the fashionable theatre before the First World War. Its smart epigrams were the talk of the town. The weekly royalties from the four plays were substantial enough to give him the freedom he had longed for.

When *Lady Frederick* opened at the Court Theatre in October 1907, its current competitors in the West End theatre included Belasco's *Sweet Kitty Bellairs, Mrs. Wiggs of the Cabbage Patch, The Thief, The Mollusc,* a revival of *The Devil's Disciple,* two forgotten plays by Sutro, *Brewster's Millions, As You Like It,* and Sarah Bernhardt in repertory. The critics were astute: they suspected that the new playwright had gone overboard to write a successful play (as he had), and they heard all the echoes. Here was an ambitious young writer who instead of examining a corner of life had looked up the traditions of the stage and provided an agreeable and clever mélange of Scribe, Sardou, Pinero, Sheridan, and Wilde. All commented on the epigrams, some fresh but others almost directly from La Rochefoucauld. Reviewers were equally shrewd when *Jack Straw* was performed shortly afterward: they praised it as diverting entertainment but commented on its comic opera plot and obvious debt to Marivaux and Molière. In *Mrs. Dot* they noted that the comic idea derived from *Much Ado About Nothing,* but that the play was otherwise twentieth-century Marivaux. These three early comedies were soon produced in New York with considerable success. Ethel Barrymore played in *Lady Frederick,* Billie Burke in *Mrs. Dot,* and John Barrymore in *Jack Straw.* All three then toured the United States with the New York companies intact, in that golden age when the American commercial theatre was not anchored to a square mile of mid-Manhattan. The fourth play, produced a few months later in 1908, was *The Explorer,* which the reviewers with justification pounced upon for its absurd notions of honor and heroism. These four plays were the only ones Maugham ever wrote to please a manager.

Not only the audiences but also the critics were hostile to and shocked by *The Unknown* in 1920. The sophisticated reviewers did not, of course, admit to shock, but attacked this vigorous play as "dull," "lacking drama," and "shallow." The idea of the play comes straight from Omar Khayyam:

For all the sins wherewith the face of man
Is blackened, man's forgiveness give—and take!

The outcry of the mother whose sons have been killed in the war, "But who will forgive God?" was the most shocking line heard on a London stage in many years.

Before the outbreak of the war in 1914 Maugham wrote five more original plays, the last being *The Land of Promise,* all of which were popular successes. Commenting on this period, he remarks without umbrage that the intelligentsia ignored him but that he was securely fixed in public favor. When we examine the plays written before 1915 we must admit that the "intelligentsia" were correct in their judgment: not one of the fifteen plays has any marked distinction. It should be remembered, however, that in the continuing history of the English stage Maugham helped revive one of its glories, the comedy of manners (*Lady Frederick, Mrs. Dot*), and along with Shaw, Hankin, Barker, and other thinking playwrights affronted the stodginess and hyperorthodoxy of the backward theatre with vigorous expression of startling, unconventional views (*A Man of Honour, Smith, The Unknown*). As is true with plays of Shaw and often with those of O'Neill, Maugham's early comedies on revival have received pleasanter notices than when they were first performed. *Caroline,* for example, a piece of fluff he wrote for relaxation in wartime Geneva, has struck reviewers as almost brilliant in its revivals in recent years.

In 1915 he wrote the first of a handful of comedies that seem certain to escape occasionally from the long, crowded shelves where the plays of nearly all the Elizabethans, Henry Arthur Jones (nevertheless, Jones's granddaughter reported in 1959 that Jones's *Silver King*, written in 1882, was still being performed in various parts of the world), Clyde Fitch, and a multitude of other dramatists have their permanent resting place. *Our Betters*, also written when Maugham was a secret agent, is a brilliant artificial comedy directly in line with the glittering comedies of manners, often barnyard manners, of the Restoration. It is cynical, heartless in its satire, rich in its vocabulary of vituperation. This excoriating yet remorselessly detached picture of the degenerate idle rich in an alien society will probably be as actable and amusing as *Love for Love* and *The Country Wife* in any age when heartless, artificial comedy is relished. If the story of *Our Betters* were not so banal, it could take a place among the notable English comedies. While a patient in a tuberculosis sanitorium in Scotland in 1919 he wrote one of the liveliest and wittiest farces since *The Importance of Being Earnest: Home and Beauty* (performed in America under the vapid title *Too Many Husbands*). It has not only a farcical situation—but not too farfetched, for soldiers reported dead or missing did sometimes return later from prison camps or regain their memory after long attacks of amnesia—but also wit and blistering satire on war profiteers and human selfishness. Like Oscar Wilde he embroiders style, wit, and elegance on an absurd plot; and in the last act, where invention flags in most farces, as in some of Noel Coward's and Kaufman's, *Home and Beauty* is at its liveliest. In 1919 the comedy was topical in its use of wartime shortages, the black market, the new rich, the scarcity and arrogance of servants. Maugham would point out that war, like suffering, brings out not only the heroic in man, but his most selfish, detestable qualities as well. *Home and Beauty,* however, is a bright comedy and as a period piece is still amusing.

Two high comedies of the 1920's have outlived their generation: *The Circle* and *The Constant Wife.* *The Circle* is already a classic, considered by many to be the best modern English comedy. Its humor is brilliant and unforced, its characterization firm, its underside of serious philosophy and ethics hard and unsentimental, disturbing to the romantic and painful to the complacently orthodox. *The Circle* impressed the first reviewers exactly as it strikes reviewers and intelligent audiences forty years later. It is the most timeless of his comedies. When John Gielgud produced it in his repertory season in 1944 (alternating with *Hamlet* and *Love for Love*) he did not allow the wit to flash so brightly, but stressed the serious implications of the play. Audiences have become more sophisticated, the more ingenuous having deserted the theatre for the cinema and television; cries of shocked protest from the gallery would be unthinkable in 1960. *The Circle* is high comedy but not artificial comedy, as is *The Constant Wife,* which is spurious in theme and "artificial" almost to the point of obsolescence in an England transformed by social revolution. The crackling repartee and salty epigrams remind one of Oscar Wilde; the dialogue of *The Circle* never does. But *The Constant Wife* is witty and irreverent, dry and unsentimental, and will be enjoyed whenever taste is wide enough to include examples of the amoral, contrived comedy of the Restoration type; it will no doubt become a costume play, like Congreve's comedies. It is a play one can laugh at and enjoy without believing a word of it.

By the late 1920's he had only four more plays in mind,

and he felt a compulsion to write them before he retired from the theatre. He was aware of changing tastes and suspected that none of the four would please a great many people, but the dramas had shaped themselves in his mind and he composed them for his own satisfaction. *The Sacred Flame* (the title is so lurid that it was not necessary to change it when the cinema version was made) was already unfashionable in 1929, a "strong" play with form and a hefty plot. It did not then nor does it now completely satisfy as either melodrama or tragedy. *The Breadwinner* is a light-hearted but acid version of *A Doll's House,* with the bored husband deserting his arty wife and his parasitical, intolerably bright children. Maugham succeeds here like Molière, Wycherly, and Congreve in transporting an odious group of people and an unpleasant situation into the realm of comedy. After the harsh opening scene with the selfish and arrogant young people, a scene so overdone as to appear false, the ingeniously written play—the action is continuous—is unfailingly diverting. *For Services Rendered* is Maugham's only grim and uncompromising tragedy. It is completely without catharsis, and the mordant irony of the final scene is harrowing.

His last play, *Sheppey,* produced in 1933, is a sardonic comedy with a kindly, lovable protagonist. It is the author's one morality play; when at the end Death, in the person of a pleasant, tweedy English girl, enters and leads Sheppey away, one is grateful, for Sheppey is one of that rare company who really are too good for this selfish world. The play baffled most of the critics, who erroneously judged it as a thesis play or a tragedy. It is neither. It is a biting comedy, striking out at bogus Christianity and medical quackery, comedy harsh and dry, like Ben Jonson's and Molière's. Even the death of Sheppey is in no way tragic. When his wife discovers him dead in his chair, she smiles and says with obvious affection, "He always was lucky." He was lucky because the next morning he was to be taken to an insane asylum; he had been certified because he attempted to behave according to the precepts of Christianity. The pervading warmth of Sheppey's native goodness envelops the play, a foil to its otherwise unrelieved mockery and the despicable opportunism of most of the other characters. It is possible that *Sheppey* is the most underrated of Maugham's plays. Sean O'Casey considers it as one of the masterpieces of the modern theatre.

Maugham has never entertained or expressed solemn and highfalutin notions about the drama. By 1927 he had made up his mind that "a prose play is scarcely less ephemeral than a news sheet," and that anyone can learn playwriting if he has the "knack" (never defined). He felt strongly that unnecessary verbiage must be ruthlessly cut out of a play and that the shrewdness and quickwittedness of the playgoer must be assumed. His professed low opinion of the lasting quality of prose drama, except, he admits, for a few comedies that have haphazardly survived a century or two, is hard to share. It is inconceivable that *Caesar and Cleopatra, Hedda Gabler, The Wild Duck,* and *Rosmersholm* will not outlive all the poetic dramas of the late nineteenth century. *Man and Superman, Major Barbara, The Three Sisters, The Cherry Orchard, The Plough and the Stars, Saint Joan,* and *The Circle* will not be museum pieces for many years to come; not one play in verse written between 1900 and 1925 approaches them in merit. Maugham's attack on the drama of ideas, although amusing and not altogether unsound (Walter Kerr would agree with it thoroughly at this late date), is in part a defense of his own limitations and tastes, like Poe degrading the long poem and novel; it also results from his failure to admit that ideas are basic in his own plays: in a shrewd treatment of a corner of society such as *Our Betters,* or an intelligent dissection of human conduct and ethics as in *The Circle.* Moreover *For Services Rendered* and *Sheppey* are charged with ideas. Time has proved Maugham justified in his harsh estimate of such palely intellectual dramatists as Granville-Barker, but his cool entombment of Ibsen and Shaw seems recklessly premature.

After forty years of playwriting he grew tired of it and also realized that the public had little interest in the kind of play he liked to and could write. When he finished *Sheppey* he felt a sense of exaltation and freedom. The impact of the vigorous, free-wheeling American drama of the 1920's and 1930's was being felt abroad, and Maugham was perspicacious enough to see that both critics and playgoers were assessing with seriousness and respect the plays of Sidney Howard, Odets, Wilder, Sherwood, Lillian Hellman, and Kingsley. Then came the more subtle drama of the new French school, particularly that of Giraudoux, Anouilh, Sartre, and Aymé. These new French plays were as popular in the London theatre as the American plays and aroused sharper, more respectful attention from the young British playwrights. Still later the grotesqueries of Beckett, Betti, and Ionesco and the rough-

neck plays of the Angry Young Men and Angry Young
Women have also failed to create in him any desire to
return to the theatre as a playwright.

Outside the theatre itself, however, Maugham has had
a vast and attentive audience in the postwar years. On the
wireless and television in Britain, and to a less extent in
America and on the continent, his plays are frequently
performed, the early comedies as well as the more serious
late plays. Even *For Services Rendered,* relentless and
hopeless as it is, was well received in an expert television
production in 1959 and struck no London reviewer as dated.
*The Letter, The Land of Promise,* and *The Sacred Flame*
( which somehow escapes censorship) are established television favorites. Even such minor and otherwise forgotten
plays as *The Camel's Back* and *Love in a Cottage* do well
enough in the new medium.

In 1957 an indefatigable team of historians of the theatre,
Raymond Mander and Joe Mitchener, made a reasonably
complete pictorial record of Maugham's plays, as they have
likewise done with the theatre of Shaw and Coward. It is
valuable for reference, and the many photographs are most
interesting. A staggering amount of industry went into
assembling the data and pictures. They even brought to
light an unperformed full-length play, *The Road Uphill.*
Maugham thought that he had destroyed all copies of the
manuscript, but he admitted that writing the play had
not been a waste of time, for later he frugally used the
theme in *The Razor's Edge.*

What place will there be for Maugham in the theatre
of the future? Will he be forced to the library shelves

along with Peele, Kyd, Greene, Dekker, Fielding, Scribe, Bulwer-Lytton, H. J. Byron, Rachel Crothers, Clyde Fitch, and hundreds of others who once filled the theatres? Will the time come when the public mood will respond to the diatribes of *For Services Rendered* (*Time* magazine in 1958 dismissed the equally bitter play *Paths of Glory* as "unfashionably anti-militaristic"), or find the trenchant satire of *Sheppey* sardonically amusing? Or is Maugham correct in prophesying that of all his plays only one or two of the high comedies will survive to please occasional audiences of the future? His own prediction is very modest: "I think that one or two of my comedies may retain for some time a kind of pale life, for they are written in the tradition of English comedy and on that account may find a place that began with the Restoration dramatists. It may be that they may secure me a line or two in the histories of the English theatre."

Although we at once think of exceptions to his bland assertion that the prose drama of the past is ephemeral, all the exceptions we can muster would not amount to more than one-tenth of one per cent of all the prose plays of the past. We must acknowledge, for example, that for one Chekhov there were hundreds of imitators of Sardou and Scribe in the European and American theatre. But it is unlikely that English-speaking audiences will ever reject the comedy of manners, for centuries a major glory of the English stage, whatever the vagaries of its popularity or reputation. *Much Ado About Nothing* still attracts largely because of its Beatrice-Benedict episodes; in 1959 John Gielgud's elegant production, possibly the best the play had ever received in its 350-year history, struck New Yorkers as a bore in everything except its high-comedy passages. *The Way of the World, Love for Love, The Country Wife, The School for Scandal, The Importance of Being Earnest, The Circle,* and perhaps *Our Betters* and *The Constant Wife* for many years to come will find appreciative audiences as well as readers.

## VII

### OTHER NON-FICTION

IN ADDITION to fiction and plays Somerset Maugham has written two books about Spain, a volume of Chinese sketches, a book describing a journey through Southeast Asia, prefaces to his own novels, short-story collections, and plays, introductions to nearly a score of books by other writers, a semi-autobiographical volume in which he defines his aesthetic and philosophic beliefs, a vast number of notebooks, a selection from which has been published, a book on France at war, a book-length account of his escape from France in 1940, two volumes concerned with reading and great books, two volumes of critical and personal essays, many articles in newspapers and magazines, and long critical introductions to five anthologies. He has published no autobiography, nor will he consent to the publication of his letters.

These books and sketches are hard to catalogue. His books of travel, for instance, are crammed with anecdote and philosophic comment, for although a great traveler he is interested in man rather than places and scenery. His *Summing Up* tells practically nothing of the external events of his life. Some of his numerous essays of literary criticism turn out to be largely accounts of authors' lives and idiosyncrasies. In fact all these non-fiction items have the out-of-fashion subjectivity of the pleasant, conversational familiar essay. Nearly all of them are shrewd and expertly written and the best of them—*On a Chinese Screen, The Gentleman in the Parlour, Don Fernando, The Summing Up,* and *Ten Great Novels,* have the mellowness of rare vintage wine: they are not only palatable but piquant and civilized. The least distinguished are *France at War,* which he was commanded to write, and some of the prefaces he composed, out of kindness, for books, sometimes mediocre, by friends.

In 1905 he published *The Land of the Blessed Virgin, Sketches and Impressions of Andalusia,* which found few readers in 1905 and not many more when reissued in 1920 and 1921. Maugham is aware of its imperfections, and it is not included in the Collected Works. It is the work of a young man in love with a romantic country, its landscapes, its folklore, its people, its sun—have any pagan people been such sun-worshipers as the English? For the most part it is an enthusiastic book, warm and agreeable, but in parts indifferently written. The author is now embarrassed by its spurts of fine writing, its superlatives, its devotion to local color. There is, however, some sly humor and an occasional foretaste of the lucid, effective style he was to perfect later. He does not romanticize his material unduly. He writes of the grotesque ugliness of the old women, of landscapes as sinister as those in Browning's "Childe

Roland"; he analyzes the national habit of lying, and his description of a bullfight is all but sickening. He is sarcastic about the self-righteous attitude of the English who are shocked by bullfights: "The English humanity to animals is one of the best traits of a great people, and they can justly thank God that they are not as others are. Can anything be more horrid than to kill a horse in the bullring, and can any decent hack ask for a better end when he is broken down, than to be driven to death in London streets . . . ? The Spaniards are certainly cruel to animals; on the other hand they never beat their wives or kick their children. From the dog's point of view I would ten times sooner be English, but from the woman's—I have my doubts." At the end of the book is an account of the arrival of a train of soldiers returning from Cuba, miserable, ill, and starving, shocking evidence of Spanish fecklessness. The Anglo-Saxon author suspects that the easy-going philosophy of the Spanish has brought national decay. In spite of its bleak ending this almost forgotten book is for the most part cheerful, the record of a happy period when the success of *Liza of Lambeth* had encouraged him to give up the medical profession and become a writer. His first gesture of liberation was to flee from Lambeth to the sun and color of Seville.

It was not until nineteen years later that his second book of travel sketches appeared. When he visited China, he meant to write an account of his journey and took notes on whatever he saw that excited his interest; but when he came home and read these notes and sketches, it occurred to him that they might easily lose their vividness if he tried to elaborate them into a connected account of his journey. So he changed his mind, and with only a few alterations published them as they were under the title *On a Chinese Screen*. During the nineteen years between the books the author had made a systematic study of English prose style and the great stylists, and had striven to improve his writing. *On a Chinese Screen* is a far better written book than *The Land of the Blessed Virgin*. It is warm but not effusive; there is humor without exaggeration and irony without bitterness; he is not altogether unsuccessful in attempting to achieve the austere simplicity and lucidity of Swift and Voltaire, and often excels them with a quiet elegance. The book contains fifty-eight sketches, some less than a page in length, only two with more than twelve pages. Some are miniature portraits, some are vignettes or brief landscapes, two or three are technically short stories, some are anecdotes, some as one would expect are less than flattering pictures of Europeans abroad. They are sketches, which in their brevity often achieve a perfection that amplification might injure.

These memorable word-pictures tell us much about pre-Communist China, but also much about Somerset Maugham. We learn that he is at times a sentimentalist. He reveals a tolerant understanding in the cameo portraits even of types that repel him. He exhibits a sensitiveness to beauty that is far deeper than the effusive outpourings of the tourist. He is sensitive, too, not only to the diverting irony of life, but also to its soul-disturbing overtones. He can feel pity and homesickness and the beauty of human goodness and kindness. Those who dismiss him as a cynic who always sees men's motives askew have not read *On a Chinese Screen*. Here are "The Fannings," a portait of a genuinely unselfish wife and mother; "Rain," a very human confession of nostalgia; "The Grand Style," a tribute to a gentleman; "Romance," which reveals a hitherto unexpected tolerance, if not understanding, of mysticism; "The Beast of Burden" and "The Song of the River," which disclose a compassion for the harassed coolies that Galsworthy could not express with more feeling; "The Servants of God" and "The Old Timer," which display his humility before the good works of the Catholic missionaries; "The Old Timer," moreover, gives a hearty picture of happy old age.

*On a Chinese Screen,* however, is by no means a sentimental book. The author tries not to distort or judge or condemn, but to report what he sees and feels. There is ugliness to report as well as beauty, cruelty as well as kindness, silliness as well as dignity. He is not overcome with respect and admiration for most of the consuls, missionaries, company managers, and army officers trying to hold the gorgeous East in fee for Lombard Street. As he discovered in the Islands and in Malaya, life in the East often brings out the worst in the colonials—intolerance, provincialism, and pompousness, qualities a narrowly circumscribed life in Bath or Shrewsbury might not have uncovered. Few of the Britons sketched in the book are admirable. A woman ignorant of Chinese art and decoration proudly and stupidly makes her living room a duplicate of hundreds of florid rooms in Tunbridge Wells. The intense ennui and the petty jealousies of the colonials are ill concealed at their boring dinner parties. A missionary is unable to conquer his hatred for the Chinese he tries to convert. An "irritable, bumptious, tiresome little man," a consul, is ignorant of fear—"If their manners were as good as their courage is great, they [the British] would merit the opinion they have of themselves." A loud-mouthed social and political liberal kicks and curses a careless rickshaw boy. A young medical missionary abandons his idealism in order to amass a fortune. A narrow-minded, puritanical missionary refuses to associate with an agent of the tobacco company. An official of the tobacco company closes his eyes and mind to the colorful, racy life about him and spends all his leisure time reading lurid American adventure magazines. The Protestant missionaries close their city missions and abandon their good works when the summer weather becomes uncomfortable. At their harshest, however, these portraits express an amused contempt; there is not the bitterness of *For Services Rendered*.

There is humor, too: the missionary lady whose conversation is a devastating cascade of platitudes; the solemn scholar of the drama who is shocked at the notion of *entertainment* on the stage. There are harrowing sketches; the taipan who sees his own grave being dug; the execution of a wretched prisoner; the miserable coolies who are literally beasts of burden. There is philosophy when a brilliant Chinese analyzes the culture of the East and the West. There is poetry: "The Rising of the Curtain," "Dawn," "The Road," "Arabesque." There is even—God save the mark—a touch of whimsy in "Rain."

An incidental reward of the book is one that never occurred to its author when he wrote it forty years ago: it is a footnote to modern Chinese history and helps one understand the Chinese revolution, just as back of

Chekhov's quiet plays one is now conscious of the dynamics of modern social and historical change.

The year 1930 was memorable for Maugham the author: it was the year of *Cakes and Ale;* the last of his drawing-room comedies, *The Breadwinner*; and one of the most charming of all travel books, *The Gentleman in the Parlour,* the author's favorite among his books. He wrote it in high spirits but with great care, for he was as much concerned with style as with content. He says in the preface, "If you like language for its own sake, if it amuses you to string words together in the order that most pleases you, so as to produce an effect of beauty, the essay or travel book gives you an opportunity." In *The Gentleman in the Parlour* he escapes for the most part, but not entirely, the dangers inherent in exercises in style—florid passages, monotonous patterns and rhythms, undue subordination of matter to method. His prose is nearly always simple, lucid, pungent. It is never languorous, rarely embroidered. (He has said that when he finishes an essay by Walter Pater he knows how a trout feels when he is taken off the hook and lies flapping on the grass.) He achieves dignity without pompousness and skillfully adjusts the character and the flow of his words and phases to the demands of the material—description, anecdote, reflection, or philosophy.

*The Gentleman in the Parlour* is not a debunking travel book like *Innocents Abroad,* for although Maugham shares Mark Twain's honesty, he also possesses what the American lacked—a great tolerance and wide culture. What would enrage Mark Twain amuses Maugham—that is, everything but downright cruelty; so far as humanly possible, he accepts life and people on their own terms wherever he goes, and if he is confronted by a mystery he cannot penetrate, he is not ashamed to be humble before it. Readers today cannot tolerate long descriptions of scenery. In *The Gentleman in the Parlour* we never lose sight of the fact that Mandalay, Saigon, Haiphong, Keng Tung, and the jungle itself are real places where men and women live, work, eat, make love, suffer, grow old, and die. "Then it seemed to me that in these countries in the East the most impressive, the most awe-inspiring monument of all antiquity is neither temple, nor citadel, nor great wall, but man. The peasant with his immemorial usages belongs to an age far more ancient than Angkor Wat, the great wall of China, or the Pyramids of Egypt." His occasional travel companions are sharply and expertly drawn; they are as real and complete as the characters in his best fiction.

The book is enlivened by a diversity of topics. Description, narration, philosophy, and even fantasy are adroitly mixed. There is a pleasant use of the unexpected. The book begins with a charming and clever discourse on Hazlitt, whose essay "On Going a Journey" provides the title of the book. There are brief familiar essays on such subjects as humor, the game of solitaire, imperialism, shyness, food, justification of evil, English prose; there are half a dozen narratives. Maugham insists that he is a bad traveler, for he has little gift for surprise and takes things for granted so very quickly that he is hardly aware of the unusual in his surroundings. "It seems to me just as natural to ride in a rickshaw as in a car, and to sit on the floor as on a chair. . . . I travel because I like to move from place to place. . . . it pleases me to be rid of ties, responsibilities, duties. I like the unknown; I meet odd people. . . . I am often tired of myself and I have a notion that I can add to my personality and so change myself a little." Consequently his subject matter is different from that of most travel books. He is never condescending or patronizing in describing native food, dress, religion, or manners. He has no eye for the merely quaint or picturesque and is not surprised by the abnormal, for he knows how rare the normal is. For example, in the account of his visit to a Buddhist monastery he mentions so casually that the monks smoked cheroots while chanting their prayers that the reader feels little surprise.

The poet latent in all men is less successfully concealed in *The Gentleman in the Parlour* than in any of the author's other books. He is fond of the decorative metaphor and similes with a literary flavor ("The village street was bordered by tamarinds and they were like the sentences of Sir Thomas Browne, opulent, stately, and self-possessed.") He comes perilously near at times to the fine writing he has always abhorred.

More characteristic are the many asides, some humorous, some iconoclastic and biting. "Lamb's emotion . . . too often suggests the facile lachrymosity of the alcoholic;" "that agreeable type that applies common sense to the accidents of life and so sees them in a faintly ridiculous aspect;" "the lot of the English and the American humorist is hard, for pornography rather than brevity is the soul of wit;" "Give a fool a uniform . . . and he thinks his word is law;" "Men are more interesting than books . . . but you cannot skip them;" "It is very difficult to put the happiness of some one you know before your own;" "I have often asked myself how the characters of Henry James in the intervals of subtly examining their situation coped with the physiological necessities of their bodies;" "I am suspicious of the sensibility of the artist, and I have often dissipated a whole train of exquisite and sombre thoughts by administering to myself a little liver pill." The book ends with a remark by an odious but generous and cheerful Jewish commercial traveler: "I'll give you my opinion of the human race in a nutshell, brother; their heart's in the right place, but their head's a thoroughly inefficient organ."

This book was written with pleasure, and recorded a happy journey, some details of which he never forgot. He was so moved by the Angkor Wat that in his eighty-seventh year he made again the tedious journey to Khmers, the ruined ancient capital city of Cambodia, in order to see once more the world's most magnificent ruins. For centuries they had been overgrown by the jungle and only in 1860 were discovered by a French explorer and partially restored. In 1960 he again visited Viet Nam, Cambodia, Burma, and Thailand.

*Don Fernando* (1935), a labor of love, found a small audience, for few people wanted to read a book about Spain in the sixteenth century. But in 1950 Maugham prepared an entirely new edition, taking advantage of criticisms of the original version made by Desmond Mac-Carthy, Raymond Mortimer, and Graham Greene. "It is not often that a writer comes across a criticism of his work that can be of use to him. When he is lucky enough to do it he is foolish not to profit by it." It was pointed out that many things in *Don Fernando* had already been said in his books and prefaces, and consequently they were omitted in the revised version. The second important objection was that it contained a long, intolerably dull passage by a minor writer of the time who wrote dialogues designed to teach English travelers useful Spanish phrases. This passage was removed entirely. On another point on which the critics animadverted he could do nothing—his statement that this book was composed of material he had gathered in order to write a novel laid in the time of Philip III. The critics questioned such a thin pretext for writing a book. Maugham declares that it is true, that he read in Spanish two hundred books about the era, tried desperately to bring his picaresque hero to life and into focus but failed. The author is thrifty, however, for he composed *Don Fernando* out of some of the material and used part of it twenty years later in his last novel, *Catalina*.

In its revised edition the book should find many readers, for it is delightful. Some readers have been discouraged by the long section near the beginning on St. Ignatius of Loyola, particularly by the extended discusison of the *Spiritual Exercises*. Maugham's story of this page boy, soldier, scholar, social reformer, and educator who became a saint is as crisp and delightful as the other thumbnail biographies in the book, and perhaps could serve the author's purpose —to picture Spain, its daily life, art, literature, theatre, eccentric personalities, and religion in the Golden Age— without the detailed analysis of the Jesuit's religious writings. But this is quibbling: there is not really a dull page in *Don Fernando*, Maugham's best written book. Even *The Gentleman in the Parlour* is inferior, largely because of a faint literary flavor that gives to certain passages a contrived, mannered air. The smooth prose of *Don Fernando* is seemingly effortless, but sharp, rhythmical, and austere or slightly colloquial as the subject matter demands.

The book is a successful mélange of discourses on art, aesthetics, drama, mysticism, picaresque fiction, and everyday life and manners of the time; and shrewd studies (here is Maugham at his most entertaining) of eminent Spaniards of the era—St. Ignatius Loyola, St. Teresa, Lope de Vega, Calderon, El Greco, Velasquez, Fray Louis de Leon, Cervantes, Espinal. He had wanted to write of Spain ever since his first golden visits in the 1890's, but he was not at all satisfied with his first attempt, *The Land of the Blessed Virgin,* which he describes as "crude and gushing." He did not want to add to the many books of travel on Spain, and found himself unable to write the novel; the essays are the result. It was a happy resolution of his problem.

It would be difficult to name a more civilized book. It combines grandeur with intimacy and subtlety with lucidity. Its short biographies make one wish that Maugham could rewrite the *Dictionary of National Biography.* He is concerned not only with famous Spaniards: from *Don Fernando* we get a vivid picture of everyday life, the houses, the eating habits, the great poverty—in Spain's Golden Age when ships brought a great stream of wealth from Spanish America, most Spaniards remained hungry and ill fed, and cold in winter—the brutal jokes and sports, the cost of living, the roads, the appearance of the cities, the magnificent churches. Maugham read twenty-four of Lope de Vega's 2,200 plays, and analyzes shrewdly this popular play-manufacturer's gift. His unorthodox judgment of El

Greco's paintings and the baroque in general is most pro-
vocative.

Although there is frequent dryly humorous comment,
the book is free of Maugham's alleged cynicism. There is
no bitterness. In 1600 it is estimated that one-third of all
Spaniards were in the church in some capacity or other, and
parasites in the general economy, whatever their good
works. The church dominated Spanish life. Maugham
treats the church and religion with tolerance and a measure
of understanding; religious idiosyncrasy disturbs him no
more than does the fantastic costume of Siam or Korea.
It is ironical that Somerset Maugham, of all people, has
provided in *Don Fernando* one of the most lucid definitions
and analyses of mysticism to be found anywhere.

No book ever written is more accurately named than
*The Summing Up* (1938). There is nothing new in it for
the reader familiar with Maugham's earlier books and his
various prefaces; it is a summing up of his ideas on literature, art, theatre, ethics, religion, and philosophy, with an
occasional reference to some event in his life. The narrative
element is exasperatingly slight. The book is erroneously
called an autobiography: he terms it a summing up of
ideas and theories that have long floated haphazardly in
the various depths of his consciousness. He asserts that
the book was written to disembarrass his soul of certain
notions which would disturb his peace of mind until they
found some sort of literary expression; he had spoken
similarly of *Of Human Bondage* and *For Services Rendered.*

His literary and most of his aesthetic theories had already
been ventilated in the six prefaces to his collected plays,

prefaces to his novels, and the introduction to *Fifty Modern English Writers*. His views of art and artists are expressed in nearly all his earlier novels and books of travel and in various prefaces. His philosophy of life and religion, or lack of it, are practically the same as Philip's at the conclusion of *Of Human Bondage* (and restated, unchanged, in the Postscript to *A Writer's Notebook*—an entry made in 1944). Neither here nor in any previous books does one find discussion of political and social questions, which seem to him of minor and temporary interest.

He did not, however, remain static through all these years. Many experiences served to confirm early beliefs and doubts, but other events forced him to abandon prejudices. He grew more tolerant, and though he became no less skeptical of altruism and man's intelligence, he was more content to accept human nature as it is. His pessimism is not absolute. He finds that superstition is gradually yielding to science, and that many cruelties and evils of former days are less common. He himself has made many mistakes, but as a determinist he does not lament them with inane regret. For all its nihilism *The Summing Up* is strangely buoyant. Here is a man who, like Thoreau, has lived curiously and intensely and has succeeded in adjusting himself to the world he lives in without sacrificing his integrity. *The Summing Up*, like *Walden*—as unlike as the books and authors are—is the report of an individualist whose experimental design for a fit life has proved successful.

His other non-fiction writings are so numerous that only bare mention can be made of them: his many prefaces to friends' autobiographies and collected works; his introduction to his friend Charles H. Goren's book on bridge; prefaces to bibliographies and letters to writers of theses; extensive critical discussions in six voluminous anthologies of which he is the editor—a strange enterprise for a busy creative writer. His first venture in this field was aptly called *The Venture,* an annual (1903-1905) of which he was co-editor with Laurence Housman. Three articles on books and reading which appeared in *The Saturday Evening Post* were published in book form in 1940 under the title *Books and You. France at War* (1940) is a forgettable book with a self-explanatory title. *Strictly Personal* (1941) is an account of his dramatic escape from France in 1940. Dr. Klaus Jonas points out that the published book contains material rejected by *The Saturday Evening Post* when it was printed serially.

Four books published between 1949 and 1958 deserve special mention, for all have enhanced the author's reputation.

*A Writer's Notebook* is a selection of entries from fifteen large volumes of notebooks he kept from 1892 to 1944. It consists of philosophical observations, comments on writers and their craft, analyses of his religious doubts, remarks on logic and ethics, anecdotes, notes of incidents and characters later utilized in stories and plays, description of islands in the South Seas and natives, a tantalizingly brief account of his experiences in the First World War, notes on trips to Russia, Central America, the United States, Malaysia, and other places. *A Writer's Notebook* is the most exasperating of Maugham's books: it is of extraordinary interest, but seems brief and stingy when one thinks of the vast amount of material he did not choose to print. There is, for example, no entry for 1895, when he was twenty-one; three pages are devoted to the lively period of his life between 1897 and 1900. Sometimes five years pass without a line. There is far too little about his First World War experiences before he was sent to Russia. It is a tribute to the excellence and absorbing interest of a book when one complains that 367 pages are far too few.

With a sense of relief after he had finished with plays and fiction, he turned to essays, which he wrote with pleasure, indifferent to their marketable value and popularity. Few things in his long writing career afforded him more enjoyment than the composition of these essays on scattered subjects. One section of *The Vagrant Mood* (1952) deals with a minor nineteenth-century writer, Augustus Hare, whom Maugham knew and visited in 1898, when he was, as he terms it, a shy young novelist. Nothing in all Maugham's work is more delightful than the fifty pages devoted to this amazing eccentric. The other essays have as subjects Zurbaran, an early seventeenth-century painter, whom Maugham believes the Spanish underrate, and whom he considers superior to El Greco in some respects; "The Decline and Fall of the Detective Story," a serious consideration of a popular literary genre, but strange in its neglect of modern French detective fiction, particularly that of Simenon; a careful study of Burke's literary style; an intelligible analysis of Kant's *Critique of Pure Reason*; and finally in "Some Novelists I have Known" personal memories of Henry James, H. G. Wells, Lady Russell, Arnold Bennett (who once told Maugham that he considered *Of Human Bondage* one of the two greatest twentieth-century novels, too modest to mention the other one—*The Old Wives' Tale*), and Edith Wharton, a rather formidable *grande dame*: Maugham would agree with Dorothy Parker that Edie was a lady.

*Ten Novels and Their Authors* (1954) was written with a purpose: "to induce readers to read the novels with which they are concerned." He pays more attention to the authors than to their novels: "To know what sort of person the author was adds to one's understanding and appreciation of his work. To know something about Flaubert explains a great deal that would otherwise be disturbing in *Madame Bovary*, and to know the little there is to know about Emily Brontë gives a greater poignancy to her strange and wonderful book." He has frankly written about these ten novels as a novelist and confesses that a completely objective approach is impossible. It may be said at once that he achieves his purpose: nearly every intelligent reader of the book feels an urge to read or reread the ten novels discussed; and the reader is prepared for a more appreciative understanding of the novels after meeting their authors on Maugham's pages. By admitting that his list is arbitrary, and that he could have chosen ten other novels and given sound reasons for selecting them, he defends himself for omitting Hardy, Gide, Lawrence, Proust, Thackeray, Hawthorne, James, Turgenev, and a dozen others.

The reader of *Ten Novels and Their Authors* feels that he achieves a familiar acquaintance with the authors, all but Emily Brontë, whom we view from a distance. We read his discussions with pleasure even when we disagree. His enthusiasm for Balzac we can share in part, but not to the extent of considering him the only real genius among novelists. He hardly convinces us that *Moby Dick* and *Wuther-*

*ing Heights* reveal strains of homosexuality in their authors. There are many who fail to agree that *Le Rouge et le Noir* "is a very great book and to read it is a unique experience." Is *Great Expectations* inferior to *David Copperfield?* Such quibbling indicates that the book does more than entertain: it makes the reader review and defend his own opinions and interpretations.

Maugham announced that *Points of View* is the last book he will ever publish (at least in his lifetime). His publisher comments, "Since he has a way of doing what he says he is going to do, we may safely assume that with this volume of essays he will take his leave of the reading public and so put an end to a relationship that with *Liza of Lambeth* began just over sixty years ago." Maugham may have taken leave of the reading public, but it will be a long time before that public ceases to read his books.

*Points of View* is not the mixture as before, for his analysis of Goethe's novels and of the prose style of Dr. Tillotson, a churchman who lived at the end of the seventeenth and beginning of the eighteenth centuries, are surprising and novel topics for a final book. "The Saint" provides a lucid portrait of an intriguing mystic who had captured Maugham's interest twenty years before. In "The Short Story" he sums up all he has already written about this literary form, and includes sharp vignettes of a number of writers, the kind of thumbnail, somewhat gossipy biographies he so expertly composes. He thinks more highly of Chekhov (in comparison with Maupassant) than he had in earlier years. He asserts that Katherine Mansfield has a small but delicate talent; that for all their elaboration, many of Henry James's stories are uncommonly trivial;

that Maupassant is justified in not copying life but in arranging it in order the better to interest, excite, and surprise; that Poe's famous advice to short-story writers—included in his review of Hawthorne's *Twice-Told Tales*—is sound; that Kipling's stories are now underrated. His essay on four French journalists, Jules Renard, Edmond and Jules Goncourt, and Léon Léautaud, comes closer to scandal-mongering than to criticism and it throws considerable light on the jealousies and bickering on the French literary scene, among a people who take literature as seriously as business and politics. The book (except for "The Saint") shares with the reader the author's knowledge and love of reading. It is not "criticism" from the contemporary point of view. It is as though one were sitting in the garden at Villa Mauresque hearing his old and wise host speak about books he has read and people he has known.

If *Points of View* is Somerset Maugham's last book, it cannot be said that he went out with either a bang or a whimper. There is not the least sign of failing mental powers. The book is written in the controlled, urbane prose of which he has been a master for half a century, rarely brilliant, but lucid and rhythmical, with just the right amount of salt. We read, for example: "It does not matter if it [personality] is a slightly absurd one, as with Henry James, a somewhat vulgar one, as with Maupassant, a brash, tawdry one, as with Kipling—so long as the author can present it, distinct and idiosyncratic, his work has life;" and a comment on a letter Tillotson wrote to a nobleman condemned to die for treason (was it much more than political dissent?): "It is the letter of a good and sincere man; but what a hideous brutality there may be in the goodness of the good!" *Points of View* is not at all the final book one would expect from the author of *Cakes and Ale, The Moon and Sixpence,* and *The Circle,* unless he remembered that Maugham years before had stopped writing fiction and drama, determined to spend his last writing years composing essays for his own amusement. These last books have been widely read and received with gratifying praise by critics. They complete the design he had made many years ago for the writing pattern of his life. He has the satisfaction of knowing he finished what he set out to do.

## VIII

## MAUGHAM AND THE CRITICS

I T WOULD be more difficult for Somerset Maugham to as-
semble his own *Schimpflexikon*, his Dictionary of Abuse,
than it was for Nietzsche or H. L. Mencken. The iconoclastic Mencken fired his broadsides of contumely and vilifica-
tion at people, books, institutions, and organizations with
such blasts that retorts discourteous, and often fighting
mad, were inevitable. Mencken with delight collected
these counterblasts, published them, and let his enemies
pay him royalties. The animadversions against Maugham
have been of a different character, but they have been
plentiful, and many have been directed against the man
himself as well as his books. He realizes that like all men
he is not universally loved. "I have long known that there is
something in me that antagonizes some persons; I think
it is very natural, no one can like everyone; and their ill
will interests rather than discomposes me. I am only curious
to know what it is in me that is antipathetic to them."

Although he has written disparagingly about the books

and personalities of numerous other writers, unlike Mencken he never comments on politicians or other figures in public life, or on specific organizations; moreover, unlike those of Mencken, his remarks about living writers have never been caustic or even mildly uncharitable. His less than flattering remarks about Edith Wharton, Henry James, the Goncourts, Katherine Mansfield, H. G. Wells, Haddon Chambers, Turgenev (he later changed his opinion of Turgenev's novels and came to think highly of them), and Gorki were not published in their lifetimes. Even *A Writer's Notebook* (1949) was not published until all the authors whose works he discussed in it were dead.

He has been taken to task, for example, for his disparaging remarks about Henry James; a few critics have thought it presumptuous of him to pass judgment on the Master. Maugham knew the Anglo-American novelist very well in England, and once stayed with him in Boston when James was spending several months there with the widow of his brother William. Since James's death in 1916 Maugham has written amusingly at various times about his pomposity and the bloodlessness of his characters in a way painful to the Disciples, but Maugham's droll remarks have seldom been of a kind to draw a return fire; they have for the most part been ignored. The serious Jamesites, if aware of him at all, are inclined to rank Maugham with Vicki Baum or Booth Tarkington. He has said that those who knew Henry James and had felt the warmth of his personality, "curious and charming and a trifle absurd," and had heard him talk— and his delightful talk was as tortuous as his writing— could best enjoy his novels and stories. They have the added pleasure of being conscious of the man back of the stately pages. Maugham probably knows James's fiction far more thoroughly than do most of the James cultists. Several years ago when he edited an anthology of stories, he reread all of James's works, for he is a thorough and conscientious anthologist and critic. Before he wrote his essay on Francisco de Zurbaran for *The Vagrant Mood,* he made three trips to Spain in an attempt to see all the pictures by Zurbaran scattered over the country, making long, arduous journeys to villages where he had been told there might be paintings by this artist. He read hundreds of detective novels before he composed his brief study of this genre. In his eighties he reread all of Goethe's prose before writing his excellent essay in *Points of View.*

In general, then, his unfavorable judgments have not been of the stinging kind to bring about rebuttals. For example, his dry comment on modern poets—"I should be content with less cleverness if only they had more feeling. They make little songs not from great sorrows but from the pleasures of a good education"—would be annoying in certain camps, but it would not draw abusive replies. Moreover it is balanced by his thorough acquaintance with, and delight in, the poetry of Yeats and T. S. Eliot. In his old age he has said that he was glad that he lived long enough to read the verse of these two major poets.

Maugham has not been so much attacked by the critics as ignored. One is reminded of Wilde's witticism that there is one thing worse than being talked about: not being talked about. Maugham maintains that he is indifferent to criticism, and it is true that he seldom reads reviews of his books, printed interviews, and critiques of his work in periodicals; he has, however, read the books written about

him, some of them with great distaste. He has evidently
read enough to lead him to conclude that the intelligentsia
think little of him. "I look upon it as very natural that the
world of letters should have attached no great importance
to my work." In the drama he found himself at home in the
traditional molds. As a novelist he went "back to the teller
of tales round the fire in the cavern that sheltered neolithic
man." Because of his indifference to experimental forms, as
well as to the obscure depths of the unconscious mind, the
social, economic, and political backgrounds of characters,
the decline of civilization, and other concerns of the "new"
novelists, he was overlooked thirty-five years ago by many
young enthusiasts for James, Galsworthy, and Wells, and
later by admirers of Lawrence, Huxley, Virginia Woolf,
Sartre, Kafka, and Camus, none of whom were content just
to be story-tellers. In the 1920's and the first half of the
following decade the leftist critics, who were loud if not
authoritative and were listened to with some attention,
seemed as unaware of Maugham's existence as were the
conservative critics who followed them.

Actually he has had considerable support from reputable
writers and critics, for example Frank Swinnerton, Cyril
Connolly, Christopher Isherwood, Alec Waugh, Richard
Aldington, and the anonymous writers for the *Times Literary Supplement*. He came nearest to winning favor with
the intellectuals over forty years ago with *The Moon and
Sixpence*, for they could not fail to recognize that this almost savage story did not pander to public taste, that it was
free of sugary sentimentalism—as if *Liza of Lambeth, Mrs.
Craddock*, and *Of Human Bondage* were guilty of sac-
charinity! The culturally advanced of the time, who

regarded Monet, Pissaro, Van Gogh, Sisley, and Gauguin as their property, were surprised at this challenge by a "popular" writer. Swinnerton says wryly that these intelligentsia regretted that Maugham did not understand the art of the novel, for *The Moon and Sixpence* shows that he might have been able to do something excellent in that form if he had known how to write fiction.

But in general the highbrows have left him alone. Twenty-five years ago in a paper read to the Royal Society of Literature, St. John Ervine said, "Earnest youths from Oxford and Cambridge and the Polytechnic, when they write assessments of modern literature, seldom deign to mention Mr. Maugham." It should be mentioned that since that time Maugham's works have afforded topics for dozens of doctoral dissertations, many of them excellent, in American and German universities, and uncounted Masters' theses. Most of these scholars have written to Maugham, who has patiently replied and attempted to answer their questions. One exception to his neglect by the intelligentsia, except in Japan and in graduate schools of American and German universities, is the *avant-garde* literary magazine *Paris Review*, in the late 1950's a favorite of eggheads in Europe and America, especially noted for its searching interviews. By 1959 interviews with Hemingway, Mauriac, Joyce Cary, Forster, T. S. Eliot, Albert Moravia, and Faulkner had been published; to appear in subsequent issues were conversations with Kingsley Amis, André Malraux, Maugham's friend and neighbor Jean Cocteau—and Somerset Maugham. This is strange company indeed for the Old Party, as he likes to call himself.

Although Maugham replies to nearly all the vast number

of letters he receives, one came to him in 1953 from a fifteen-year-old school girl in Devonshire that he found himself unable to answer:

> Dear Mr. Maugham,
>
>  I have read nearly all your books and have liked them, but my daddy says I am only wasting my time because they are only a potboiler and will be forgotten as soon as you are dead. Are you a potboiler?
>
> Yours affectionately,<br>Rosemary

He did not know how to answer Rosemary without appearing to be immodest. "Of course I am a professional writer— I have never made a secret of it as some people do—but I don't look upon myself as a potboiler, because I have never [well, hardly ever] written anything I didn't want to write."

The accusation of writing "potboilers" he can shrug off easily, for it is quite undeserved, but there is another often used word that rankles: "competent." One would suppose that this is an adjective of approval, but critics have applied it to Maugham's writing with the same deprecatory meaning that they put into "well-made" in describing a certain kind of contrived, formula-constructed play. Unconcerned with criticism as he considers himself, he has been stung to reply to the charge of competence brought against him. The imputation of being "readable" is also frequently leveled at him. His defenders have said that to describe Maugham as "readable" is as silly as describing Chopin as "tuneful."

Is it this "competence," his old-fashioned predilection for the well-made narrative with a beginning, a middle, and an end, with recognizable characters and appropriate dialogue, simply and clearly told, that makes him seem unimportant to many critics? The fact that he introduced no notable innovations in the structure or the technique of the novel, and his failure to show concern for isms and movements, have also made him seem lacking in significance. For years he was a contemporary of Shaw, Wells, and Galsworthy, all of whom were deeply concerned with social problems and indirectly with politics—poverty, class distinctions, exploitation of the underdog, flaws in the legal system, war, the social conscience in general. They were all serious writers, but often more concerned with man's world than with man himself. To write of people just as people, stressing only slightly their entanglement in the network of current social complexities, was Victorian. In an interview in 1958 with Philip Toynbee, Maugham said, "What you have to remember about me is that I am a relic of the Edwardian era. It may seem very old-fashioned to you but I believe in *story-telling*." He said further that fiction is no place for propaganda, either political or philosophical. When Toynbee reminded him that *Liza of Lambeth* was occasioned partly by the young medical student's attitude toward poverty and slums, Maugham replied that it was all a matter of the writer's conscious intention, and he assured Toynbee that his was always a dramatic intention, not political or sociological. "I am not my brother's keeper," he says in *The Summing Up*. This anti-socialistic, if not antisocial, statement assigns him unconditionally to his place among the novelists of the center, which for advanced critics is a barren, dull no man's land.

It has been wittily, or captiously, suggested by his apologists that the highbrows might have noticed him if only he had shown a little influence by Wyndham Lewis, or even by Ernest Hemingway. He is considered by many as merely a rewriter of the Victorian novel; he cannot be modern, for he is too imitative and repetitive. If only he were as difficult to read as Kafka and Joyce—or Faulkner, whose confused and disorderly writing sometimes seems to approach the sadistic. Has there ever been a literary period such as ours when lucidity was so disregarded as a quality of good writing, and dullness so ignored as a flaw?

In most studies of the modern novel he is rarely criticized adversely, but is treated with condescension, damned with faint praise, or ignored. The excellent critic David Daiches in *The Novel and the Modern World* writes at length about *Sons and Lovers* (1913) and *Portrait of the Artist as a Young Man* (1916), but does not mention *Of Human Bondage* (1915) or any other novel by Maugham. In G. A. Ellis's long study, *Twilight on Parnassus,* and V. S. Pritchett's *The Living Novel* he is not mentioned. Gerald Bullett in *Modern English Fiction* writes at length about H. G. Wells, but says nothing about Maugham, not even in the section on the short story or in the apologetic final chapter, "Summary of Omissions." In a recent analysis of the modern novel Walter Allen is less than flattering. He notes that Maugham has always been an admittedly professional writer ("professional" is as defamatory as "competent" and "readable;" Alexander Pope was possibly the first of the inferior breed of professional writers) whose strength has come from his knowledge of his own limitations. Therefore, says Allen, he has confined himself to a narrow range of subject and character, but unfortunately he lacks a compensatory excellence of style to make up for his shortcomings. Walter Myers in *The Later Realism* devotes half a line to Maugham and includes none of his books in his suggested reading list.

In Ernest Baker's monumental ten-volume *The History of the English Novel* there are only two brief references to Maugham. Joseph Warren Beach omits discussion of his fiction in his long *Twentieth Century Novel* because "he does not stand for anything specially distinctive in the evolution of technique." In *Modern Fiction* the able critic H. J. Muller puts Maugham in his place of no great importance by grouping him with "novelists of the center." Elizabeth Drew in *The Modern Novel* (1924) complains that *Of Human Bondage* is heavy and monotonous, and she ignores *The Moon and Sixpence*. Pelham Elgar in *The Art of the Novel* accuses Maugham of offending good taste in his use of Gauguin and Hardy as models for characters.

In Edward Wagenknecht's *Cavalcade of the English Novel*, six hundred pages long, Maugham is granted recognition in one footnote, and in the Appendix he is mentioned in another note in which the literary historian acknowledges Maugham's *competence* but deplores the absence of philosophy, poetry, and imagination; "and like all materialists he finds no significance in life." Charles Angoff explains that Maugham is not loved but respected, and deplores his unchivalrous view of women, his lack of lyricism and ecstasy, and his "frigid indifference." Since he obviously loves no one and nothing, his readers cannot possibly love him. Angoff predicts that his readers will desert him altogether. John Brophy finds the style of *Cakes and Ale* too informal, and as a result the writing is full of clichés and hackneyed phrases. Harrison Smith found *The Razor's*

*Edge* written with "superb and contemptuous arrogance."
This novel was scathingly reviewed by Malcolm Cowley
for *The New Republic*. He declared that Maugham is
quite unsuited by temperament to write a religious novel,
and as a result, *The Razor's Edge is* "the old Maugham
cocktail with an ineffectual dash of holy water." Cowley
wonders why Maugham, who, during a career of nearly
fifty years, has produced so little first-class work, is still
read and reviewed seriously. Then the critic makes a most
unworthy speculation, facetiously one hopes: that
Maugham may have seen the sales reports of *The Keys of
the Kingdom, The Song of Bernadette,* and *The Robe,* the
best selling novels of 1941, 1942, and 1943 respectively, and
proceeded to write a novel with a religious theme to be
the best seller of 1944.

Maugham has aided and abetted his detractors by saying
many deprecatory things about himself, such as "My own
native gifts are not remarkable;" "My writing is a harmless
habit that happens to be profitable;" "I know just where
I stand; in the very front row of the second-raters." Yet a
vast amount of *Schimpf* has been hurled at him because
the critics themselves are not able to place him in the
front row of the first-raters. They become irked about what
they consider his failure to reach the stature of Joyce,
Lawrence, and Proust; others are irritated by the respectful
attention he has received by a number of reputable British
and American critics, as well as by Paul Dottin and Suzanne
Guéry in France, Helmut Papajewski in Germany, and
Yoshio Nakano in Japan, all of whom regard him as a writer
of considerable importance.

Perhaps the most ill-humored and acrimonious attack

*Allan G. Chappelow, M.A., F.R.S.A.*

Entrance to Villa Mauresque, showing the sign against the evil eye discovered by Maugham's father.

The swimming pool at Villa Mauresque.

ever made on Maugham was incorporated in Edmund Wilson's review of *Then and Now*. To be sure it is not a very good novel, one of Maugham's least distinguished, but Wilson judges it very harshly. Maugham himself has pointed out that every writer trips now and then, and he gives as an example the feeble episode of the lost handkerchief in *Othello*. We do not judge Bernard Shaw by *Buoyant Billions*, Galsworthy by *The Fugitive*, Sinclair Lewis by *Prodigal Parents*, Joyce by *The Exiles*, and so on. Maugham wonders why critics expect writers always to do as well as they should have done. Wilson, a first-rate critic with taste and acumen, found *Then and Now* all but unreadable, its plot handled in the inept way one would expect to find in a dull prep-school magazine, the language banal, a tissue of clichés—the entire novel hardly beyond the skill of a schoolboy. In his fifty years as a novelist Maugham had never received a more blistering notice.

To some extent Wilson was justified in his harsh appraisal of *Then and Now*. In the review, however, he took advantage of the opportunity to let fly at Maugham in general, exasperated by the novelist's repeated failure over the years to produce anything approaching "literature," and irritated by the current tendency (in the late 1940's) to elevate Maugham into the higher ranks of English fiction. Wilson says flatly that he had never been able to convince himself that Somerset Maugham was anything but second-rate. Maugham had just presented the manuscript of *Of Human Bondage* to the Library of Congress, and the solemn ceremony of presentation and grateful acceptance struck Wilson as a conspicuous sign of the general decline in American literary standards. To him, Maugham lacks the "métier," he is not really a writer at all. His use of words is undistinguished, he has no personal rhythm (even clumsy Dreiser has a compelling rhythm), he cannot create for his readers a poetic world (like that of Hecate County?). Wilson complains that Maugham as a writer has remained the perpetual schoolboy, whereas he might have pursued a normal career in medicine, diplomacy, law, or politics. Wilson admits that Maugham may have written better novels than *Then and Now*, but declares that he was never a literary artist or first-rate critic of morals.

Like some other critics Wilson is incensed by Maugham's disposition to take advantage of his popularity "for the purpose of disparaging his betters." Although Maugham is always pointedly modest in referring to his own claims to literary excellence, he "manages to sound invidious" when he speaks of his first-rate contemporaries. Wilson was particularly annoyed by Maugham's critical comments in his anthology *Introduction to Modern English and American Literature*, and in addition to his patronizing remarks he included selections by such mediocrities as Katherine Brush and Michael Arlen. How presumptuous, how insolent of a second-rater to say that Henry James never came to grips with life, that Joyce's *Ulysses* is too long, that Yeats though good company was vain and pompous, that when we reread Proust we are inclined to skip the philosophical disquisitions, that Bergson's philosophy is now largely discredited. (Maugham seems to be correct here. Bergson's centennial in 1959 did not receive the notice that such anniversaries ordinarily inspire in France, and although there were some articles, no attempt was made to place him among the great philosophers. In one of the popular weeklies a long article about Bergson was devoted entirely to his imminent conversion to Catholicism at the time of his death.) Wilson's attack is brilliant, but admirers of Maugham's books will shrug their shoulders; some may recall the old Eastern saying, "The little dogs barked, but the caravan passed on."

A much more amusing attack was made by a humorless physician who fancied himself a literary critic and who more than a generation ago was listened to with deference by those who took Coué seriously and let Henry Van Dyke and William Lyon Phelps suggest their reading. Dr. Joseph Collins was especially furious at *The Moon and Sixpence*. He denounced Maugham for masquerading as a psychiatrist and "animadverting" on love and the sexual appetite in such a way that it "becomes obvious that he knows little about biology, psychiatry, or art." About sex Dr. Collins declares that all Maugham's remarks are "heavy platitudes." His is no soft impeachment. "It is disgusting and nauseous, atavistic in implication"—Dr. Collins's language has a high specific gravity. *The Moon and Sixpence* he finds "primitive and bestially suggestive," tending to undermine faith in the fundamental goodness of human nature. "It is radicalism and realism carried to the $n^{th}$ degree." He finally condemns the novel because no one could be better or happier for reading it. Dr. Collins was also shocked by *The Way of All Flesh*, and blamed Bernard Shaw for popularizing Butler's foul novel. Without Shaw's drum-beating *The Way of All Flesh* would never have corrupted more than a handful of readers.

Joseph Wood Krutch dismisses Maugham as an unimportant writer. The London *Times* reviewer found *Christ-*

*mas Holiday* dull. *The Painted Veil* received hostile notices: "Too much paint and too little veil," "Mr. Maugham knows people, the wrong sort of people," "These joyless debauchees are not typical of humanity." *The Bookman's* review of *Of Human Bondage* deplores the lack of color and humor, the unnecessary ugliness of the conflict between Philip and his uncle. The reviewer hoped that Maugham would find a more robust subject for his next novel. *The Bookman* in fact was consistently hostile to Maugham's fiction and plays: *Liza of Lambeth*—"painful, depressing, hopeless;" *The Bishop's Apron*—"irresponsible flippancy;" *Mrs. Craddock*—"repellent." *The Bookman's* most amusing pronouncement was that "Miss Thompson" is a failure as a short story and will never interest readers. If Maugham had read the reviews of his books through the years he might have noted that he has often been praised for what he considers his flaws and censured for what he regards as his virtues.

As a dramatist he had something of the experience of Shaw, who said that according to the critics all his plays were good except the last one. Drama critics have nearly always been kinder to Shaw and Maugham revivals than to the original productions. Perhaps if he had continued in the "new-drama" vein of *A Man of Honour* ("inspissated gloom," "sordid," a popular London daily said of it), he might have won greater critical favor, but would he have gained audiences? He had no desire to be a hole-and-corner dramatist like St. John Hankin or Granville-Barker, for he wanted his plays to be seen by many and large audiences. The frank admission that he wanted to make money in the theatre antagonized the critics, who found and still find difficulty in equating popularity with excellence. With amusing inconsistency, however, the intellectuals are delighted when T. S. Eliot, Graham Greene, or Archibald MacLeish writes a play that gains popular favor.

Of all his plays only *The Circle* won unqualified approval in its first London production and has pleased critics in its many revivals. *Lady Frederick, Mrs. Dot,* and *Jack Straw,* the three comedies which catapulted him overnight into notoriety, were pronounced diverting but contrived and imitative. Yet when *Lady Frederick* was revived in the austere 1940's, critics were well disposed toward this "period piece." How pleasant to see a comedy "moving with leisured elegance in a confidently frivolous world, where luxury is taken for granted!" In 1911, fifteen years before the appearance of *Elmer Gantry,* Sinclair Lewis's jolting novel about a hypocritical clergyman, *Loaves and Fishes,* a comedy about a parson who is a transparent humbug, horrified the reviewers. Admitting that the audience was continuously moved to laughter, the *Times* reviewer moralized, "Laughter is not enough, especially when coupled with irreverence toward the clergy." *Loaves and Fishes* was written only two years before he started writing *Of Human Bondage,* when the idea of the novel and memories of his clergyman uncle and his uncle's clerical friends who came to the vicarage were big in his mind. None of the plays before *The Circle* pleased the critics, except to some extent *Home and Beauty. Caroline* was "preposterous;" *The Land of Promise* "unbelievable, sordid, nauseous;" *Caesar's Wife* "old stuff;" *Love in a Cottage* "insincere;" *The Unknown* "blasphemous."

After *The Circle* he had twelve years of playwriting, but

only one play was well received by the London critics, *The Sacred Flame*. In 1923 reviewers admitted being greatly entertained by *Our Betters* but they gave it uncomplimentary notices. Of all his plays *The Constant Wife* has received the harshest treatment, more so in England than in America. "It gave me several hours of acute depression," "tedious throughout," "devoid of wit" were typical comments. The *London Mercury* reviewer left at the end of Act Two, disgusted. "Dismal theme," "epigrams in a teacup," "no more shocking than a bowl of goldfish swimming coldly but in an elaborate pattern, after one another's decorative tails," were other next-morning judgments. Although *The Constant Wife* with Ethel Barrymore as Constance fared better in America, it received unflattering notices. Stark Young found it "without shine and without wings." Its revivals have never pleased the critics. In 1946 the London *Times* dismissed it as a second-rate problem play. A popular revival in America several years later with Katharine Cornell rather preposterously cast as Constance drew this stricture from Harold Clurman: "Old-fashioned without being delightful because of it. The whole evening an epigram with wool in its mouth."

Near the end of his playwriting career he felt impelled to write four plays for his own satisfaction, indifferent, so he declared, to their reception in the commercial theatre. *The Breadwinner, For Services Rendered,* and *Sheppey,* cast with the most skillful performers in the English theatre, and each play probably one of the best new plays of the year, all received cold notices. Only *The Sacred Flame,* the least distinguished of the four, pleased a number of the London critics. All four are still very much alive in theatres all over the world, except in England and America.

In critical studies of the modern drama Maugham is nearly always handled with condescension or ignored entirely. The high-brow weeklies and quarterlies think no more of his plays than of his fiction. One drama quarterly recently consented to print an article on his plays if the obstacle of his not being "modern" could be overcome in the critique. To such highest-browed critics as Eric Bentley and Francis Fergusson, Maugham seems to be vaguely grouped with Denham Thompson, Sardou, and H. J. Bryan. Even his friendly admirer St. John Ervine in *The Theatre in My Time*, published in 1933, the year Maugham completed his playwriting, mentions him only twice: one brief reference to *The Unknown* and one to the weekly cost of the production of *For Services Rendered*.

Maugham has no doubt supported this tendency to belittle and undervalue his plays. As early as 1908, when he was much interviewed after his sudden success, he said with sincerity, although his statement was received as mere flippancy, "I must say there is a tremendous amount of nonsense talked about the serious drama. All that hifalutin chatter about ideals!" Naturally such a cavalier statement would not endear him to journalists whose métier is writing about the "serious drama." Moreover, in the excellent prefaces to his collected plays and in *The Summing Up* he consistently refuses to place drama, except the few masterpieces of the Greeks and Renaissance Europe, among the higher art forms. If he subscribed to a cutting agency and read the reviews, no one would be less surprised than he at his treatment by serious drama critics.

Some admirers of Maugham are certain that he has now

lived through the period of scoffing patronage by the intellectuals and the little cliques, a period which befalls nearly
every important writer who has made his writing pay. Such
obloquy came to Anatole France, Galsworthy, Wells, and
Bennett after their deaths, but it came to Maugham early
in his lifetime. It is doubtful that it has withered away as
much as Glenway Wescott, Frank Swinnerton, and other
supporters declare. Waspish references to the enormous
sales of his books, his love of comfort, his undisputed position as the Grand Old Businessman of English letters, his
description of the Ritz (New York) as a quiet family hotel,
his employment at Villa Mauresque of the best cook in
France, his luxurious means of travel are almost as frequent
as ever.

Irresponsible journalists through exaggeration and downright fabrication have created the impression that he is
a Sybarite and gourmand, a character out of Huysmans or
*The Picture of Dorian Gray.* There have been references to
his yacht, for example. He never owned one. He has no
"liveried servants." Villa Mauresque is a villa, not a manor
house or country seat, and it is a "show place" (as it is
usually described) only for those who appreciate civilized
taste, comfort, and an easy, unaffected way of life. For
the price of one of his Renoirs he could have installed a
few fountains, floodlighting, a brace of costumed foot-
men, and other fripperies of the tasteless rich. For some
time Pablo Picasso has been trying to purchase from
Maugham two of his (Picasso's) best pictures, which adorn
the entrance hall and the dining room of the villa. Picasso
wants these 1904 paintings as an investment for his family
and offers Maugham a sum sufficient to purchase a yacht

of impressive grandeur. There is not even a piano or television set at Villa Mauresque. When the composer of the music for a proposed musical version of *Of Human Bondage* came to the villa and prepared to play for Maugham the melodies he had written, he was astounded to find that there was no piano in the house. (If this musical is never produced, most admirers of *Of Human Bondage* will be able to bear their disappointment with fortitude.) On the rare occasions where there is something on the wireless he wishes to hear, Maugham borrows the cook's radio.

Maugham has been a professional writer for over sixty years. Every morning, whether at home or away, he has devoted, and still devotes, to reading and writing. Only a hard-working writer could produce more than twenty novels, more than thirty plays, books of travel, numerous anthologies, several volumes of essays, a score of introductions to others' books, and fifteen large volumes of journals. And he is a worker to the end, writing a partial autobiography, a memoir of a celebrated friend, and other items for posthumous publication. Moreover, he has tried always to write well, to satisfy his own standards. "One fusses about style. One tries to write better. One takes pains to be simple, clear, and succinct." Then recalling that the four greatest of all novelists, Dostoievsky, Tolstoy, Dickens, and Balzac, sometimes wrote badly, he could only conclude that if a novelist can tell a story, create living characters, be inventive and sincere, "it doesn't matter a damn how he writes. All the same, it's better to write well than ill."

Nevertheless the fact that nearly forty million copies of his books have been sold has disconcerted the critics.

(What would the champions of modern art say if every resident in Levittown installed a statue by Henry Moore on his lawn?) Published statements concerning Maugham's wealth and annual income are guesses or inventions by imaginative journalists. Some published figures are of course valid: that one book store alone, the Times Book Shop of London, has sold nearly 300,000 copies of his books; that the sales of *The Razor's Edge* are approaching five million; that his collected short stories published a few years ago have sold half a million copies; that *Of Human Bondage* has outsold all other items in the popular Modern Library series; that Maugham has been for years the most popular author writing in English; that in his eighty-sixth year the total sales of his books were as great as they had ever been. But neither Maugham nor his secretary announces the annual income from royalties on books, radio, theatre, film, and television.

What does such popularity imply? He is a best-seller in South America, Turkey (where his books have sold several hundred thousand copies, but Maugham has never received a penny of royalty), Japan, Italy, and Spain. His complete works have been translated into Japanese, and he has a tremendous following in Japan—even among the intellectuals. In 1959 more than forty thousand people, mostly students and teachers, crowded for ten days an exhibition of Maugham's works in Tokyo's leading book store. On his eighty-sixth birthday, January 25, 1960, the Maugham Society was inaugurated in Japan, with fifty scholars of English literature as founders. As soon as the announcement was made, more than two thousand applications for membership were received; over two hundred of the applicants were university professors. Not only is Maugham the most widely read foreign author in Japan, he is also regarded as a major literary figure. In more than one Japanese editorial he has been ranked second to Shakespeare among English writers. After years of publishing his books illegally in Russia, often under phony authorship and titles, the state printing houses are bringing out a complete new edition of his works under his name and with his titles. As recently as 1946, however, *The Circle* and *Caroline* were banned in the U.S.S.R. because of their "deleterious influence on home life."

He has been too canny a professional writer to run into many censorship difficulties. It is true that his threatened publishers had him change certain proper names in *The Painted Veil*, but none of his books have been officially suppressed, except *Ashenden* in Nazi Germany and some for a time in Russia. Librarians have been known to keep certain items off the open shelves, and in at least one girls' school in England his stories are not permitted in the library or in the possession of the pupils. His books were never banned in Fascist Italy; they are widely circulated today in Poland, Czechoslovakia, Spain, and other totalitarian countries.

Obviously such world-wide popularity in itself does not spell greatness, but neither does it imply mediocrity. To those like Swinnerton and Harold Nicolson who consider Maugham an important, underrated literary figure, the paradox of his writing career is that he has attained such popularity while refusing to write down to the supposed medium-low mentality of the bulk of novel-readers; even more of a paradox is the fact that many of his stories and plays lack all the obvious elements that make for popular favor.

Whether or not he achieves the excellence of style he strives for, one suspects that the millions read his stories and novels in English and a dozen other languages for a reason other than literary artistry. They read him because he is concerned with the drama of human relations, and because they can read him with ease. Maugham was pleased when an American serviceman wrote to him that he "read all of *The Razor's Edge* without having to look up a single word." The genesis of a story in his mind was always a particular situation between individuals. They read him because, as he says, he believes in story-telling.

He entertains his readers. "Why are people so ashamed of being entertained?" he asks, noting that the great pictures were painted to give pleasure, that the great plays, including those by Sophocles and Shakespeare, were written to entertain. He has repeatedly declared that he has always found pleasure in writing, and he suggests that that might be the reason he has given pleasure to readers. "Reading must be primarily a pleasure, not a chore. . . . All literature is escapist. That is its charm. . . . The novel is a form of art and the purpose of art is to please. . . . There are pleasures of the spirit as well as of the senses. . . . There are intelligent and unintelligent pleasures, and the reading of a good novel is among the most intelligent pleasures a man can enjoy." Such remarks would probably seem banalities to the New Critics, and would be received with indifference by most of the forty million buyers of his books. But they help explain why his books are read with pleasure.

When he was eighty he confessed that one of the pleasant compensations of being old is that he has no illusions about his literary position. He is able to bear with equanimity the fact that many critics do not take him seriously. "I have seen essays by clever young men on contemporary fiction who would never think of considering me. I no longer mind what people think." One cannot help suspecting, however, that he has been at least slightly nettled by the failure of the New Criticism to consider him a peer of Lawrence, Joyce, and Proust. Has he protested too much? Is his use of the phrase "no longer" significant? As he looks back on a very long literary career, he feels that on the whole he has done what he set out to do. He notices with amusement that when he was eighty and again when he was eighty-five, many more people took him seriously than when he was a youthful seventy. His advice to writers is: live a long time. "I have found that longevity counts for more than talent." He said in an interview in 1958, almost quoting from *Cakes and Ale,* "you know how funny the English are about old age—once they take some one to their hearts, they are loyal to the last, whether it's a singer who has lost his voice or an actor who forgets his lines. That seems to have happened to me!"

According to a Talk of the Town paragraph in the *New Yorker* in 1946, Maugham had a preview of the post-mortem depreciation that his literary reputation will undergo. When interviewed by a reporter for the *Herald Tribune*, he gave the man a message to take back to the editor. Somehow Maugham had got hold of the obituary notice already set up and ready for use in the *Tribune* the morning after his death. It was not flattering. "Tell your editor that I regard it as very cool. Very cool indeed."

Although Maugham continues to be patronized or ignored by nearly all the New Critics and their scholarly journals, he has for the most part enjoyed a gratifyingly good press for more than half a century. Among his supporters have been many eminent and respected critics and creative writers. It is noteworthy that Maugham is highly regarded by other novelists and dramatists. At the end of a long writing career of nearly sixty-five years he enjoys a critical reputation greater than ever before.

In 1920 Sir Desmond MacCarthy started his campaign to persuade critics and readers that Maugham was a major writer. Some serious attention had been paid to him earlier. As early as 1908 Walter Pritchard Eaton, an authoritative dramatic critic of the day, called attention in America to the brilliant new London playwright, and at the same time Max Beerbohm was writing enthusiastically for British readers about Maugham's early comedies. In 1915 came Theodore Dreiser's memorable review of *Of Human Bondage*: ". . . a novel or biography or autobiography or social transcript of utmost importance." Four years later Maxwell Anderson welcomed *The Moon and Sixpence* with equally high praise.

In 1931 Mark Van Doren hailed *Cakes and Ale* for its wit and wisdom, as did William Rose Benét, who declared, "Maugham is one of the world's leading writers of fiction . . . his mind is agreeable, amusing, and entirely civilized." A vastly popular but superficial critic of the 1930's, Alexander Woollcott, wrote for his many thousands of readers,

"As an example of the story-teller's art, *Cakes and Ale* is a masterpiece, unsurpassed in our language in our time." The novel was also favorably reviewed by Cyril Connolly and V. S. Pritchett. *Cakes and Ale* during the past thirty years has received much more ungrudging praise than has *Of Human Bondage.*

It is notable that Theodore Dreiser's golden opinion of *Of Human Bondage* was formed without aid of hindsight. Since 1915 the praise of this novel has become widespread. Carl Van Doren wrote in 1925: "There are critics prepared to call it the triumph of its generation. It is perhaps the most brilliant of the many autobiographical novels which the present century has seen." According to V. S. Pritchett, "*Of Human Bondage* did for its time what is more popular in French literature than in English . . . the honest portrait of a young man;" Burton Rascoe thought it "one of the greatest novels of all time." S. P. B. Mais called it "one of the few absolutely sincere documents I have ever read." Although H. J. Muller finds the virtues of *The Moon and Sixpence* and *Cakes and Ale* scarcely solid or deeply significant, he praises *Of Human Bondage* as a wholly earnest and important novel. "It is in some ways superior to *The Way of All Flesh* . . . much more than a forum or slaughter-house of decrepit conventions . . . it deals with the problems that eternally torture sensitive and thoughtful men. It considers the terms of life in this or any age."

Of the later novels only *The Razor's Edge* has pleased a number of critics, but it was dismissed as insignificant by many reviewers. Cyril Connolly wondered at the uncharitable reviews and concluded that the British are incapable of recognizing excellence when they see it: "*The Razor's*

*Edge* appears at a time when decline of literary quality is fairly matched by the decline of literary taste": why cannot critics see, he asks, that "Maugham's writing is delightfully flexible, vivid and easy?" *Christmas Holiday,* which appeared in the uneasy year of 1939 and which is the only one of Maugham's novels to touch on current social and political problems, left most critics uncertain. Glenway Wescott, however, considers *Christmas Holiday* the most significant novel of the decade just before the outbreak of World War II. Maugham's last novel, *Catalina,* was charitably received as a pleasant trifle, expertly done.

Perhaps his short stories have aroused more general acclaim than his novels. Christopher Morley nominated Maugham as the most readable author of our time: ". . . [his short stories] are delightful entertainment, which, as Mr. Maugham says, is fiction's true aim." Harold Nicolson calls him the greatest master of the short story, and Cyril Connolly agrees: "He is the greatest living short-story writer."

Ashley Dukes said of his plays in 1924 that they "are not only invented, but felt—they flow from an emotional reservoir one must respect. . . . A resolute intellectual integrity gives them [his characters] whatever dignity they possess." *The Circle* (1921) was his first play to persuade critics that he was a serious and important dramatist, capable of brilliance and thought as well as of clever entertainment. W. A. Darlington in the *Times* called it "one of the most brilliant of English comedies." James Agate said of *The Breadwinner* that it was impossible to be dissatisfied with it as entertainment; and Agate (as hard to please as George Jean Nathan) lauded *For Services Rendered*:

"For sheer playwriting our stage has seen nothing so good for a very long time. The piece is put together like an Ibsen puzzle in which every bit fits. It is the work of a man possessed of something like genius." Ivor Brown wrote approvingly of Maugham's last play, *Sheppey*: "brave, expert, unforgettable, brilliant." St. John Ervine has said that he has always read Maugham's plays with pleasure. Carl and Mark Van Doren assert that neither Wilde nor Shaw provides examples of the comedy of manners as brilliant as Maugham's.

The books of travel and those of an autobiographical nature (except *A Personal Record*) were reviewed with almost unanimous approval. *The Summing Up, Don Fernando, A Writer's Notebook,* and his collections of essays received from the reviewers little or none of the carping criticism and even abuse that sometimes greeted his plays and novels. Edward Weeks says of *The Summing Up,* "There is no better book on writing in the English language." Frank Swinnerton praises the lucid style of the essays and concludes, "Of all modern authors Maugham is the man who most nearly says, hardly as if it were opening his mouth, precisely what he means to say." J. B. Priestley considers him "an essayist of extraordinary merit." It must be most gratifying to Maugham that the two books which he wrote in his old age solely for his own pleasure, *A Vagrant Mood* and *Points of View,* pleased nearly every British and American reviewer.

To the charge of professionalism often brought against Maugham, John Brophy repeats the answer given by the author himself in his introductory note to *The Mixture As Before*: nearly always the professional is more expert than the amateur. As to Maugham's place in the future, Glenway Wescott expresses the confidence of many readers. This novelist-critic asserts, with some excess in his enthusiasm, that Maugham is the only writer who for more than a generation has held the respect and admiration of an "elite of highly cultivated, sophisticated readers, and of a sufficient number of good fellow writers." He adds that at the same time Maugham has pleased and made sense to and even affected the lives of a million of ordinary readers. He declares that eight or ten of his books are better than almost any one's today and will continue to be read for many years to come. "There is no 20th century novelist who will be so widely read in the 21st century."

Although denied the supreme accolade bestowed by the New Criticism on Joyce, Proust, Faulkner, Kafka, Camus, and James, Somerset Maugham can be proud of his admirers: W. H. Auden, Frank Swinnerton, Theodore Dreiser, Max Beerbohm, Christopher Isherwood, Desmond MacCarthy, St. John Ervine, Carl and Mark Van Doren, Richard Aldington, Mary Colum, Cyril Connolly, Harold Nicolson, Glenway Wescott, V. S. Pritchett, William Rose Benét, S. N. Behrman, and many other fellow writers. Perhaps he is equally proud of the fact that his books have afforded pleasure to hundreds of thousands of intelligent readers who know or care little about literary criticism. They feel that W. SOMERSET MAUGHAM on the cover of a book provides all the endorsement necessary.

## IX

### THE FINAL YEARS

IN THE AUTUMN and winter of 1959-1960 Maugham made a long journey to the Far East, by ship, to visit once more some of the countries he had known thirty-five and forty years earlier. Everywhere he was received like a reigning monarch, especially in Japan. Great crowds were at the pier when his ship docked in Yokohama, a Maugham exhibition at the world's largest bookstore, Maruzen's in Tokyo, drew thousands of visitors, and the Japan Maugham Society was formed. It joined the two other large literary groups in Japan devoted to English authors, the Shakespeare Society and the Hardy Society. Maugham was greatly pleased by this honor, especially since more than fifty university professors, all scholars of English literature, formed the nucleus. He had never been so honored in England or America. The Japanese are probably the world's greatest readers (there are more bookstores on one street, appropriately named Bookstore Street, in Tokyo than in all of New York and Chicago combined), and Maugham is the most widely read foreign author in Japan—in 1964 Thomas Hardy was the second most popular foreign author. Maugham's books are extensively used in the schools and universities of this literate country, and he is fortunate to have such scholars as Yoshio Nakoma, Natsuo Shumuta, and Mutsuo Tanaka to translate and edit his books, and contribute to the impressive journal of the Society, *Cap Ferrat*. After his death only two literary periodicals brought out special Somerset Maugham issues; both were Japanese.

Again he saw the Angkor ruins in Cambodia— he once said that he made this last trip just to see them one more time, and such favorite cities as Bangkok, Singapore, and Colombo. The trip was a success in every way. He met with a great, and to him, moving reception everywhere he went, and his good health persisted. In Bangkok he was feted on his eighty-sixth birthday by students who performed an elaborate Siamese birthday ceremony. He did not revisit the South Sea Islands, the setting of his most popular stories in the 1920's and 1930's.

After his return to Mauresque he enjoyed over two years of good health and serenity, and was able to visit again his favorite European cities of Munich, Venice, and London. The Soviet government sent him urgent invitations to visit the U.S.S.R. and he was eager to accept, but his physician forbade such an expedition because of the distance and strain; he was then in his eighty-eighth year. A sizable fortune had accumulated for him in Soviet banks from royalties but they could not be spent outside Russia. He retained his love of reading, good food, bridge, and conversation. He was greatly pleased by two honors bestowed on him in 1961. In May he journeyed to London to become one of the first five writers to be named by the Royal Society of Literature as Companions of Literature, "to be limited to ten writers who have brought exceptional honors to English letters." The other four were Winston Churchill, E. M. Forster, John Masefield, and G. M. Trevelyan. When asked to say a few words at the presentation, Maugham, with a touch of humor, began, "I did not expect to be called upon to speak or I would have spent three or four hours this morning devising an impromptu speech." Since 1961 Edmund Blunden, Aldous Huxley, Edith Sitwell, Evelyn Waugh, Elizabeth Bowen, C. Day-Lewis, Osbert Sitwell, Rebecca West, Ivy Compton-Burnett, Compton Mackenzie, and John Betjeman have been made Companions.

In June 1961 Maugham traveled to Heidelberg, where he was made Honorary Senator of the University during a ceremony marking the 575th anniversary of the founding of the oldest university in Germany. He was the first Englishman ever so honored. He was especially pleased, for he had received—one wonders why—very few honorary degrees, only from Oxford and the University of Toulouse. He was never a registered student at Heidelberg.

In 1962 his very last publication as a book appeared, and it is of such a nature that it does not belie his assertion that *Points of View* (1958) was his last *book. Purely for My Pleasure* is a handsome volume containing thirty-seven full-color plates, reproductions of his favorite pictures on the walls of Mauresque. In a brief introduction Maugham remarks that his collection took him more than fifty years to make, "fifty years of delight. I have bought pictures purely for my pleasure." He did not buy pictures as investments. He has a paragraph with each picture, and when possible he tells in a sentence or two his personal relationship with the artist. Among the painters represented are Matisse, Gauguin, Léger, Laurencin, Renoir, Rouault, Monet, Utrillo, Toulouse-Lautrec, Picasso, and Boudin. When at Deauville with his mother, Maugham saw Boudin making rapid, inexpensive portraits of vacationists on the sands. Most of the pictures reproduced in *Purely for My Pleasure* were sold later in the same year at Sotheby's.

By 1962 Maugham had grown tired of the burden of his great collection of paintings. Because of audacious thefts of pictures all along the Riviera, every time he went on a journey, at least twice a year, he had the paintings carefully crated and taken to Nice, where they were stored in a vault until his return. Moreover he paid regular fees to what he bluntly called "The Thieves' Union," a racketeering group on the Côte d'Azur which for decades had been exacting "protection" money from the well-to-do who had settled there. Maugham once said after greasing the palm of a local official to have the residence permit of a foreign member of his staff extended, "It must be very inconvenient living in a country where there is no corruption."

He arranged with Sotheby's of London for the auction of thirty-five of his paintings. One he had given to the city of Nice. Again he was the victim of petty gossip: that the sole purpose of the sale was to prevent his heirs from inheriting the pictures. In reality he had in mind safeguarding his estate and adding to the sum he was to leave to his favorite charity. His determination to provide a substantial sum of money for the Royal Literary Fund to help struggling and aged writers in need had become almost an obsession, which, ironically, was partly responsible for his rash actions during his last three years.

The sale aroused considerable excitement, whetted by exuberant free publicity in the press, and on the day of the auction Sotheby's rooms were crowded. Among the items was the famous Gauguin door, for which he had paid four hundred francs and which sold for £13,000— actually a great bargain for the purchaser. Two Renoirs brought £48,000 each. Lady Beaverbrook bought Lepine's "River Scene" for the Beaverbrook Art Gallery in Fredricton, New Brunswick. The total sale amounted to nearly £525,000.

The sale proved to be a tragic turning point in Maugham's final years. His daughter, Liza, Lady Glendevon, had claimed some of the pictures before the sale, declaring that her father had given them to her. After the auction a claim for £331,250 for nine pictures was made against Sotheby's by her solicitors, who contended that by deed of settlement the pictures were hers. She had some legal justification, for several years earlier Villa Mauresque had been made into a trust, "a limited company," with Liza one of the trustees, or shareholders. "Why did I ever do such a thing?" Maugham asked later. The probable explantation is that the awkward arrangement was made to avoid what the family regarded as excessive death duties. The press the world over reported the sordid details of the family quarrel, which ended temporarily when Liza accepted a cash settlement.

The London *Times* complained that on his ninetieth

birthday in 1964 not a single play by Somerset Maugham was brought back to the West End, but praised the Ashcroft Theatre in suburban Croydon for its revival of *Home and Beauty*. The drama critic blamed capricious public taste for the neglect of Maugham's skillful and entertaining comedies. "With a little luck, however, it will spring in the other direction, for this production serves a timely reminder of the indestructible stageworthiness of Maugham. . . . Maugham in the final analysis may have very little to say, but how well he says it!" When one remembers *Sheppey, For Services Rendered*, and *The Unknown*, it would seem that the critic could omit *very* from his judgment of the playwright.

In 1963 a new film version of *Of Human Bondage* was made, the third, but before the long period of editing was completed—it is hard to believe that this pruning task occupied a year and a half—and the film was released, the author of the novel was ill and unable to have any interest in it, indeed was only intermittently and dimly aware of the new film. It was an undistinguished production, partly because the overzealous surgery of the film editors had removed too many good things as well as weakening the beginning and the end. Laurence Harvey's Philip, however, was much closer to the Philip of the novel than was that of Leslie Howard a generation earlier. Howard, a Hungarian by birth, who was universally regarded as a typical Englishman, had made Philip too ingratiating and lovable. Kim Novak refused to use the cockney dialect in her portrayal of Mildred; Bette Davis was much praised for her use of it in her memorable performance in the first version. Miss Novak was right: nowhere in the novel is

Mildred described as a cockney. The vulgar waitress lives in a shabbily genteel suburb of London, far from the sound of Bow bells. Both Laurence Harvey and Kim Novak made a long and thorough study of the novel before the filming began.

In *Points of View* Maugham writes, "What makes old age hard to bear is not a failing of one's faculties, mental and physical, but the burden of one's memories." As a generalization it is a questionable statement, but it was unfortunately true to a degree for Maugham; it was equally true, though, that serious loss of health added to the blight of his last years. The deplorable and futile strife with Liza aggravated the burden of his memories. As his physical condition deteriorated, he was more and more haunted by events in his past—his unhappy marriage, into which he believed he had been tricked, his conviction that he was not the father of Liza, bouts of remorse for his responsibility in the cold-blooded killing of enemy foreign agents in the First World War when he himself was a secret agent, and ever the heartache when he thought of his mother's death and the unhappy years that followed. In addition to corroding memories was the growing fear that his fortune would never reach the charitable organization as he had planned. In the rare intervals of freedom from fears and tormenting memories, he wrote a series of autobiographical sketches called *Looking Back*. It is probable that he got most of the material from his notebooks, all of which were eventually destroyed. Its publication in a London Sunday newspaper and in an American magazine shocked many who read it, caused the loss of some old friends, and equally sad, a loss in public respect.

*Looking Back* is so interesting and readable—Maugham's severest critics rarely reproached him for dullness and un-readability—although tasteless and embarrassing in one passage, that one regrets its failure to be a notable autobiography. But he declared that he wrote it to relieve his memory of tortuous obsessions, not for publication until many years after his death, and not even then if publishers decided that he was too nearly forgotten. These fragments of autobiography do not add up to an impressive opus.

How often did he declare that he succeeded in ridding himself of a problem by writing it out? He had no religious faith to offer an outlet, and his philosophy of life, as usefully as it had served him for nearly seventy years, proved inadequate to dissolve his most oppressive remembrances of things past. He maintained that he wrote *Of Human Bondage* "to relieve himself of unhappy recollections." He repeats in *Cakes and Ale:* "Whenever he [an author] has anything on his mind, he has only to put it down in black and white, using it as the theme of a story or a decoration of an essay, to forget all about it." How could one of his intelligence and rationalism depend upon such a simplistic device? It seems to be a case of self-deception, but it may at times very well have provided some peace of mind. *Of Human Bondage* did not drive out memories of an unhappy childhood or ease the anguish of his mother's death. His identification with Philip persisted. When someone facetiously suggested *Worst Foot Forward* as a title for the proposed musical version of *Of Human Bondage,* he was not amused by the flippancy. He was pained by it. *Cakes and Ale* had no therapeutic or psychological task to perform: by 1930 Maugham's affection for "Rosie" was already a happy memory, and he wrote the novel with gaiety and a light heart. The writing of *Looking Back* did not purge his failing memory of bitter resentment and hatred but deepened them and possibly aggravated his illness.

Maugham's literary reputation would have suffered if *Looking Back* had been published as a book. When it is read in installments Sunday by Sunday or month by month, its haphazard organization, its lingering over the relatively trivial, and its disregard of many significant occurrences and influences in his past, its scrappiness in general are less noticeable. Nevertheless this disappointing work possesses the supreme virtue of Maugham's talent as a writer: it holds the reader's interest. It is doubtful that anyone who possessed the newspaper or magazine installments failed to read every page. Garson Kanin expresses the response of just about every devotee of Maugham the writer: "These revelations are shattering . . . sordid, embarrassing, and absolutely enthralling." Not many would agree with Kanin, however, that "it is the best writing he has done in years."

Although it is futile to regret that *Looking Back* is not a fully realized, complete autobiography, one cannot help being disappointed by his omission of entire segments of his past and his failure to render an account of many of the remarkable people whom he at one time or another had known well. He tells us little about his parents and other members of his family. He barely mentions his youthful adventures in Italy and Spain, and his apprentice years in Paris. There is hardly any mention of his association with Norman Douglas, Henry Arthur Jones, Matisse, Adlai Stevenson, Ethel Barrymore, Arnold Bennett, S. N.

Behrman, Noel Coward, Compton Mackenzie, and a hundred others.

His defense of such a fragmentary story of his life might have been that his experiences on the Continent which he had utilized in his stories and novels, his boyhood and young manhood are preserved under a thin coat of fiction in *Of Human Bondage*, and his memories of "Rosie" are secure in *Cakes and Ale*. When asked, as he frequently was asked, why he did not write his autobiography, he always replied, "I have put my life into my books." He more than once expressed regret, however, that he had not kept a day-by-day journal; as a result he had no record of the thousands of hours passed in the company of writers, artists, and statesmen of Europe and America over a period of sixty years.

Nevertheless *Looking Back* is a noteworthy achievement for a man of eighty-eight, written, he candidly admitted, when his memory was not always reliable, and when looking for the right word became an onerous task. Moreover the physical strain, the downright pain of writing was considerable; it was caused by writer's cramp, a trivial phrase that does not adequately describe an ailment so painful that when writing he had again to wear a corset-like gauntlet bound to his wrist and part of his hand, a heavier and more cumbersome device than he had worn when writing *Points of View*. With his erratic memory certain people and events in his past were completely blacked out, whereas others remained vivid and alive. He recalls many details of his long association with Winston Churchill. The two remained close friends until they were near ninety. Their last meeting, not reported in *Looking Back*, was pathetic.

They lunched in Churchill's hotel suite in Monte Carlo. Both were very old, and Churchill was pathetically dotardy (the press voluntarily omitted mention of his senility in his last years); both were a bit querulous. Their entire conversation consisted of a half dozen crotchety remarks about the food and drink they were consuming.

The writing in *Looking Back* does not have the grace and distinction of that in *The Summing Up* and *Don Fernando*, but it is straightforward and lucid, and exhibits in its sentences the euphony and balance he had always striven for. We must believe him when he declared that he wrote it for himself, not for publication, and therefore it did not undergo the careful revision and refining that he had lavished on his stories and essays. The only bad writing is a long, vapid letter—he says, not very convincingly, that he found a rough sketch of the original among his papers—to Syrie, in which he sentimentally and verbosely analyzes the collapse of their marriage. Nothing he ever wrote for publication was so banal.

In spite of unofficial announcements, mostly in gossip columns, of imminent publication, *Looking Back* never appeared in book form, but was published serially in the London *Sunday Express*, and in the short-lived, not widely read American monthly *Show*. The few friends who read it in manuscript advised him to destroy it or place it where it would be hidden for many years to come—as he had planned to do. One evening when Lord Beaverbrook was dining at Mauresque, Maugham said to him, somewhat to his secretary's consternation, "I have just finished a rough draft of my autobiography. I'd be glad if you'd read it and give me your opinion." Beaverbrook took the manuscript home and after he had read it asked if he might publish it in his *Sunday Express*. To the dismay of the few who knew about it, Maugham consented and could not be dissuaded. "It can do me no harm," he said. Beaverbrook evidently obtained foreign rights as well, for a London literary agent telephoned the editor of *Show* that he was sending over the manuscript of "Somerset Maugham's latest and probably last book. . . . Mr. Maugham specifically requested that *Show* get the first look." One wonders whether the author ever made such a request.

The newspaper and magazine publication resulted in much notoriety because of the vituperative attack on Syrie. Whether or not Maugham was accurate in narrative details or in his dissection of Syrie's character and personality, she was not living to defend herself, and the *fin de siècle* damning word *cad* was resurrected and used by many Britons to denounce Maugham's conduct "unbecoming a gentleman." He received many abusive letters, and some old acquaintances broke off their association with him. Noel Coward was one old friend who castigated him for the vicious attack on Syrie. Later Coward was able to understand Maugham's views, and the friendship was renewed. The most publicized defense of Syrie was a letter to the press written by her friend Oliver Messel, uncle of Lord Snowdon. The forceful letter ended, "I can think of no one who was more fun to be with or who had more understanding and tenderness on occasions when one needed a friend most." One of Maugham's most devoted American friends, Garson Kanin, writes, "the Syrie I knew was a quiet, diffident, sweet lady." He also points out that Syrie was thirty-seven and Maugham forty-two at the time of the marriage. "The drama was entirely adult."

*Looking Back* begins with a detailed account, which he had related before and is included in his published *Notebooks*, of why he did not write a final novel about Bermondsey to bring his novel writing to full circle, his last as well as his first to be a novel of slum life. He then determined that his last book would be a haphazard collection of essays, and *Points of View* was published in 1958. But the habit of writing was too strong to drop and he was conscious that there were still things to write: stories that he had told which obviously had amused his guests and others, portions of autobiography he had refrained from writing, portraits and profiles of some of the hundreds of noted people he had known, and religious and philosophical thoughts he had been disinclined to express. One wonders what they were.

In this capriciously organized chronicle there follows an excellent essay on growing old and on funerals, and then a sudden shift to an account of childhood holidays in Deauville with his mother, who, he tells us, was not free of the upper middle-class snobbery of the early 1880's. After mentioning his happy days with French playmates in Paris, he is off on a tangent about his mother's closest friend, Lady Anglesey, and her broken marriage. What follows seems a compendium of the early chapters of *Of Human Bondage:* the deaths of his parents, his unhappiness at the vicarage and at King's School, the mind-stirring year at Heidelberg, and finally his five years at St. Thomas's Medical School. He reminds us that he was never poverty-stricken, to use one of his favorite trite expressions. He had a legacy of £150 a year, which had a substantial buying power in the 1890's. He writes of Ellington Brooks, whom he met first in Heidelberg, and who introduced him to the pleasures of reading the great writers. Since his fondness for the great works of literature endured for more than seventy years and indirectly spurred him on to writing, Brooks must be regarded as an important influence in his life.

Maugham then points out the importance of chance: a brutal schoolmaster had driven him from King's School; otherwise he would have finished preparatory school and gone on to Cambridge like his brothers; and with his stammer closing the law and most other professions to him, he conjectures that he might have stayed on at the university and devoted his lifetime to dull *(sic)* scholarship.

There is only a brief mention of his years in medical school, his *Wanderjahr* in Spain, his writing years in London before moving on to Paris, his dreary, loveless affairs with waitresses and shopgirls. Then through the modest success of his fourth novel, *Mrs. Craddock*, and the publicity attending his unconventional play *A Man of Honour*, which enjoyed two performances, he entered a heady kind of society with more invitations to dinners and balls than he could accept. In this smart set he met "Rosie" and began the affair that was to last eight years.

At this point he abruptly returns to the theme of the role that chance plays in human life and the fortuitous events that rearranged the patterns of his own life; as minor examples he tells of the origin of the stories of "Rain" and "Before the Party." He is easily diverted into a discussion of determinism. He then tells of his first meeting with Winston Churchill and their subsequent association. Again he turns to "Rosie," her refusal to marry him, and her marriage to the son of a peer. The original of Rosie, who moved in the highest circles of society—she even entertained the Prince of Wales at dinner—is easily disguised as a barmaid in *Cakes and Ale.* He read of her death in the late 1940's. "She must have been well over seventy. [She was nine years younger than Maugham.] I still think of her with tenderness. . . . She had the most beautiful smile I have ever seen on a human being and, notwithstanding her moral looseness, was a very good and very sweet woman." According to those who knew her she was gay and charming. Once when her ailing father was indulging in a vast amount of self-pity, he ended his lamentations with "And I've got one foot in the grave." She replied, "Yes, and busy kicking the earth in with the other." Her father laughed for the first time in weeks. The author of this book possesses a photograph of "Rosie" when she was seventeen; however, with her long black skirt, voluminous shirtwaist, and piled-up hair she looks at least twenty-five. But the famous smile is missing: her slight frown gives her a sullen beauty, not at all as Maugham describes her or as the artist who painted her portrait several times depicts her. Maugham tells of the pleasure he experienced in writing *Cakes and Ale* and again denies that Driffield is a portrait of Thomas Hardy. "An author must be credited with some invention," he concludes.

He tells of his first meeting with Mrs. Syrie Wellcombe, "a very pretty little woman," in 1913. She was then separated from her husband, Henry Wellcome, who was later knighted, a wealthy manufacturer of pharmaceutical products. The firm was still operating in 1969. Maugham describes his unhappy affair with Syrie, the birth of their child in 1915, and her overdue divorce from Wellcombe.

While waiting for the divorce to become absolute, he journeyed to Tahiti to gather material for *The Moon and Sixpence*. His traveling companion was Gerald Haxton, who figured in their divorce case ten years later. On their return from the South Seas Syrie and Maugham were married. Ethel Barrymore said some time later that she was present at the ceremony in New Jersey, but Maugham does not mention her presence.

Soon after their marriage he was pressed into government service again and given the preposterous and futile assignment in Russia. Much of the middle section of *Looking Back* is devoted to their wretched marriage, his long absences (she disliked travel), and finally the divorce. The cruelty of his portrait of Syrie can be excused only by his certainty that the material was not for publication and by his hope that the writing would ease his mind.

The last section begins with a long account of a forgotten book reviewer and comments on the press in general. He then outlines his religious views, unchanged from those he attributed to Philip Carey nearly fifty years before, and he takes Bertrand Russell to task for disparaging Christ's character, showing a surprising familiarity with the four Gospels. He adds nothing to what he had said before concerning religion and philosophy. Critics who regard Maugham as second-rate and who have characterized his agnosticism and philosophical pessimism as sophomoric, or even more disdainfully as adolescent, will be gratified to learn that for more than seventy years he would occasionally read with pleasure quatrains of the *Rubaiyat*, to which Ellington Brooks introduced him in Heidelberg in 1892.

Then follows an acute analysis of Churchill's character

and personality. It was long rumored that Maugham was
writing a substantial memoir of the statesman, but if he
was, it was destroyed with all the other manuscripts.
*Looking Back* ends abruptly with brief remarks about his
pleasant years at Mauresque before the outbreak of the
Second World War, a bare mention of his wartime adventures, the death of Gerald Haxton, his return to his badly
damaged villa in 1946, and a tribute to Alan Searle, who
made his old age endurable. In a surprising postscript he
relates a near-mystical experience in 1958 in the Academia
in Venice. While seated in front of Veronese's large painting "The Feast of the House of Love," to his amazement
he saw "Jesus turn his head" and look directly at him.
He admits that it was an optical illusion. Why did he close
these disorganized snatches of autobiography with this
strange story?

Although it is futile to do so, one cannot help regretting
that the account of a long and interesting life is so fragmentary. Why has he been so reluctant to relate his early
adventures on the Continent, except at Heidelberg? One
regrets, too, that his years with Syrie are recollected not
in tranquillity but in rancor that became more intense in
his old age. An autobiography of Somerset Maugham with
the precision and dimension of Santayana's or Bertrand
Russell's could be an invaluable chronicle of the period
from 1880 to 1960.

His first infirmity of old age was a frequent failure of
memory. All remembrance of some intimate friends was
erased entirely. This writer saw him last in late November
of 1964, two months before his ninety-first birthday. He
had been warned that the aged writer might have no idea

who he was. Fortunately he was recognized, called by name, and courteously and warmly greeted. The day passed agreeably, almost as in former years. Maugham was not seriously frail physically, and he drank his martinis before eating a hearty lunch. His stammer had returned, but he talked a great deal—about Henry James, a seven-weeks sojourn in Greece, the Greek royal family, his triumphant reception in Heidelberg, his love of Venice. But that day in November was almost the last of his good days, and thereafter his decline was rapid. It is regrettable that Robin Maugham in his engrossing *Somerset and All the Maughams* fails to stress sufficiently his uncle's illness.

He suffered from loneliness now, for the time came when it was inadvisable to have any more guests at Mauresque. He was depressed, too, by the absence of his paintings from the walls of his home, and equally depressed by the absence of most of his books, which had been removed to King's School. To be sure pictures were on the walls, his collection of theatre prints, water colors, and oils, a collection second only to that of Charles Mathews, now the property of the Garrick Club in London. In 1948 Maugham had given his collection to the Trustees of the National Theatre, and eventually the pictures were to hang on the staircase and other walls of the structure to be built on the South Bank. When his paintings were taken away to Sotheby's, the National Theatre Trust graciously returned the theatre collection to Maugham's possession for his lifetime. But the Zoffanys, DeWildes, and Reynolds were no substitute for his Impressionist and other canvases. Weakening eyesight took much of the enjoyment from his greatest source of pleasure, reading, but he never entirely stopped reading until his fatal stroke.

He could not be restrained from ill-advised legal actions which brought an ugliness into his last years: his attempt to disinherit Liza, denial that he was her father, and other inept and embarrassing moves. Eventually a family reconciliation was effected, and the press let him alone.

For some time Maugham underwent rejuvenation treatments by Professor Paul Niehans in Vevay, Switzerland. Most physicians viewed the professor's regimen with suspicion, but many famous people who could afford it went to his clinic in hope of postponing the distasteful traits of old age, among them, it was reported in the press, Georges Braque, Ibn Saud, Fürtwangler, Gloria Swanson, and Adenauer. Some have wondered whether the treatment might help physically but be unable to retard the mental impairment common to nearly all people of extreme old age. Certainly in his last two years Maugham maintained astonishing physical vigor. To the end he ate heartily and smoked eighty cigarettes a day. Once when he was ninety years old he dropped nine feet from the garden wall to the road and started running. Eight months before his death he collapsed and was taken to the British-American Hospital a few miles from Cap Ferrat. Friends the world over awaited the inevitable bad news, for after all, he was ninety-one years old, but to their astonishment a few days later newspaper photographs showed him walking out of the hospital toward his car to be taken home. Earlier Maugham had undergone geriatric treatment by an eminent Austrian physician, Dr. Max Wolf, who had migrated to America. Maugham pointed out that Dr. Wolf kept Elsie Mendl alive for years.

The final year of Maugham's life was a year of distress for Searle, who had promised the nonogenarian to take care of him personally, without the aid of male or female nurses. At the end of one particularly ghastly day he fell and cut his head badly. The next day he fell again, and when Alan picked him up, he said, "Why, Alan. I want to say thank you and goodbye." These were his last words. He suffered a stroke immediately afterward on December 11, 1965, and never regained consciousness and died on December 16. He had asked that his ashes be buried in England.

There was no ceremony at the cremation in Marseille, but there was a semiprivate service in Canterbury, with all the members of his family present, at the burial of his ashes on December 22 by the wall of the library he had given King's School. Alan Searle, who did not share Maugham's agnosticism, chose the burial site. Permission could not be secured for burial in the Cathedral precincts, but the spot against the Maugham Library is most fitting. There was a procession of clergy, his daughter and four grandchildren, his nieces and nephew, and about forty boys of the school who had returned from Christmas holiday for the occasion. Over the ashes of the agnostic the committal sentences were said by the Dean of Canterbury, and prayers were offered by the headmaster of King's School. The famous photograph of the writer's mother was buried with the ashes.

In *Looking Back* Maugham says that he has directed in his will that there be no memorial (burial) service, "an ugly feature of contemporary manners." In one of his last interviews he said to the journalist, "All the interviewers want me to say that with death at hand I want to make peace with the Maker. I'm afraid not." Then he said, somewhat irrelevantly, "But at the risk of sounding banal I must add that the ultimate virtue for me is loving-kindness, what some people call goodness." The burial rites of the Anglican Church struck no one as inappropriate or incongruous; at least the newspapers, even the flippant columnists, made no ironic comments. There was a dignity, even beauty, in this final attention paid to the memory of a man who had brought, and would continue to bring, pleasure to millions of people the world over.

The Headmaster of King's School wrote to the *Times* after the burial: "It is true that if we may judge by *Of Human Bondage* that the memories of King's School 1884-1889 were not particularly happy. But the wheel came full circle. In his later years he was a fairly frequent visitor to the school, of which he became a governor, and this enabled him to find an outlet for the altruism, sentiment, and affection which was also a part of his nature." Maugham last visited the school when he was eighty-eight years old. It is interesting to note that he never returned to St. Thomas's Medical School, though he kept in touch through the school's magazine, which he read regularly. He never gave the school anything or remembered it in his will. Yet he was happier at St. Thomas's than at King's School.

The books he gave to King's School are of great interest, variety, and financial value. There are many volumes of poetry, drama, literary criticism, fiction, religion and philosophy, psychology, science, and biography, as well as dictionaries and encyclopedias. Some he had acquired while in medical school. A volume of Shaw's plays is inscribed "Christmas 1911. Much love, from Syrie." Many are gifts from the authors with expressions of admiration and affection: from S. J. Perelman, "For Willie, with unfaltering fealty and love"; twenty-eight volumes of H. G. Wells, Volume One inscribed "To Willie, God bless him"; from Jean Cocteau and Colette, both inscribed "Cher voisin." A French scholar, the leading Maugham authority in his country, Professor Joseph Dobrinsky of Montpellier, made a study of the books Maugham read just before he wrote each of his novels before 1919. Maugham wrote the date of acquisition in the flyleaf of each book.

Not all his library went to King's School. Many presentation copies by Norman Douglas, D. H. Lawrence, the Sitwells, and others were left to his secretary with the other contents of the villa. There are priceless "art books," collections of reproductions of paintings by Dufy, Picasso, and Matisse among them. They are priceless because the artists made original sketches on the blank pages of the presentation copies. In these books are original Matisses, Dufys, and Picassos.

The secretary was also left a considerable sum of money and the income from copyrights for the rest of his life. Copyrights continue longer in Britain than in the United States. After his death the income goes to the Royal Literary Fund for aged authors in need. This income will be considerable, for Maugham's books in the years following his death enjoyed a greater sale than ever before. Moreover, his plays are constantly performed, not on Broadway and rarely in the West End of London, but in the many repertory theatres of Britain and on the Continent and elsewhere. Although *The Constant Wife, Rain,* and *The Circle* are often revived, the most frequently produced are *Home and Beauty* and *The Noble Spaniard.* There is still a considerable income from radio and television, especially from adaptations of the short stories.

The novels and collections of short stories continue to have a very big sale in Europe, the Americas, and the Far East—all except three or four of the very early ones. *Liza of Lambeth*, published first in 1897 when the author was twenty-three, is one of the best selling nineteenth-century English novels. *Of Human Bondage*, partly because of its wide use in the schools of Britain, Scandinavia, and the United States, has had an enormous sale: it was estimated in 1965 that over ten million copies had been sold by that time. The Royal Literary Fund, like the three beneficiaries of Bernard Shaw's literary estate, will enjoy a substantial income for many years.

On the day of Maugham's death Mr. A. S. Frere, Chairman of the author's British publishers, Heinemann's, announced that absolutely no manuscripts finished or unfinished remained to be published. The holocaust the author staged in 1959 destroyed nearly all the unpublished notebooks, plays, stories, and other manuscripts. Perhaps the most shocking burnt offering on that October day was fourteen of the original twenty Ashenden stories, six of which were published in 1928. All twenty were written at the same time, within a year or so. They were read in manuscript by Winston Churchill, who advised—insisted, rather —that fourteen of them not be published. Why? Did they in some way strike Churchill as unpatriotic? Did he fear that they revealed state or military secrets? The few who read them agree that the fourteen lost stories were superior to the six in *Ashenden*. *Ashenden*, incidentally, in the years following Maugham's death had a more extensive sale than ever, possibly because of James Bond and the plethora of spy stories on film and television.

Alan Searle found it impracticable to keep for his own

use the contents of the villa, and so at Sotheby's most were auctioned off—eighteenth-century and Regency furniture, Aubusson and Chinese carpets, a few paintings, African wood carvings, and books. The sale of the books realized £10,000 and that of the furniture £31,000. The few remaining original manuscripts of published books and essays were also sold, those of *Creatures of Circumstance*, the essays on Augustus Hare and Kipling, and *Ten Novels and Their Authors*. The money realized at the sale was added to that to be bequeathed to the Royal Literary Fund.

Immediately after Maugham's death, actually beginning on the day he died, sensational, gossipy accounts of his bisexuality, penny-pinching meanness, and other alleged frailties appeared in the press, and soon thereafter in one hurriedly written book by a writer who had enjoyed the famous hospitality of Villa Mauresque. This defamatory book was rejected by thirty-two reputable American publishers before a little-known paperback concern accepted it. As to his sexual tastes, whatever they were, they are of little or no relevance, for they exert no discernible influence on his plays and stories. As to his meanness, like most people he had his pet economies, which are always amusing in the wealthy. He objected to tipping, for example, and often tipped not at all although he frequented hotels and restaurants where substantial pourboires are expected. He paid his secretary an absurdly small salary. In New York he would sometimes wait for a bus on a cold street corner rather than hail a taxi. Of course he had been the victim of gossip for sixty years; few famous men escape it. It was said repeatedly that he liked only the rich and successful, that he was a horrendous snob, that he was a thorough hedonist and materialist, that he was unpatriotic because he preferred to live abroad, that he traveled so much because long absences from Mauresque reduced his French taxes, that he dropped old friends who became failures, and so on. The post-mortem attacks probably equaled in viciousness any ever leveled at a well known literary figure.

But he was a deeply generous man. He set up large trust funds for his daughter and his grandchildren. He responded so generously to begging letters that his staff made sure that the unworthy ones, that is, most of them, did not reach him—as Charlotte Shaw and Blanche Patch daily extracted similar solicitations from Bernard Shaw's mail. Once when Maugham was a guest in Simenon's home in Switzerland, it was discovered that both Maugham and Simenon had just received identical letters from a "beggar." They wondered how many others had received the same letter. Maugham gave his school a boathouse, science building, and library, and endowed a scholarship. He set up funds for grants to young writers. Much of the distress of his last years resulted from his attempts to preserve his fortune for his charity and prevent its inheritance by those who he knew had no need of it. These kind impulses never quite disappeared. The few who saw him in his few days of relatively good health in the last year of his life agree that he was kind and gentle, exhibiting in these few good moments the quality he admired most in people—loving-kindness.

The brilliant and of course unsigned obituary in the London *Times* stresses the nearly faultless efficiency of performance of Maugham the writer, "which seldom belongs to literature at its most creative," a civil way of agreeing with Maugham that his place is in the top layer of the second-raters. It is true that his "perfection of performance" is often merely skillful manipulation of plot and character. For the less critical reader, however, the result is gratifying: a good story well told with believable characters. "As a novelist he would ask for no better epitaph than 'He told stories supremely well.'" The writer of the obituary would not place him in the very first rank because of what he considers an all too often balanced contrivance of plot, his narrow range of social observation, a too great degree of worldliness, and, except in *Of Human Bondage*, a refusal to dig deep into himself for a "passionate sense of humanity."

Two very readable books about him appeared the year after his death, *Remembering Mr. Maugham*, by Garson Kanin, and *Somerset and All the Maughams*, by Robin Maugham, the son of the Somerset Maugham's brother Frederick. The latter is the more valuable for Maugham students, more amusing and perceptive. Kanin's book is in the form of a diary in which Maugham figures in every entry, nearly every one of which Kanin declares he wrote down immediately after he had been with Maugham. The reader becomes a bit dubious and uneasy when he comes across solid paragraphs of Maugham's uninterrupted talk, sometimes an unbroken passage of four hundred words, by one who stammered and was never verbose. But the gossip and anecdotes are of constant interest. Kanin has a sense of style and maintains an admirable objectivity in spite of the deep affection he and his wife, Ruth Gordon, had for their old friend.

Noel Coward's introduction to *Remembering Mr. Maugham* is clever and racy but shallow and surprisingly unperceptive for one who was "indebted to him for nearly fifty years of kindness and hospitality." Those who knew Maugham will find it imposible to agree with Coward that he had one major illusion, that "people were no good." "He rarely drew a sympathetic character" would apply more to Coward's fiction and plays than to Maugham's. He should reread the fiction and travel books. Maugham was not an idealist: he never expected things or people to be as he wished them to be. He accepted man as he found him: imperfect, rarely genuinely altruistic, often hardened and made cunning by the struggles of life, but capable at times of touching human-kindness. Coward might examine the books in the Maugham Library in Canterbury and read the inscriptions by the well-known and unknown donors of books, many of them testimonies to his kindness and the affection he engendered. Jean Cocteau, H. G. Wells, G. B. Stern, Osbert and Edith Sitwell, Charles Goren, Aldous Huxley, and others could hardly be so devoted to an arrant misanthrope. Maugham more than once declared that because of his own serious faults he had learned to be indulgent of others.

Nor can this writer agree with the repeated allegation in books, articles, and interviews (in which his pessimistic statements were often quoted out of context) that Maugham's was a lifetime of unhappiness. We might recall Bernard Shaw's withering scorn of "happiness," his doctrine that life has far greater things to offer—excitement, thought, productive accomplishment, all of which to be sure bring incidental gratifications. Shaw's characters such as Octa-

vius in *Man and Superman* who mewl about happiness are
always figures of comedy. After Maugham left King's
School and lived an independent life in London, he no
doubt was as "happy" as the average young man. He had
a small but sufficient income, he made friends among artists
and writers, he enjoyed his internship, and he was able
to write evenings. When he discovered that his first love
was not medicine, but writing, he was able to take the risk
of changing his profession after university, as most men
are not able to do. His *Wanderjahre* were educational and
exhilarating. His ten years with too little success as a
writer were discouraging, and he must have questioned
his decision to leave the medical profession. But he spent
most of this decade at the turn of the century in the most
dynamic city in the world for artists and writers, associ-
ating with Gerald Kelly and other struggling painters as
well as with would-be authors. Phenomenal success in the
theatre in 1908 freed him from all financial worry.

Before he was twenty he had learned the delight of
reading, and for more than seventy years he spent hours
daily on what to him was the most civilized and satisfying
of pastimes. He read all the great and hundreds o' the not
so great novels of the world, as well as drama, poetry, philosophy, science, history, biography, comparative religion,
psychology, and even some law. He read with equal facil-
ity English, Spanish, Italian, German, and French. For
more than half a century he was an ardent bridge player,
and played with visitors and Cap Ferrat neighbors until
he was near ninety. He once remarked that bridge is one
of the crutches of old age. He liked travel and change of
scene, and was able to go when and where he pleased in

peacetime. Even when very old and ill he insisted on one more journey to Venice—and the Gritti, a disastrous mistake. He liked comfort, company, good food (he may have had just about the best in the world: his cook, Annette, was reputed to be the best in France, and the best cook in France should be one of the world's best). His knowledge and love of painting were substantial, and he could buy the pictures he chose to live with. He was able to drink moderately and smoke immoderately until his final collapse. Until his last few years he visited regularly friends in Germany, Switzerland, America, and England, and his home was seldom without interesting and stimulating visitors. He relished the honors bestowed on him by the Royal Society of Literature, the University of Heidelberg, and the Queen of England.

Robin Maugham's book is well worth reading. Many will be only faintly interested in the family ancestry, but when the writer comes to his greatgrandparents, especially remarkable Greatgrandmother Snell, and his grandparents (Somerset Maugham's mother and father) and their life in Paris, the book becomes absorbing. The infrequent confrontations of the novelist with his brother Frederick, the Lord Chancellor, who detested Willie's books as well as the triviality of his way of life, are salty high comedy. Although Robin may exaggerate the strength of the tie that bound him and his uncle together, the accounts of their meetings strike the reader as free of invention and hold his attention completely. The author of *Somerset and All the Maughams* (the title is from a droll couplet by Noel Coward) engaged in an enormous amount of research and unearthed hundreds of interesting facts about the

Maughams, not all of them, to be sure, very significant. We learn, for example, that the site of the Maugham apartment in Paris is now 25 Avenue Franklin D. Roosevelt; that Somerset Maugham was not born in his parents' apartment, but in the British Embassy to avoid French citizenship, which would have been automatic had he been born on French soil; his brothers were also born in the Embassy. Of interest to readers of *Of Human Bondage* is the fact that Uncle Henry came from Whitstable to perform the marriage ceremony of Maugham's parents. Robin talked with a very old woman, a Mrs. Hammersley, who knew the Paris Maughams very well, and remembered Willie as a boy. She declared that he did not stammer then. We learn, too, that Maugham told Robin that he once refused a knighthood. The unworthy suggestion is made that Maugham may have given his old school so much in order to outdo Hugh Walpole, also a benefactor of the institution. Ironically the Junior School to which the vicar first brought his eight-year-old nephew is now named Walpole House.

Because of the eminence of the Maughams in our century it is surprising to learn that the family came from middle-class stock, and that only in 1968 did the family acquire a coat of arms, which in that year appeared in *Debrett's Peerage*. Robin, Lord Maugham upon the death of his father, used as his crest the symbol discovered by his grandfather in the Atlas Mountains; it is said to ward off the evil eye, and is possibly Christian in origin, a cross-hilted sword. The crest was already world-famous, having been used by Somerset Maugham on the cover of all his books (and nearly all books about him) and on his stationery; and it is carved over the front door of Villa Mauresque and into the gateway into the grounds of the small estate. Now it passes into the symbols of British heraldry.

Although "lifetime of unhappiness" is an exaggeration, "lifetime of happiness" would be even more hyperbolic. The advantages and amenities of what is usually considered the good life were unable to erase the painful experiences: unrequited love, which he speaks of in *The Summing Up* and elsewhere, his frowned-upon sexual tastes, his unfortunate marriage, the lack of warmth and affection in his family after the death of his parents, the tendency of first-rate critics in general to ignore his work, his excessive love of his mother for eighty-three years, a love that brought more pain than peace of mind. Only a week or so before his death he was discovered crying before her picture, his head on the bedside table.

Moreover his utter belief in determinism had hardened into a hopeless kind of pessimism. He once advised a troubled young relative not to have psychiatric treatment, which he declared useless since it is impossible to change one's essential nature. He saw man as a product of genes and chromosomes and was convinced that all he could do is "supplement his deficiencies," for there was no hope of fundamental change.

But to declare that he was an unhappy man all his life is nonsense, for he probably got as much satisfaction from his days as does the average person. He had with him always the medication to end his life whenever death seemed preferable to staying alive under certain conditions, but he never used it. It occurred to him in 1940 when the Germans started to overrun Unoccupied France that he might have to do so, since he was on Goebbel's black list. For all his dramatic remarks about longing for death, he dreaded it. He did not fear it, but he wished to postpone as long as possible the final hour which he believed would bring utter oblivion.

*Somerset and All the Maughams* was widely reviewed, often by young critics who did not know the aged author and certainly knew nothing about his illnesses after 1963. They found the details of the wretched last years titillating, to say the least. Generalizations and even gossipy invention appeared in some reviews. In one of the most respected American newspapers the assertion was made that Maugham's generosity was always selfishly calculated, that Gerald Haxton's death broke whatever was left of his heart, that he was the unhappiest man in the world, etc. A review in a Chicago newspaper stressed his lack of enduring affections, his "ineffable unhappiness" and his turning into "a nasty old man"; the reviewer suggests that his Riviera villa was an escape, not a home (whatever that means); and the review ends "he was heroically hateful." In a more staid English review Maugham is described as a "tortured kaleidoscope of neuroses and guilt complexes." His nephew's failure to describe more exactly Maugham's breakdown in health is partly responsible for such allegations. For example, at the very end of the book the writer tells of the aged man's outbursts of rage against his guests —"his eyes glittered with hatred"—but he fails to mention that Maugham was gravely ill at that time.

Four months after his death a group of his close friends talked of him at a meeting of the Friends of the University of Southern California Library. Clare Boothe Luce spoke

The Final Years 293

of his warmth and generosity, and of his painstaking aid and advice when she began writing. "I found him very generous," said George Cukor. Ruth Gordon spoke of his "loving friendship and generosity," and added, "When people said, 'Oh, he's difficult, he's cold, he's cruel,'" she admitted that she knew what they meant, but to her the protective exterior could not conceal from her his kindly nature, goodness, and capacity for friendship. It was suggested that the loneliness of his last years—perhaps most very old people suffer from a great loneliness—resulted from his ceasing to write after having been a constant and systematic writer for nearly seventy years. A longtime friend described his final visit with him during Maugham's sojourn in Venice—his faded memory, his old brilliance in his best moments. Dr. Aerol Arnold expressed the belief that he was terribly hurt when a child, and when a very young man he developed a "premature stoicism, which was really a defense against pain."

The author of this book would like to relate one of Maugham's many kindnesses to him. In preparing an introduction to the Modern Library paperback edition of *Of Human Bondage*, he wrote down a list of twenty or more questions concerning Maugham's early years—family, religious beliefs, and other matters—gave the list to Maugham's secretary, and asked him to find any answers he could, and as tactfully as possible. Maugham got hold of the list, wrote out an answer to every question in his angular handwriting, and spent hours in doing so, for he checked dates and other details. This writer knows of many such acts of kindness. For example, Guy Bolton tells of a bridge game on shipboard after which Maugham learned that the heavy loser (the stakes were high) was a woman who could ill afford it and whom he had never seen before the bridge game. Later on in London he sent her on her birthday a George III silver tankard, which more than compensated for her loss at cards.

If this writer has seemed to stress unduly Somerset Maugham's severe illness at the end of his long life, it is for an obvious reason: to make more understandable the bizarre and sometimes deplorable occurrences of those years. It is doubtful, however, that the sensational and defamatory reportage and *on-dit* in the public press, much of it exaggerated and some entirely fabricated—for example the newspaper story that he sued to recover gifts made to Liza years before—and in one lurid book, reduced in any way his stature as a writer. The tumult and the shouting soon died, and his books continued to be read more widely than ever. It is a tribute to his literary eminence that none of the tags that have been employed to designate his place in literature are satisfactory, especially those that would fix him in an age: "Edwardian," "The Last Romantic," "Post-Victorian," "Modern." Somerset Maugham is a writer for all seasons.

**BIBLIOGRAPHY**

Place of publication London unless otherwise noted.

*NOVELS*
*Liza of Lambeth* (1897)
*The Making of a Saint* (1898)
*The Hero* (1901)
*Mrs. Craddock* (1902); new and revised edition (1928)
*The Merry-Go-Round* (1904)
*The Bishop's Apron* (1906)
*The Explorer* (1907)
*The Magician* (1908)
*Of Human Bondage* (1915); new edition with "A Digression on the Art of Fiction," an address by Maugham in the Coolidge Auditorium, Library of Congress, on presenting the original manuscript to the Library (1946)
*The Moon and Sixpence* (1919)
*The Painted Veil* (1925)
*Cakes and Ale* (1930)
*The Narrow Corner* (1932)
*Theatre* (1937)
*Christmas Holiday* (1939)

*Up at the Villa* (1941)
*The Hour Before the Dawn* (1942) New York
*The Razor's Edge* (1944)
*Then and Now* (1946)
*Catalina* (1948)

*SHORT STORIES*
*Orientations* (1899)
*The Trembling of a Leaf* (1921)
*The Casuarina Tree* (1926)
*Ashenden* (1928)
*Six Stories Written in the First Person Singular* (1931)
*Ah King: Six Stories* (1933)
*Cosmopolitans* (1936)
*The Mixture As Before* (1940)
*Creature of Circumstance* (1947)

*MAJOR COLLECTIONS OF SHORT STORIES*
*Altogether* (1934); published in the United States as *East and West* (1934)
*The Complete Short Stories*, 3 vols. (1951)

*PLAYS*
*A Man of Honour* (1903)
*Mrs. Dot* (1904)
*Lady Frederick* (1911)
*Jack Straw* (1911)
*The Explorer* (1912)
*Penelope* (1912)
*The Tenth Man* (1913)
*Landed Gentry* (1913)
*Smith* (1913)
*The Land of Promise* (1913)
*The Unknown* (1920)
*The Circle* (1921)

*East of Suez* (1922)
*Caesar's Wife* (1922)
*Our Betters* (1923)
*Home and Beauty* (1923)
*The Unobtainable* (1923); also produced under the title *Caroline*
*Loaves and Fishes* (1924)
*The Letter* (1927)
*The Constant Wife* (1927)
*The Sacred Flame* (1928)
*The Breadwinner* (1930)
*For Services Rendered* (1932)
*Sheppey* (1933)
*The Noble Spaniard* (1953)
*The Plays of W. Somerset Maugham*, 6 vols. (1931-1934)

*OTHER NON-FICTION*
*The Land of the Blessed Virgin* (1905)
*On a Chinese Screen* (1922)
*The Gentleman in the Parlour* (1930)
*Don Fernando* (1935); new and completely revised edition (1950)
*The Summing Up* (1938)
*Books and You* (1940)
*Strictly Personal* (1942); published in the United States in 1941
*A Writer's Notebook* (1949)
*The Vagrant Mood* (1952)
*Ten Novels and Their Authors* (1954) (a revision of *Great Novelists and Their Novels*, published in the United States 1948)
*Points of View* (1958)

*ANTHOLOGIES EDITED BY MAUGHAM*
*Traveller's Library* (New York, 1933)

*Teller of Tales* (New York, 1939)
*Modern English and American Literature* (New York, 1943)

BIBLIOGRAPHIES

*A Bibliography of the Writings of William Somerset Maugham,* by Frederick T. Bason (1931)
*Maughamiana,* by Raymond T. Stott (1950); revised (1956)
*Bibliography of the Writings of W. Somerset Maugham,* by Klaus W. Jonas, published in the United States in 1950
*More Maughamiana,* by Klaus W. Jonas, published in the United States in 1950

BIOGRAPHY AND CRITICISM OF MAUGHAM

Brophy, John. *Somerset Maugham* (1952)
Cordell, Richard A. *Somerset Maugham* (Edinburgh, 1937)
Dottin, Paul. *W. Somerset Maugham et ses romans* (Paris, 1928)
————*Le Théâtre de Somerset Maugham* (Paris, 1937)
Guéry, Suzanne. *La Philosophie de Somerset Maugham* (Paris, 1933)
Jonas, Klaus W. *The Maugham Enigma* (1954)
————*The World of Somerset Maugham* (New York, 1959)
MacCarthy, Desmond. *W. Somerset Maugham, The English Maupassant* (1934)
Mander, Raymond, and Mitchenson, Joe. *Theatrical Companion to Maugham* (1955)
Nakano, Yoshio. *Japanese Maugham Studies: An Anthology* (Tokyo, 1954)
Papajewski, Helmut. *Die Welt, Lebens- und Kunstanschauung William Somerset Maughams* (Köln, 1952)
Pfeiffer, Karl. *Somerset Maugham, A Candid Portrait* (New York, 1958)
Ward, Richard H. *W. Somerset Maugham* (1937)

## BOOKS CONTAINING MATERIAL ON MAUGHAM

Connolly, Cyril. *Condemned Playground* (New York, 1946)

Dukes, Ashley. *The Youngest Drama* (Chicago, 1924)

Lewisohn, Ludwig. *The Drama and the Stage* (New York, 1922)

Nichols, Beverley. *Are They the Same at Home?* (1935)

Sawyer, Newell W. *The Comedy of Manners from Sheridan to Maugham* (1931)

Swinnerton, Frank. *The Georgian Scene* (1934)

Van Doren, Carl and Mark. *American and British Literature Since 1890* (New York, 1925)

### SUBSEQUENTLY PUBLISHED

## BIOGRAPHY AND CRITICISM OF MAUGHAM

Kanin, Garson, *Remembering Mr. Maugham* (New York, 1966)

Maugham, Robin, *Somerset and All the Maughams* (New York, 1966)

## OTHER NON-FICTION

*Purely for My Pleasure* (1963)

# INDEX